From the Library of.
Ed Bussard.

A Popular

HISTORY *of*
CHRISTIAN
EDUCATION

By the Same Author

A Popular

HISTORY *of* CHRISTIAN EDUCATION

By

C L A R E N C E   H.   B E N S O N

Formerly instructor in History of Religious Education at the Moody Bible Institute of Chicago

Secretary of the Evangelical Teacher Training Association

Editor of the All Bible Graded Series

Editor of the Superior Summer School Series

MOODY PRESS
153 Institute Place
CHICAGO

Printed in the United States of America

Dedicated to my students in the Christian Education Course who have taken the journey with me and have come to appreciate the importance of reaching and teaching and saving the children

FOREWORD

This volume is more than a textbook. It has a peculiar personal interest. The contents have already had a marked influence on the life of the author. Being a son of the manse, it was only natural that his life contribution should follow the line of a ministerial ancestry. He served in five pastorates and when he left Japan in 1922, it was with every expectation of continuing this work. But while man proposes, God disposes.

The author had never been to the Moody Bible Institute and only knew the president, Dr. James M. Gray, through correspondence. Moreover, God had already set his seal of approval upon a pulpit ministry and it seemed unthinkable that it should be set aside for the classroom. But while the invitation to the Moody Bible Institute was pressing, other doors were strangely closed. It was with considerable reluctance, therefore, that the pastor consented temporarily to become a teacher. In a year or two, he thought the way would be opened for his return to the pastorate. Little did he dream that influences would be at work which would entirely change his ministry and keep him at the Institute for twenty years.

The first interest in Christian education came with the assignment of classes in Child Study, Pedagogy and Sunday School Administration. Then, at a Founder's Week Conference, a representative of the American Sunday School Union demonstrated the futility of evangelism without education. He provided statistics for churches of one county in Ohio to show that in thirty-five years eighteen hundred evangelistic campaigns had been held with a net loss of five hundred members. This woeful record was offset by the success of a layman, Frank L. Brown, who made every Sunday School teacher an evangelist and in the same number of years (thirty-five) added no less than six thousand pupils to the membership of the Bushwick Avenue Central Methodist Church of Brooklyn. In 1924 the author was requested to become director of the new Christian Education Course at the Institute. The informing and inspiring subjects that were added to his teaching schedule had a strong influence in determining his life work. Of these, History of Religious Education was to prove the most fascinating. H. Clay Trumbull's marvelous assembly of facts in *Yale Lectures on the Sunday School* was especially effective in impressing the sadly neglected teaching ministry.

In addition to arousing the Church to its neglected teaching ministry, this volume has a patriotic mission. The Sunday School is as much an American institution as the public school system. While it originated in England, it saw its greatest development in the free soil of the new world. The Sunday School has truly made America just as much as America has made the Sunday School. Its international and interdenominational character has made it the most satisfactory supplement to our non-religious public schools. Certainly every Christian patriot must view with alarm the declining prestige and power of the Sunday School in recent years, and the unparalleled crime wave that has arisen in consequence. How long can the moral integrity of the Republic be maintained when seven out of ten of its future citizens are growing up without any religious instruction? Protestants cannot agree on many things, but the most serious difference today is the indifference to 37,000,000 children and adolescents who are growing up without any religious education.

A great loss has been sustained in the passing of the old-time Sunday School convention with its thrilling enthusiasm for reaching and teaching and saving the children. In some way we must regain that early convention enthusiasm that sent teachers back to their classes with the realization that their work was the biggest task on earth. Where can we find that flashing eye and that burning heart today? In so many Sunday Schools the fire has been permitted to go out or the flame is being used to light the mind rather than heat the soul. But it is heat that the world needs quite as much as light. It is the life on fire that kindles a light. If this volume will help arouse the nation to a new appreciation of the Sunday School as "the most indispensable institution in America," its preparation certainly will have been worth while.

C. H. B.

CONTENTS

HISTORY *of* CHRISTIAN EDUCATION

1

JEWISH EDUCATION

HOW insignificant are the annals of the Jewish nation in comparison with those of the contemporary civilizations about them! How little that nation has contributed to the pages of world history when measured by Egyptian, Babylonian, Grecian and Roman population and power.

But while these world dominions have either passed into oblivion or lost their former prestige, the insignificant Jew still remains a force to be reckoned with, and his contribution to civilization exceeds that of all other nations. The Romans gave the world its law and the Greeks its literature and art, but the Jews provided Christianity, which today dominates all other religions of the globe.

This is remarkable considering the failure of the Hebrews to appreciate and appropriate fully what has so greatly influenced other peoples. The explanation of this marvelous power of Christianity lies not only in its divine origin, but also in the divine plan for its propagation. The progress and permanency

13

of Christianity has been dependent upon a program of education.

H. Clay Trumbull has well summed this up in his *Yale Lectures on the Sunday School:*

> From the beginning, in short, all the way down the centuries, the history of the Christian Church shows that just in proportion as the Bible School has been accorded the place our Lord assigned to it in the original plan of His Church, has substantial progress been made in the extending of the membership, and in the upbuilding of the body of Christian believers in the knowledge of God's Word and in the practice of its precepts. And just in proportion as the Bible School agency has been lacking, or has been ignored, has the Church failed in retaining or continuing the vital powers of its membership.

The program of education that Christ laid down for the furtherance of His Church was only the enlargement and the improvement of God's plan for His chosen people Israel. Had they faithfully adhered to that plan, the Old Testament would not have had to record their tragic failure as a nation. Their crowning mistake, the rejection of their Messiah, would hardly have been possible had they fully known and understood the Scriptures that were written concerning Him.

But even with their defeat and final dispersion to the ends of the earth, these remarkable people have not been annihilated or assimilated by the nations. While other governments have come and gone, without a king or a country the Jews have remained a distinct people throughout the centuries. This miracle which is perpetuated before the eyes of the world is to be accounted for not only because the last chapter of Jewish history has been prewritten in Scripture, but because of their adherence to faithful instruction in that Scripture.

I. The Divine Plan

Israel was highly favored in receiving from God not only a code of laws for the prosperity and permanence of the nation, but also a divine plan of instruction in these laws. The Mosaic code was one of the most comprehensive, powerful and permanent bodies of legislation ever enacted. It was a political, civil, religious, and domestic code all in one. This is remarkable in the light of the variance that is to be found today in regulations for homes, municipalities, churches, and even states and provinces. There is little uniformity of law such as the Hebrews enjoyed. Their legislation was definite and absolute, and was enforced by the strongest penalties. It regulated the whole life of the Jew—his house, dress, food, employment, domestic arrangements, the distribution of his property, politics, and civil and religious life.

While reading and writing were rare attainments in that day, it is significant that from the first this legislation was reproduced and preserved in manuscripts. The stones upon which the Decalogue was written fitly symbolized the enduring character of its substance and of the whole legislation of which it is a part. But it is not the nature of the Law so much as the divine provision for the knowledge and mastery of its content that is the concern of the moment. The legal discipline of the nation was enforced by the most powerful agencies.

1. Parents

Fathers and mothers were enjoined in the most impressive manner to teach the history, the precepts, and the ordinances of the Law to their children.

> He established a testimony in Jacob, and appointed a law in Israel, which he commanded our fathers, that they should make them known to their children: that the generation to come might know them, even the children which should be born; who should arise and declare them to their children (Ps. 78:5, 6).

> These words, which I command thee this day, shall be in thine heart: and thou shalt teach them diligently unto thy children, and shalt talk of them when thou sittest in thine house, and when thou walkest by the way, and when thou liest down, and when thou risest up (Deut. 6:6, 7).

> Therefore shall ye lay up these my words in your heart and in your soul, and bind them for a sign upon your hand, that they may be as frontlets between your eyes. And ye shall teach them your children, speaking of them when thou sittest in thine house, and when thou walkest by the way, when thou liest down, and when thou risest up. And thou shalt write them upon the door posts of thine house, and upon thy gates (Deut. 11:18-20).

Jewish education began with the mother. The very household duties that she performed molded her children in accordance with the divine program of instruction. "The Sabbath meal, the kindling of the Sabbath lamp, and the setting apart of a portion of the dough from the bread of the household—these are but instances with which every child, as he clung to his mother's skirts, must have been familiar."

One of the first things to arrest his attention was the parchment fastened to the door post, which was reverently touched by those who went in and out because on it was written the name of the Most High. His mind would also be indelibly impressed with the prayers and domestic rites of the household, especially with the midwinter festive illumination in his home. At his mother's knee he heard the oft-repeated stories of patriarchs and prophets, of poets and patriots, of kings and national heroes. Timothy was the son of a Greek father and was removed from the training of any Jewish school or synagogue, but he had a thorough knowledge of the Scriptures, as Paul declared, because of the painstaking instruction of his grandmother Lois and his mother Eunice (II Tim. 1:5). As teachers of their children, the women of every country may learn lessons from the mothers of Israel.

Jewish fathers also assumed their responsibility for teaching. Indeed, they considered it an honor and everything else gave way to this most important task of their lives. As soon as the child could speak, his religious education began. He was early taught his birthday text—some verse beginning with, ending with, or at least containing the letters of his Hebrew name. Since to know the law was primarily the ability to repeat it accurately, much attention was given to the cultivation of the memory. Forgetfulness was as reprehensible as ignorance. Large portions of the Scriptures were cast in poetry and proverb to be easily learned, and each father served as a drill master for his children.

Not only did the parent impart the precious knowledge of the Law with unwearied patience and intense earnestness, but he also kept before his children the purpose of it all. Sin was shown in its repulsiveness. Industry, honesty, sobriety, and espe-

cially obedience, were constantly set forth as virtues
to be attained, while the fear of the Lord was ever
reiterated as "the beginning of wisdom."

2. Priests

Domestic discipline was ably reinforced in the divine plan by the provision of public teachers. The
purpose of the Jewish priest was to instruct. The
holy order taught the people not only in the details
of the temple service, but in the Law itself.

> And Moses wrote this law, and delivered it unto the
> priests the sons of Levi, which bare the ark of the cove-
> nant of the Lord, and unto all the elders of Israel. And
> Moses commanded them, saying, At the end of every
> seven years, in the solemnity of the year of release, in
> the feast of tabernacles, when all Israel is come to appear
> before the Lord thy God in the place which he shall
> choose, thou shalt read this law before all Israel in their
> hearing. Gather the people together, men, and women,
> and children, and thy stranger that is within thy gates,
> that they may hear, and that they may learn, and fear
> the Lord your God, and observe to do all the words of this
> law: and that their children, which have not known any
> thing, may hear, and learn to fear the Lord your God, as
> long as ye live in the land whither ye go over Jordan
> to possess it (Deut. 31:9-13).

One cannot help but be impressed by the plan
for providing public teachers for Israel. The position
was not elective. The tribe of Levi was set apart to be
the national educators. These teachers were not
called upon for military service, and they were not
apportioned land for agricultural purpose. Their
whole time, indeed their whole life, was devoted to
their God-chosen profession, their support coming
from the tithe. In other words, the religious teachers

and religious schools of the Jews were as well provided for as the tax-supported public instructors and
institutions of today. While it is true that the tax
is now recognized as obligatory and the tithe was
voluntary, nevertheless with the Jew there was no
difference, since the command to support the Levites
was as binding as any other law. "Take heed to
thyself that thou forsake not the Levite as long as
thou livest upon the earth" (Deut. 12:19). The
fact that there was no penalty prescribed for the
violation of this law made it much easier to evade
and called for this special exhortation of Moses.

3. Religious festivals

The most significant instruction of Israel's public
teachers was in connection with religious festivals
when the priests appeared in an official capacity.
There was a cycle of public feasts and fasts, most
of which lay within the observance of the child.
There was the Feast of Purim, the Feast of Taber-
nacles, the Feast of the New Year, the Day of Atone-
ment, and the Passover, which were never-to-be-forgotten occasions.

That the divine purpose for these religious festivals
was instruction is plainly recorded in connection
with the institution of the Passover. After the description of this festival and the command for its
faithful observance each year, we read:

> And it shall come to pass, when ye be come to the
> land which the Lord will give you, according as he hath
> promised, that ye shall keep this service. And it shall come
> to pass, when your children shall say unto you, What
> mean ye by this service? That ye shall say, It is the sacri-
> fice of the Lord's passover, who passed over the houses

of the children of Israel in Egypt, when he smote the
Egyptians, and delivered our houses (Exod. 12:25-27).

4. Government support

The political leaders of Israel were charged to
make a study of the Law for its national observance.
In the instruction laid down for kings we find this
injunction:

> And it shall be, when he sitteth upon the throne of
> his kingdom, that he shall write him a copy of this law
> in a book out of that which is before the priests the Le-
> vites: and it shall be with him, and he shall read therein
> all the days of his life; that he may learn to fear the
> Lord his God, to keep all the words of this law and these
> statutes, to do them (Deut. 17:18, 19).

That the rulers were expected to actively support
all religious education is plainly indicated by the
national revivals of public instruction under Jehoshaphat and Josiah. These good kings of Judah discovered that the national calamities were the result of
neglect of the teaching ministry. When powerful nations threatened to invade the southern kingdom,
Jehoshaphat sent out his princes with the Levites and
priests "to teach in the cities of Judah." And it was
after "they went about throughout all the cities of
Judah and taught the people" that we read:

> And the fear of the Lord fell upon all the kingdoms of
> the lands that were round about Judah, so that they made
> no war against Jehoshaphat (II Chron. 17:10).

It is evident that religious education was also an
important factor in accounting for the prosperous
reign of the good king Hezekiah, for it is recorded
that he "spake comfortably unto all the Levites that

taught the good knowledge of the Lord" (II Chron. 30:22).

In the national revival of religion under King Josiah, he encouraged the priests in the service of the house of the Lord as well as the Levites "that taught" all Israel (II Chron. 35:2, 3).

These instances are recorded only in connection with the good kings of the southern kingdom, which leads us to infer that government support of religious instruction was not given by the other rulers, who constituted the vast majority that "did that which was evil in the sight of the Lord." The northern kingdom did not have any Levites to teach the Law nor any good kings to enforce it, while only a few of the rulers of the southern kingdom concerned themselves with the divine program of instruction.

II. Israel's Tragic Failure

The history of Israel is the tragic story of failure to adhere to God's plan for His chosen people. The failure of the priests to perform their duties as teach-ers, the failure of the people to give their financial support to the priests, and the failure of the rulers to enforce and encourage the educational program were important contributions to the downfall of the nation.

1. The school of the prophets

Probably nothing reveals the ineffectiveness of the teaching ministry of the priesthood so much as the supplementary service of the prophets, which was apparently brought into existence to substitute an appointed agency that failed to function. This fol-lowed shortly after the corruption of the priests' office by the sacrilegious sins of Eli's sons (I Sam.

3:13). As the prophetic order practically ceased to exist in New Testament times, evidently it was only a temporary agency that was specially instituted when the regular means of national instruction failed.

As the first of the prophets, Samuel inaugurated a system for religious training similar to the Bible In-stitute movement of today. Young men were in-structed under his immediate supervision (I Sam. 9:19; 10:5, 10; 19:20; II Kings 2:3-5; 4:38; 6:1). They studied the Law and its interpretation, made copies of it, became teachers and preachers who denounced national, family, and personal sins. They even became proficient in the use of musical instru-ments (I Sam. 10:5). At first the prophets were *forthtellers,* or evangelists, and it was not until the declining days of the kingdom that the *foretellers,* or prognosticators, appeared upon the scene.

Not all the students who enrolled in these schools possessed the predictive gift. It is also true that there were inspired prophets who were not graduates of these institutions. Amos was a notable exception. Although called to the prophetic *office* he did not belong to the prophetic *order* and had not been trained in the schools of that day (Amos 7:14, 15).

The first school of the prophets was at Ramah (I Sam. 19:19, 20). Others were established later at Bethel (II Kings 2:3), Jericho (II Kings 2:5), Gilgal (II Kings 4:38), and elsewhere (II Kings 6:1). Into these schools, or Bible institutes, were gathered con-secrated and promising students who were trained for the office they were destined to fill.

So successful were these institutions that from the time of Samuel to Malachi there seems never to have been wanting a supply of men to keep up the line of official teachers. The enrollment appears to have differed from year to year. At times the students were numerous (I Kings 18:4; II Kings 2:16). One elderly or leading prophet presided over them (I Sam. 19:20), called father (I Sam. 10:12), or master (II Kings 2:3).

Their teaching was an oral rather than the symbolical instruction of the priests, and gradually supplanted it. This method was employed because of the constant need to rebuke a nation whose persistent disobedience was fast hastening it to its end.

> Yet the Lord testified against Israel, and against Judah, by all the prophets, and by all the seers, saying, Turn ye from your evil ways, and keep my commandments and my statutes, according to all the law which I commanded your fathers, and which I sent to you by my servants the prophets (II Kings 17:13).

The prophets, then, were at first exhorters rather than instructors of the Law. As forthtellers they called the people back to the divinely appointed schools and teachers. When it became evident that the kingdoms of both Israel and Judah would go steadily downward, the prophets became better known as foretellers who recorded their predictions that a faithful remnant might be reminded of a coming Messiah and a future period of restoration and blessing.

2. Lessons of the exile

There were three great lessons that the Jews learned during their years of captivity. When their seventy years of exile were over and they returned to Jerusalem, they were no longer idolaters. This crowning sin of the nation, which the prophets had so frequently reproved, was not again to appear among these chastened people. They had witnessed the downfall of all the polytheistic nations whose gods they had worshiped, and they had learned that only the God of Israel was able to restore His people.

Not only did the Jew of New Testament times repudiate idolatry, but drunkenness as well. No exhortations of our Lord or of the apostles were required for this besetting sin of pre-exilic days. Timothy was so scrupulously temperate that Paul had to prescribe "a little wine for thy stomach's sake and thine often infirmities" (I Tim. 5:23). Even to this day the Jews advocate and practice temperance as a national virtue.

The most important reform brought about by the Babylonian exile, however, was the new emphasis upon religious education. That Israel's painful suffering had come through their persistent neglect of the divine plan for instruction was attested both by facts and by maxims.

> The people that knoweth not the law is accursed.
> A town in which there is no school must perish.
> Jerusalem was destroyed because the education of the children was neglected.
> Get thyself a teacher.
> Make the study of the law thy special business.
> An ignorant man cannot be truly pious.

"During the seventy years of captivity on the banks of the Euphrates," it has been said, "a profound change occurred in the character of the Hebrew nation. Prophecy had ceased. The priest had lost all of his authority. There was a great revival of religious instruction, it is true, but it was the beginning of a new order of things rather than the restoration of the Mosaic program. The new organization made Judaism, as a system, firmer and stronger than it had ever been before. The new system included a cycle of schools co-extensive with the nation and highly exalting the teacher. It constituted the most efficient organization of human training that the world has ever seen, and its worth is well proved by the fact that it has been maintained to this day."

III. Post-Exilic Education

1. The Jewish teacher

The man of importance in the new order of education was the rabbi. He was also known as doctor, teacher, reader, and lawyer. Ezra was the first rabbi. He was "the man who was heard and obeyed with respect; the man of the book; the scholar, who knew the ancestral records, and could teach the principles of the Law, the violation of which had brought upon the nation such great trials."

The honor shown to a teacher bordered on that given to God. To dispute with a rabbi, or to murmur against him, was as sinful as to murmur against God. The Jew gave preference to his teacher over his father; the one gave him temporal life, the other eternal life. The highest and most honored profession to which a Jew could attain was to be a rabbi or teacher. Wealthy merchants with marriageable daughters were accustomed to visit the schools to discover some bright student whose tuition they would gladly defray that they might be honored in having a rabbi for a son-in-law. From the time of Ezra the rabbi has been the man of supreme importance among the Jewish people, the man who is heard and obeyed with respect.

2. The Jewish school

"Eighty years before Christ," says Deutsch, "schools flourished throughout the length and breadth of Palestine." Ginsburg finds added proof of the growth in prominence and favor of these schools. "So popular did they become," he says, "that while in the pre-exilic period the very name of 'schools' did not exist, we now find in a very short time no less than eleven different expressions for 'school.'" These included such terms as house of instruction, house of learning, house of the book, house of the teacher, and house of the master.

Synagogues were largely used for instruction. In the estimation of the Jews, the purpose of the synagogue was for the study and teaching of the Law rather than for worship. The latter service was reserved largely for the temple.

The Jewish child, from five to ten years of age, studied in these schools. Primary instruction was arranged with a view to giving the child a knowledge of the Hebrew text of the Bible and of prayers, together with their translation into the vernacular. The Bible itself was put into the hands of the Jewish child, and it was the Bible that shaped and molded his mind and heart. The book of Leviticus was chosen as the first subject of instruction in the Bible—the law being regarded as of greater importance than the history of Israel.

Every province and city was required not only to provide these schools, but also the teachers. Instruction was given the children all day and a part of the night, to accustom them to learn at all hours. No vacations were granted except the afternoon preceding the Sabbath or a holiday, and the holiday itself. On the Sabbath nothing new could be learned, the time being spent in reviewing the lessons of the week. One teacher had to be secured for every twenty-five pupils; where there were forty, an assistant was engaged.

In addition to these elementary schools, there were more advanced institutions of learning in connection with every local synagogue. In some cases these were held in the houses of the rabbis.

The regular Sabbath service of worship in the synagogue included afternoon Bible study for old and young, with an intermission between the morning and afternoon sessions, for dinner. So important was this afternoon service of instruction in the estimation of the rabbis, that the saying arose, "The righteous go from the synagogue to the school," or as might be said today, "The good man goes from the church to the Sunday School." And the duty of bringing the children from one service to the other was explicitly enjoined by the rabbis. One of the services was not considered enough by itself without the other to complement it.

Synagogues were found in all the towns and villages of Palestine and in many other cities of the Roman Empire where there was a sufficient number of Jews to support this combination of church and school. In Jerusalem, according to one authority, there were at one time four hundred and eighty synagogues.

That the Jews regarded these schools indispensable to the stability and permanence of their national existence is proved by such proverbs as, "The true guardians of the city are the teachers"; "If you would destroy the Jews you must destroy their schools"; "He who teaches a child is like one who writeth with ink on clean paper; but he who teacheth an adult is like one who writeth with ink on blotted paper."

3. The Jewish method

The method of instruction was interlocutory. The idea of attempting to instruct passive hearers by a prepared discourse never appealed to the Jews. It was the teacher's part to listen and the pupil's part to question. Often the instruction began in the answer to a question that was raised by the teacher's assistant, but the pupil's chief gain lay in the questions he asked. Ginsburg says:

> The method by which instruction was communicated was chiefly catechetical. After the teacher had announced his theme, the scholars in turn asked different questions, which he frequently answered by parables or counter questions. Sometimes the teacher introduced the subject by simply asking a question connected with the lesson of the day. The replies given constituted the discussion, which the teacher at last terminated by declaring which of the answers was the most appropriate.

Many indications are given in the Talmud which suggest how fundamentally important this interlocutory method was regarded. One rabbi testifies: "Much I have learned from my teachers; more from my colleagues; but most of all from my scholars." A pupil admitted that because he did not study aloud, he forgot in three years all he had learned in the school. A common saying was, "He who teaches without having the lesson repeated back to him aloud is like one who sows without reaping." In modern terminology we would say that instruction without an opportunity for expression is likely to be forgotten.

The ability of the Jewish teacher was judged entirely by the pupil's response. "If a lesson is not understood by the pupil, the trouble is not so much with the pupil as with the teacher, who fails to make the lesson clear." It was said of a certain rabbi that he was ready to repeat his teaching a hundred times to his pupils, if that were necessary to their understanding of it. The effect of such teaching was evident in the interest the pupils took in their lesson. A proverbial caution of the rabbis was: "At the coming of the teacher the pupils should not overwhelm him with questions."

---

1. What is the teaching of Church History regarding the importance of a program of education?
2. What Old Testament passages placed teaching responsibilities upon the parents?
3. Who were the public teachers of Israel and how were they supported?
4. Point out the educational values in the religious festivals.
5. How was a war averted by a national revival of religious instruction?
6. What was the purpose of the school of the prophets?
7. How do we know that the Babylonian exile affected education?
8. Describe the Jewish elementary school of the post-exilic period.
9. What synagogue service took the place of the modern Sunday School?
10. Explain the interlocutory method of instruction.

2

EDUCATION IN THE EARLY CHURCH

JESUS was a master teacher. It is surprising and unfortunate that so little attention has been given to His methods. Not only have comparatively few books been written about Jesus as a teacher, but the impression seems to have prevailed in some quarters that only His instruction is of importance and there need be no concern as to the methods He used to impart that instruction.

A careful study of the Gospels will furnish abundant evidence that Jesus regarded Himself as a teacher. In sharp contrast, it is to be noted that John the Baptist was a preacher—rare indeed in that day. While there were occasions when our Lord did address great multitudes, for the most part His time was spent with individuals or the group designated as His disciples or pupils. In all these contacts He exercised the functions of a teacher.

Evidence might be multiplied that Jesus regarded Himself as a teacher. "Teaching in their synagogues" and similar expressions occur repeatedly in the Gospels (Matt. 4:23; 9:35; Mark 1:21; 6:2; Luke 4:15; 6:6; 13:10; John 6:59). At the close of His Sermon on the Mount, it is said that the people marveled, "for he taught them as one having authority, and not as the scribes" (Matt. 7:29). A singular expression occurs in Mark 1:21 where it is said, "They went into Capernaum; and straightway on the sabbath day he entered into the synagogue, and *taught*." Jesus acknowledged Himself to be a teacher when He said to His disciples, "Ye call me Master and Lord: and ye say well; for so I am" (John 13:13). The entire Gospel record assumes that Jesus so regarded Himself. Everywhere Jesus permitted others to address Him by this title and He seems to have welcomed it.

It is also evident that others recognized Jesus as a teacher. Of the ninety times our Lord was addressed in the Gospel record, sixty times He was called rabbi or teacher. Only rarely did His disciples address their Lord by any other title. Even under unusual circumstances, this title still clung to Him. When He was asleep in the boat which was being buffeted by the winds and the waves, the disciples cried out, "Teacher, carest thou not that we perish?" That Jesus should be addressed by such a title in these trying circumstances indicates how deeply the teaching idea was imbedded in the disciples' minds and hearts.

Not only the disciples but others insisted upon giving our Lord this title. Perhaps His disciples (literally meaning pupils) would naturally acknowledge their instruction in this way. But Nicodemus, who was himself a teacher, reflected the general opinion held in Jerusalem concerning Jesus when he said, "Rabbi, we know that thou art a teacher come from God." The rich young ruler came to Jesus anxious to know the way of eternal life, saying, "Teacher, what good thing shall I do, that I may have eternal life?"

Even the scribes and the Pharisees, who were unwilling to credit Him with the training and authority
of a teacher, were forced by public opinion to address Him as such. "They send unto him certain
of the Pharisees and of the Herodians, to catch him
in his words. And when they were come, they say
unto him, Master, we know that thou art true, and
carest for no man; for thou regardest not the person
of men, but teachest the way of God in truth"
(Mark 12:13, 14).

I. The Disciples as Teachers

Christian education in the early Church began
with the disciples, who literally obeyed the Lord's
Great Commission. We are accustomed to speak
of the Great Commission in connection with the
great missionary enterprise, and perhaps overlook
the fact that it was a teaching commission. In any
event, we must recognize that the command was to
teach and not to preach. The word "teach" is found
twice in this farewell address and the instruction
was to teach "them to observe all things whatsoever
I have commanded you." From this we see the place
and importance of a Bible school in contrast to the
adoption of a pulpit for this program.

As the Jews understood that command and as we
have reason to believe our Lord meant it, Bible
schools were to be organized everywhere as the very
basis of the Christian Church. Grouping pupils in
classes under skilled teachers for the study of the
Word of God—that was the starting place as Christ
founded it. And it would seem that this was the
way the Great Commission was carried out by the
apostles and their immediate successors. We read

that every day in the temple and in the homes they ceased not to teach and to preach Jesus as the Christ. These apostles were Jews before they were Christians and it was as Jews they had learned how to teach. That they realized the difference between teaching and preaching is evidenced in their frequent antithetical use of the one term over against the other, and if anything, the teaching ministry predominated.

II. Paul a Master Teacher

The most influential figure in human history next to Jesus of Nazareth was probably the apostle Paul. He was the greatest missionary of all time, as can be seen by noting the difference between the foothold Christianity gained in Europe and in Asia. Christianity originated in Asia, but Paul introduced it into Europe, and through his efforts, it there soon out-distanced its greatest progress in Asia.

The library of Harvard University possesses more than two thousand volumes dealing with the life and letters of this remarkable man, more than one for every year since his time. In addition, there are multitudinous commentaries and histories in which the teaching of Paul has an important place. On the Epistle to the Galatians alone, there are at least 108 exegetical commentaries that have been written since the Reformation.

But not only was Paul one of the greatest personalities of all time, whose ministry accomplished more than the greatest of conquerors and statesmen, but he was also an extraordinary teacher. While he did not discuss pedagogy or lay down any laws for instruction, it is evident from a study of the Acts and the epistles that he was a master teacher—second in greatness only to our Lord.

1. Paul's training

Paul did not enjoy the same privileges as did the disciples. He did not sit at the feet of the Master Teacher. Perhaps for that reason he received exceptional educational advantages. In fact, it is no exaggeration to say that no one was better prepared to be a teacher than the great apostle to the Gentiles.

First of all he had the distinct advantage of belonging to a nation that reverenced the teacher and that laid great stress upon his ministry. As we have already seen, the Jews had a very high regard for their instructors, and the teaching profession was the highest office to which they could attain. Moreover, the sum and substance of all their teaching was religion. It was a heathen philosopher who thus commented: "The Jews look on their Law as a revelation from God, and are taught in their very swaddling clothes by their parents, masters, and teachers, the holy laws and unwritten customs."

Not only did Paul have the benefit of these racial influences, but he was also brought up in a highly instructive environment. Life among the Hebrews, as we have already seen, was a series of object lessons. Their rites and ceremonies provided valuable instruction. Parents, seizing a moment of excited curiosity, imparted to the child knowledge that was dear to themselves. The repetition of precept upon precept, line upon line, made these impressions permanent.

Furthermore, the teachers of Paul's day were pedagogues in every sense of the word. They were not content merely to impart knowledge, but trained their pupils to self-activity by goading, overseeing and guiding, and exemplifying industry. Painstaking application was required on the part of the pupil. Master teachers of religion specialized in individual pupils. This was the relationship of Paul to the great teacher Gamaliel. Paul was his prize pupil, and undoubtedly was prepared to be his successor. In Gamaliel, religion and its handmaiden education were exhibited to Paul as the concern of one's life.

Paul also had distinct advantage in the scholastic atmosphere of the city in which he was born and reared. The inhabitants of Tarsus were so zealous in the pursuit of philosophy and Greek study that they surpassed even the Athenians and Alexandrians. This was well brought out at the time of Paul's arrest. He was taken into custody as a Jew, and when he addressed his guard in Greek, the astonished captain asked, "Canst thou speak Greek?" Instead of replying in the affirmative, Paul said, "I am a Jew of Tarsus," just as though one could not live in Tarsus without knowing Greek.

2. Paul's ministry

Paul always insisted upon calling himself a teacher as well as an apostle. He seems well justified in doing so. His active life was one teaching situation after another. He taught in the synagogue, in the market place, by the riverside, in prison, in the courthouse, in private and in public. He taught Hebrews, Greeks, Romans, friends, foes, and strangers. He taught whenever an occasion presented itself, wherever he happened to be, and whoever came within range of his influence. To be sure there were occasions when he delivered public addresses, but for most of his contacts and intercourses, these would have been impossible, even if desirable. The situations in which he found himself called for a teacher, and he was marvelously qualified to answer that call.

We make a mistake when we think of Paul as an itinerant evangelist. He introduced the gospel through teaching rather than preaching. The substance of his instruction can be easily determined not only from the content of his epistles, but also from the book of Luke. Luke, it will be remembered, was Paul's private physician and amanuensis. Undoubtedly his Gospel was largely a reproduction of what he had seen and what later he had heard Paul teach. The summary of this teaching Luke states in the first verse of Acts: "The former treatise have I made, O Theophilus, of all that Jesus began both to do and teach, until the day in which he was taken up."

It is undoubtedly true that Paul remained long enough in each place to fulfill our Lord's commission "to teach all things whatsoever I have commanded." This took time. It was necessary to stay more than one week and have more than one service.

We read that Paul and Silas "came to Thessalonica, where was a synagogue of the Jews: and Paul, as his manner was, went in unto them, and three sabbath days reasoned with them out of the scriptures, opening and alleging, that Christ must needs have suffered, and risen again from the dead" (Acts 17:1-3). In addition to the services on the Sabbath, the Jews met on Mondays and Tuesdays, so that there were at least nine sessions in which there was interlocutory instruction.

At Berea, we read, Paul did a similar work. Berean hearers were commended "in that they received the word with all readiness of mind, and searched

the scriptures daily, whether those things were so."
Here the class was encouraged to investigate the
sources of teaching material.

At Athens Paul reasoned or discussed with the
Jews in the synagogues. He did the same thing "in
the market daily with them that met with him." In
these instances he must have used the interlocutory
method of teaching and learning, which was the es-
sence of the Jewish educational system.

In the same way Paul started his ministry in Cor-
inth. When the Jews drove him out of the synagogue,
he started a new school in "a certain man's house,
named Justus." The fact that "he continued a year
and six months, teaching the word of God among
them" is quite significant. Paul occupied himself
similarly "in his own hired dwelling" in Rome for
two years, and found it necessary to spend three
years in Ephesus in order to complete his course of
instruction.

In his writings, Paul speaks of teachers as recognized workers of the Christian Church. An essential
qualification of a bishop was that he should be "apt
to teach" (I Tim. 3:2). In his epistles to Timothy,
Paul was very explicit regarding the teaching ministry. The young bishop of Ephesus was commissioned not only to teach but to train teachers: "And
the things that thou has heard of me among many
witnesses, the same commit thou to faithful men,
who shall be able to teach others also" (II Tim.
2:2). Timothy was to be a teacher of teachers as
well as a pastor.

3. Paul's teaching methods

Paul used both the discourse and the discussion
method of instruction. A good illustration of the

discourse method was the teaching situation in the synagogue at Antioch of Pisidia (Acts 13:14-52). To many this would appear as a sermon, but a closer examination of the text reveals the teacher and his class taking as their theme "Jesus is the Christ." The teacher focused each point as he made it to this conclusion (Acts 13:23, 25, 27, 28, 30, 33, 38).

But before announcing his theme, which would not have been favorably received by his prejudiced pupils, like a good teacher, he first adapted himself to the situation. He made his point of contact with his Jewish constituency by presenting himself in their synagogue on the Sabbath day. Moreover, he sat down, as was the custom of all teachers of his time (Acts 13:14). But in order to engage their attention, he did the unusual thing of standing up and beckoning with his hand as a solicitous gesture. His first words were a sympathetic appeal, "Men of Israel" (v. 16). Later he used a similar endearing appellation, "Men and brethren, children of the stock of Abraham" (v. 26).

Not only did he arouse interest and hold undivided attention throughout the lesson, but what is significant, when he had finished he was invited to return the next Sabbath. In fact, his presentation was most effective. He had appealed to everyone, and consequently he received a remarkable response: "And the next sabbath day came almost the whole city together to hear the word of God" (v. 44).

The Epistle to the Romans may be regarded as a typical example of a teaching situation carried on by the discussion method. The theme "Justified by Faith" is undoubtedly one that Paul had taught again and again. Now he was writing to the church in Rome which he had never visited. It was only natural that he should put into writing the lesson that he would undoubtedly have taught had it been possible for him to be present in person.

Observe from a study of the first eight chapters of Romans the large number of questions that are asked. These are not to be regarded as rhetorical questions of the teacher, but rather inquiries from members of the class. Paul seems to imagine himself face to face with a group with whom he discusses and answers arguments that are raised in the course of his instruction. He permits the class to divert his attention from a direct discourse in order to reply to inquiries and objections.

Paul's influence on early education has been summed up by Seeley in *History of Education:*

> The apostles and Church Fathers were foremost in all educational matters. They caught the spirit of the Master and sought to instruct the head as well as the heart. Men like Paul, Origen, Chrysostom, Basil the Great, and Augustine did much good not only in building up the Church, but in promoting education, the chief handmaid of the Church.

III. The Large Use of the Catechetical Method

That the teacher was the central figure of the first century Church is suggested by the method they employed in imparting the message entrusted to them. It is hard for us to realize how successfully the apostles and their successors carried on by an oral ministry. Textbooks were unknown, and even the words and works of the Lord Jesus Christ were not committed to writing until thirty years after His resurrection. But the apostolic school was a burning expression of great personalities. The world's contact with their lives and not with their books made an indelible impression upon it. Nevertheless, the method employed for this indelible imprint must also be recognized as an important factor in the success of the early Church. While it is true that the catechumen was the object of the teacher's affection as well as his instruction, it may be said that the continent of Europe was a conquest of catechumens. The method of preparing the catechumen was of great importance. He was the evolution of the catechetical method of instruction in the early Church.

Many writers make no distinction between the interlocutory and the catechetical method; nevertheless, it needs to be pointed out that the former was distinctly Jewish and the latter Greek. The interlocutory method required as a prerequisite for admittance to the congregation in which there was a free-for-all discussion, thorough instruction in the home and in the school. This we have already seen was supplied by the parents and the primary school. When at the age of twelve the Jewish child became *bar mitzvah* (son of the law), he was admitted to the synagogue and was recognized as being sufficiently well qualified for hearing and answering questions. It was not unusual, then, that our Lord at the age of twelve was found in the temple engaged in a discussion with the doctors. It was the character of His answers and questions that aroused astonishment (Luke 2:46).

On the other hand, the catechumen had no early Christian education, and even if an adult, he had to pass through a period of instruction before he was admitted to the assembly. This was true of nearly all the Gentile converts except those who had previously become Jewish proselytes.

The catechetical, or question and answer, method closely followed the Socratic plan that was prevalent in the Greek schools. All of the Greek converts were familiar with it, and the well educated Christians received their secular instruction in this way. The Socratic method was based on the thought that instruction does not consist in imparting information to be stored in the memory, but in the development of ideas in the mind of the pupil. Beginning with that which was near and present to the senses, and proceeding by means of an interesting conversational method, it sought to permit the pupil at each step to discover for himself the new or added element of truth. In the Jewish training of the child, facts and truths were given to be memorized. The Socratic method led the pupil to discover these facts or truths for himself. This was done by means of skillful and appropriate questions which stimulated mental self-activity and led to independent thinking.

The period of preparation required two and sometimes three years. During the introductory period, the pupils were called *catechumens,* and the teaching itself *catechetical,* from the careful and systematic examination by which their progress in the faith was effected. The content of this instruction varied with the time of their discipleship. It advanced from the most simple principles of natural religion to the peculiar doctrines of the gospel.

When first admitted to the assembly they were called *hearers,* from the permission granted them to attend the reading of the Scriptures and sermons

in the church. Afterward, being allowed to remain
during the prayers and to receive the imposition of
hands as a sign of their progress in spiritual knowledge, they were called *kneelers*. Lastly, some short
time before their baptism, they were taught the
Lord's Prayer, were entrusted with the knowledge
of their creed, and were destined for incorporation
into the body of believers, receiving the title of *the
chosen*.

The Alexandrian school, perhaps the greatest of
all institutions of learning in the early Church, was
specifically known as a catechetical school. It was
a pattern to the churches in its diligent and systematic preparation of candidates for baptism. As a
simple and natural consequence of circumstances,
Christian teaching in this celebrated school very early
assumed the form of regular catechetical instruction.

Frequent conversation with educated pagans, often
philosophers and scholars, made it necessary to en-
trust the instruction of catechumens only to scholarly, educated Christians. Converted philosophers
were frequently chosen for this purpose. The discussions of these teachers were heard not only by
educated pagans, but also by Christians who wished
to have a scholarly exposition of Christianity. No pay
was given for the instruction, but rich catechumens
usually offered presents, though many teachers declined to accept them. The instruction was given in
the house of the teacher, where the students gathered from early morning until late at night. Taught
individually by means of the catechetical method,
the students received instruction beginning with the
Old Testament story of creation and continuing on
to the most practical details of the Christian life.

According to tradition, the Alexandrian school was founded by Mark the evangelist, but the first teacher we know with certainty to fill that office in this school, was Panataneus. He was followed by his pupil, Clement, who in turn was succeeded by Origen. As the Christian Church grew and came to have a larger place in the political control of towns and communities, the Bible became a part of the curriculum of the schools. When Gregory entered upon his work in Armenia, at the beginning of the fourth century, he adopted a compulsory system of Christian schools for the children in every city there. "It would seem," says H. Clay Trumbull, "that at that period, as also earlier, there were public schools for the training of both heathen and Christian children in the knowledge of the Scriptures, in Mesopotamia, Cappadocia, Egypt, and elsewhere." In all of these Christian schools, as in the earlier Jewish educational institutions, it was the Bible text itself which was the primary subject of study and teaching.

Thus it is clear that the early Church not only understood the purpose of the Great Commission, but carefully followed the method as well as the content of the instruction that was entrusted to it. The Church organized Bible schools far and near as a means of instructing its converts and of training its membership.

IV. Church Buildings Favored Teaching

The emphasis laid upon the catechetical plan was reflected in the type of churches built in that period. Instead of large auditoriums, the buildings were divided into apartments best suited for the interlocutory and catechetical plan of teaching. While there

was a considerable number of Jews admitted to the
churches, we have no record that synagogues were
used for the Christian assemblies. When the gospel
was proclaimed and the Christian leaders were
driven out of the Jewish sanctuary, they held their
gatherings in private homes. For instance, there is
reference to the church in Rome which met at the
house of Priscilla and Aquila (Rom. 16:3-5). Likewise the church of Laodicea was first held in the
home of Nymphas (Col. 4:15); while the church
at Colosse held its services in the commodious dwelling of the influential Philemon (Phile. 2). In these
smaller rooms every person present had an opportunity to ask and answer questions.

In times of persecution any place at all became
a place of worship—a field, a desert, a ship, an
inn, a jail, and a tomb. For a long period the cata-
combs of Rome were the church of the Roman congregation, the place of their teaching and their worship. It was not until the third century that independent church buildings, that is, edifices erected
or set apart for the services of the congregation,
existed. The frail character of these structures is
proved by the fact that during the persecution of
Diocletian, the famous church of Nicodinea was lev-
eled to the ground by the Praetorian guard in the
course of a few hours.

Not only were the church buildings such as to
favor the teaching ministry, but there is also direct
evidence that the preaching in this period was sub-
servient to the teacher. Paniel, in his pragmatic *History of Christian Oratory and Preaching,* says:

> Public edifying was a mode of instruction which arose
> from the familiar colloquy of members of the congrega-

tion. This method was the dialogue. The preacher was only one of the speakers, though the principal one. Several co-speakers prompted the chief speaker in his message. Even when the ministry was transferred to a special class, the right to join in the conversation was not wholly surrendered by the congregation.

This testimony from one whose purpose was to emphasize preaching is most important. As Dr. Trumbull says:

If the Christian Fathers felt the need of this interlocutory method of instruction in the pulpit and yet ignored it in the teacher's chair, they must have been as contrary-minded in their processes of instruction as Herodotus says the Egyptians were in their religious and social customs.

The free use of the question and answer form of statement which permeates the religious writings of the Christian Fathers shows how familiar this method was to them as an element in the ordinary teaching process. Like Paul in his Epistle to the Romans, they practically lived over a teaching situation in their writings.

V. Success Recognized by Great Leaders

1. Julian the Apostate

The Roman emperor Julian was a son of Constantius, the younger half brother of Constantine, the first ruler to give Christianity national standing. Julian was educated in the Christian faith, but he became an apostate, and the most conspicuous feature of his short reign was his attempt to restore paganism as a national religion. Not only were Christians excluded from all public offices, but the Church lost all of its privileges. It was bereft of support from the State, and in some cases even compelled to pay back what it had received in earlier times. The clergy was again made subject to taxation and conscription.

But the hardest blow was the school law. The emperor recognized that the continuation of Chris-tianity pivoted on the school idea. Therefore he or-dered that all candidates for the position of teacher should obtain the confirmation of secular authori-ties, that is, indirectly from the emperor himself. Such a law could not fail, in the course of time, practically to exclude Christians from the schools and from all higher education. Fortunately, Julian did not live long enough to seriously check the prog-ress of Christianity. But this action of the govern-ment was the highest testimony to the success of Christian teachers in bringing about the nominal ac-ceptance of Christianity throughout the Roman Empire. The great pagan critic Celsus asserted that Christianity was propagated most successfully among the young children in pagan homes, and Origen in his celebrated reply did not deny this insinuation.

2. The Church Fathers

The most outstanding of the Church Fathers rec-ognized the importance of the teaching ministry. Clement, the head of the Alexandrian school, testi-fied of his indebtedness to the teaching methods of his instructor. Origen, the representative scholar of his age, was a great teacher. He used the Socratic method of instruction, and one of his pupils thus speaks of his manner: "He probed my soul with questions." Eusebius says that Origen devoted him-self to the instruction of one pupil at a time. Augustine, perhaps the greatest of the Church Fathers, is credited with the saying that the pupil must be watched and questioned and carefully dealt with individually, so that he may be caused to know rather than merely to hear the truth.

As a summary of the evidences of Christian education in the apostolic period, consider the significant statements of Baron Bunsen, Philip Schaff and H. Clay Trumbull.

Baron Bunsen says in *Hippolytus and His Age*:

> The apostolic Church made the school the connecting link between herself and the world.

The counsels of Tertullian, the eminent Church Father, concerning the relation of Christian teachers to heathen literature while engaged in the work of popular instruction, are illustrative of this truth.

The survey of this period by the outstanding Church historian, Philip Schaff, is most significant:

> It is a remarkable fact that after the days of the apostles no names of great missionaries are mentioned until the opening of the Middle Ages. There were no missionary societies, no organized effort in the anti-Nicene age; and yet in less than three hundred years from the death of St. John the whole population of the Roman Empire, which then represented the civilized world, was nominally Christianized.
>
> To understand this astonishing fact we must remember that the foundation was laid strong and deep by the apostles themselves. Christianity once established was its own best missionary. It grew naturally from within. It attracted people by its very presence. While there were no professional missionaries devoting their whole lives to this specific work, every congregation was a missionary society and every member a missionary. Celsus scoffingly remarks that Christianity was brought first to women

and children. Women and slaves introduced it into the
home circle. The gospel was propagated by *living* preaching and by personal intercourse. By the end of the third
century the name of Christ was known, revered, and
persecuted in every province and every city of the empire.
Maximilian, in one of his edicts, says that almost all had
abandoned the worship of their ancestors for the new
sect. One-tenth of the population was Christian, or ten
million.

H. Clay Trumbull, in commenting upon this remarkable statement of Schaff's, says that this was
brought about "because the divinely approved plan
of child-reaching and child-teaching was adhered to
by the immediate successors of the apostles of our
Lord."

----

1. What passages in the Gospels reveal not only
   that Jesus regarded Himself as a teacher but was
   so recognized by others?
2. What evidences prove that the teaching ministry predominated in the early Church?
3. Why was Paul the most influential figure in
   human history?
4. How did Paul's training prepare him for the
   teaching profession?
5. What marks of a teacher did Paul reveal in his
   ministry?
6. State and illustrate the discourse method Paul
   employed.
7. Explain and give an example of his discussion
   method.
8. Distinguish between the catechumen and the
   bar mitzvah.

9. What was the difference between the interlocutory and the catechetical methods?
10. Describe the catechetical instruction of the Alexandrian school.
11. In what respect were the church buildings of the first centuries adapted for the teaching ministry?
12. What does Paniel say as to early public edifying as a mode of instruction?
13. What was Julian the Apostate's estimate of Christian education?
14. Give the testimony of Clement, Origen, and Tertullian regarding Christian education.
15. How does Philip Schaff explain the remarkable growth of the early Church?

3

EDUCATION IN THE DARK AGES

I T IS clear that the early Church was not unfaithful to its trust. Faithfully it carried out the requirements of the Great Commission. The missionary spirit has never since been as enthusiastic nor has the teaching ministry ever occupied as large a place.

But from the time that Constantine gave Christianity state recognition and Christians no longer were persecuted, this all-important task became more and more neglected. As the Church grew in worldly prominence and lost in spiritual life, it changed its instruction methods. "Teaching gained in proportion as ritualism lost," says DePressense, and conversely, teaching lost as ritualism gained. As long as instruction continued, Christianity kept spreading. The prime cause of decay so undeniably apparent in the fifth century was the lack of Christian nurture. The emphasis on rites and the reign of the papacy were the factors most largely responsible for the neglect of the reaching and teaching ministry.

When Gregory became Bishop of Rome in 590 he initiated a long line of popes. This was the beginning of the Dark Ages. While missionary work revived under Gregory's direction and the northern barbarians were made acquainted with the gospel, the Church was already dying at heart. The priesthood was declining into self-indulgence and incredible ignorance.

Although the councils issued decrees from time to time, requiring bishops and priests to establish schools, only a handful complied. In many instances the church leaders themselves were too ignorant to teach, even if they had had any desire to do so. The curse of illiteracy and indolence blighted the clergy, and there seems to have been no ambition or aspiration for self-improvement. The Archbishop of Rouen could not read. His brother, of Treves, had not been ordained. According to Robert Hastings Nichols, "It is not too much to say that throughout Europe those of scandalous and shameful life outnumbered those of worthy life. Not only ignorance and neglect of duty were frequent, but also luxurious living, gross immorality, robbery, and simony; that is, buying of clerical offices. This was the regular and recognized way of obtaining a bishopric, and for some bishoprics there was a fixed price. The wickedness and misery of the mass of men in these ages was appalling."

It was a world of corruption, war and ignorance. The ancient Greco-Roman culture had been wellnigh extinguished by barbarian invasion. Knowledge even of the most elementary subjects was the possession of only a few. One of the few bright spots in these Dark Ages was Charlemagne's revival of learning in the middle of this millennium.

The impotence of the Church is best shown by the rise and spread of Mohammedanism. It seems almost unbelievable that this counterfeit religion should have taken such deep root and spread with such amazing rapidity after the Christian Church had been sufficiently strong to conquer the Roman Empire. Had the Church leaders been as concerned about furthering the missionary movement in Asia and Africa as they were about determining whether Rome or Constantinople should have the primacy, all medieval history might have been changed. As it was, the Christian nations were obliged to resort to the sword in order to repel the Mohammedan invasion of Europe. The great decisive battle of Tours might never have been fought had the Africans been converted to Christianity before they contacted Mohammedanism.

Aside from the revival of learning under Charlemagne, there were two agencies which helped preserve through these Dark Ages the message and the methods of the apostolic Church.

I. The Persecuted Sects

One of the factors that characterized the Dark Ages was the large number of small groups which withdrew to inaccessible places where they could continue their Christian worship and instruction as they believed the Church had received it from the apostles. In fact, all that kept the New Testament truth from well-nigh universal deflection were these sects that adhered not only to the apostolic message, but also to their methods of instruction and training.

1. Albigenses

In the south of France was a congregation of believers who met apart from the Catholic Church. They were called Albigenses, from Albi, the district in which many of them lived. Pope Innocent III required of Count Toulouse, who ruled the province, that these heretics be banished. But this would have meant the ruin of the country, since the Albigenses were industrious workers. The result was a hopeless

political quarrel with the Pope, who in 1209 proclaimed a crusade against the count and his people.
A twenty-year crusade led by Simon de Montfort,
a military leader and a man of boundless ambition
and ruthless cruelty, changed the most beautiful and
cultivated part of Europe into a scene of unspeakable
horror and desolation. The Inquisition later finished
what the crusade of Simon de Montfort had left
undone.

Many of the Albigenses fled to the Balkan countries. Others were scattered throughout the neighboring lands, as the independent provinces of the
south were incorporated into the kingdom of France.
However, these people for several centuries were able
to maintain their faith through Bible instruction by
parent and teacher, and later, even though scattered,
made their contribution to the growing strength of
the Reformation.

2. Waldenses

In the Alpine valleys of Piedmont there had been
for centuries congregations of believers calling themselves Brethren. They came later to be known as
Waldenses, though they did not themselves accept
the name. They traced their origin back to apostolic
time. From the period of Constantine there had continued to be a succession of those who preached and
taught the Bible uninfluenced by the relations existing at that time between the Church and the State.
This accounts for the large groups of Christians
found in the Taurus Mountains and Alpine valleys
who were well established in the Scriptures and
free from the idolatry and other evils prevailing in
the Church. They considered the Scriptures both for
doctrine and church order to be binding for their

time and not rendered obsolete by change of circumstances. It was said of them that their whole manner
of thought and action was an endeavor to hold fast
the character of original Christianity.

For centuries these Brethren in the valleys had
been unmolested, but from the fourteenth century
on, their beautiful country was invaded and the people were required to negotiate with surrounding
rulers. To the Princes of Savoy, who had had the
longest dealings with them, they could always assert
without fear of contradiction the uniformity of their
faith from father to son, even from the very age
of the apostles. To Francis I of France they said,
in 1544, "This confession is that which we have
received from our ancestors, even from hand to hand,
according as their predecessors in all time and in
every age have taught and delivered." When they
came in contact with the reformers in the sixteenth
century they said, "Our ancestors have often re-
counted to us that we have existed from the time of
the apostles. In all matters, nevertheless, we agree
with you, and think as you think. From the very
days of the apostles themselves we have been very
consistent respecting the faith."

Apart from the Scriptures they had no special
confession of faith; and no authority of any man,
however eminent, was allowed to set aside the authority of the Scriptures. Throughout the centuries
and in all countries they confessed the same truths
and had the same practices. Regular individual reading of the Scriptures, regular daily family worship,
regular instruction of the children, and frequent conferences were among the most highly prized means
of maintaining their spiritual life. They valued edu-

cation as well as spirituality. Many who administered the Word among them had received a degree at one of the universities. Pope Innocent III bore a double testimony to them when he said that among the Waldenses, educated laymen undertook the work of teachers and preachers; and again, that the Waldenses would only listen to a man who had God in him.

The comparative peace of the Waldensian valleys was broken in 1380 when Pope Clement VII sent a monk as an inquisitor to deal with the heretics. In the next thirteen years about 230 persons were burned and their possessions divided between the inquisitors and the rulers of the country. In the winter of 1400 the scope of the persecution was enlarged, so that the Waldenses were required to take refuge in the higher mountains, where most of the children and women and many of the men died of cold and hunger. A bull of Innocent VIII gave authority to the Archdeacon of Cremona to extricate the heritage, and 18,000 men invaded the valleys. The Waldenses who were not destroyed were scattered throughout Europe; but, like the Albigenses, they rallied when the call of the Reformation sounded.

3. Lollards

A third group who held to the purity of the apostolic message and method was found in England. These people were given the derisive name of Lollards, which means babblers. It had not been the habit in England to persecute what was deemed heresy so violently as on the continent, but early in the reign of Henry IV the growth of this group reached such proportions that death by burning was decreed as a penalty.

John Wycliffe, the most eminent scholar in Oxford, became the leader of the Lollards. His translation of the Bible wrought a revolution in English thought. Wycliffe found writing and circulating popular tracts and organizing bands of traveling teachers and preachers to be the most effective means of spreading the teachings of Scripture. So great was his influence, all the power of his bitter enemies could not accomplish more than to drive him from Oxford to his retreat in Leutterworth, which became a center from which instruction and encouragement went out over the country. Although summoned to appear before the Pope, he refused, and his prestige was sufficient to prevent his enemies from turning him over to the Church of Rome. He died in peace in Leutterworth on the last day of the year 1384. Persecution followed, however, and his ashes were later unearthed and scattered to the winds by his enemies. But the preservation of the apostolic message and method by the Lollards was destined to be the foundation of the Reformation in England.

4. Hussites

One of the foreign students who listened to Wycliffe in Oxford was Jerome of Prague. He returned to his own city full of enthusiasm for the truths he had learned in England, and taught boldly the principal doctrines of the New Testament. One of his hearers was John Huss, theological director and preacher in Prague and confessor to the Queen of Bohemia. His sincere faith and striking abilities, with his eloquence and charm of manner, made him a natural leader among the people already prepared by the labors of the Waldensian teachers who had been before him.

The Pope, through the Archbishop of Prague, ex-communicated Huss, but the King of Bohemia and the majority of the people supported him and his teaching. Finally a council was called at Constance, which drew together an assemblage of ecclesiastical dignitaries and political rulers who were in session for three and one-half years. Huss was invited to be present and Emperor Sigismund gave him a safe con-duct, assuring him security from molestation if he would come. At the council, Huss was subjected to every kind of persuasion and ill treatment to in-duce him to retract what he had taught, but with humility and with rare courage and ability, he stead-fastly refused. Despite the imperial promise, he was seized and sentenced to be burned. Jerome of Prague soon followed the same fiery way.

The Hussites, however, had grown to such strength that under the leadership of Jan Zizka they carried on a vigorous and successful warfare. The Pope raised crusades against them, but the invading armies were utterly routed and the Hussites pene-trated and occupied all the surrounding countries.

With the death of General Zizka the Hussites lacked a military leader, and in a decisive battle of White Mountain they were completely defeated. Twenty-seven Protestant noblemen were publicly beheaded.

Murder and violence of every kind was let loose on the land. Thirty-six thousand families left Bo-hemia and Moravia. The population of Bohemia was reduced from three million to one million. Bohemian independence, that had been enjoyed while the Prot-

estants were in power, disappeared, but the Hussites maintained their faith elsewhere. Although most
of the writings of their leaders were burned, some
did escape. Among these was a work by Peter Chelt-
schizki, entitled *The Net of Faith,* which preserves
much of their teaching. He wrote:

> Nothing else is sought in this book but that we, who
> come last, desire to see the first things and wish to return
> to them insofar as God enables us. We are like people
> who have come to a house that has been burned down
> and try to find the original foundation. This is the more
> difficult in that the ruins are grown over with all sorts of
> growths, and many think that these growths are the foun-
> dation. It is much more difficult now to restore spiritual
> ruins so long fallen down, than to get back to the former
> state for which no other foundation can be laid than
> Jesus Christ, from whom the many have wandered away
> and turned to other gods and made foundations of them.

As the number of Hussites grew, increased
changes took place. Persons of education and position
decreased and the leadership passed from the simpler
brethren to the men of higher education. Hymn
writing and music flourished among them. Their
close adherence to the teaching ministry not only
explains the purity of their message but the success
of their movement.

Dr. Trumbull, in summing up the valuable contribution these outstanding groups made to the Reformation, says:

> It was not the pure liturgy, nor yet the faithful pulpit
> of the Waldenses, the Albigenses, the Lollards, and the
> Hussites, but the divinely appointed Bible school which
> was the distinctive means of their preservation from well-
> nigh universal deflection.

II. Monasticism

1. History

When Christianity became the official religion of the Roman Empire and worldliness crept into the Church, men conceived the idea of separating themselves from the materialistic atmosphere and retiring to secluded spots. They thought that they could best escape the temptations of the world by living a solitary life, and through consecration and self-denial increase their own holiness and godliness. Jesus taught denial of self, and many thought this was the way to obey His commands. No doubt these men were sincere and earnest and their intentions were genuine. But they forgot a fundamental truth—one must let his light shine to glorify his Father in heaven. They did not realize that to be a Christian one must be very much in the world though not of it. But so popular did this movement become that multitudes of people fled to sparsely settled localities where the climate was warm and their needs were few. Caves, dens, mountains, and deserts were thronged with thousands.

The earliest of these hermits was St. Anthony of Egypt, born in A. D. 257, and called the patriarch of monks. His life was a sample of others. At the age of twenty his parents died. He and his sister were left a fortune, but following Jesus' instruction, "Take therefore no thought for the morrow," he gave away all of his wealth. He lived on bread and water in a little hut, and spent his time in meditation and prayer.

The most perverted of the hermits were the stylites or pillar-saints, so named for Simon Stylites of Syria (A. D. 420). For thirty years he made his

home on a pillar sixty feet high, near the city of
Antioch, from which he preached to others. Thousands followed his example, and many of the pillars
were made even higher.

After the practice of these hermits had grown
into a mass movement, solitude was destroyed, and
we next find them organized on a social basis.
Cloisters were built and little colonies of hermits
lived under a single roof according to a rule or code
of law which brought about uniformity of life. The
monks ate, prayed, and worked together. Each house
was independent of every other. Those for the men
were called monasteries; those for the women were
called nunneries. Each house was under the direction
of either an abbot or an abbess.

2. Discipline

At first each monastery formulated its own rules.
But as the movement grew, the Church recognized
the importance of some standard of uniformity. In
529 Benedict, an ardent monk, drew up a set of
rules, and through the influence of the popes, these
were quite generally adopted. The distinctive feature of the Benedictine rule was insistence on manual
labor of some kind, added to the implicit obedience
which the monk was compelled to render to the
abbot in the performance of this work. Indolence
was termed the enemy of the soul. To guard against
this, at least seven hours a day were to be given to
some kind of toil.

It is noteworthy that this Benedictine rule is the
first recognition of the value of manual labor in
education. From this provision came most of the social benefits of monasticism. It introduced new proc-

esses for craftsmen in wood, metal, leather, and cloth. It gave new ideas to the architect. It offered asylums to the poor, to the sick, the injured, the distressed. It drained swamps and improved public health and public life in almost every way.

The Benedictine rule also specified that two hours of each day should be devoted to reading. It indicated portions of the Bible and writings of the Church Fathers that were to be read each day, and through minute rules prevented these times for reading from being wasted in idleness, sleeping and talking. All these forms of discipline were for the sake of spiritual growth. It was thought that the latter could only be obtained by the discipline of the physical nature. As Paul Monroe states it: "The ideals of monasticism were usually summed up in the three ideals of chastity, poverty, and obedience, or more technically, conversion, stability, and obedience."

3. Education

Monasticism became in a larger sense an educational force of great importance to society as a whole. In fact, the monasteries were the sole educational institutions of that period.

a. Students

Every monastery either authorized indirectly or commanded directly the study of literature. "Love the study of the Scriptures and you will not love vice," was a common motto. The Scriptures, however, included all religious writings related to the Bible. Moreover, study was never an end in itself, but simply a disciplinary agent. The instant study became an end or a pleasure in itself, the very purpose of its introduction was negatived. To most

monks the study of the classical literature of Greece
and Rome represented distinctly the interests and
temptations of the world, the desire for such study
being distinctly hostile to the idea of asceticism.

b. *Schools*

Except for the self-improvement of the monks or
the training of those who wished to enter the cloister,
the monasteries in their early history made little provision for education in general. Boys not yet in their
teens were accepted and subjected to prolonged
schooling and discipline. This education was distinctly religious, and outside of these monastery
schools there was no opportunity for education.

But under Charlemagne the value of the monasteries as an educational agency was recognized and
some provision was made for the education of youth
not intended for monastic life. However, as Monroe
points out, "it was not until the eleventh century
that there was any education to speak of outside of
monastic schools, and not until the thirteenth century
were there any marked changes in the character of
education given in any institution."

Thus we see that the education of the Middle
Ages was under the Church, and therefore distinctly
religious. More than that, it was provided for comparatively few. The mass of people during these centuries was little more than barbarians, more interested in warfare and manual occupation than in mental discipline and literary accomplishments.

c. *Manuscripts*

Another important service of the monasteries was
the copying of Scripture manuscripts. Whether this
was entered upon as a form of monastic discipline

or through real interest in learning, it is nevertheless true that most of the writings of the past in
our possession today were reproduced in the cloister
to prevent their disappearance into oblivion.

Not only did the monks copy manuscripts, but
they collected them. While the majority of the monasteries possessed but few books and these were of
a strictly religious character, others made a business
of accumulating hundreds and even thousands of
volumes. The institutions especially noted for their
learning had large libraries and gave particular attention to the collection of books through the ex-
change of duplicates. But with the founding of universities and finally with the invention of printing,
monasteries ceased to give attention to this activity.

---

1. What conditions in the Church were responsible for the decline of Christian education?
2. Who were the Albigenses?
3. How did the Waldenses preserve the method as
   well as the message of the apostolic Church?
4. What was the contribution of Wycliffe and the
   Lollards to Christian education?
5. Describe the Hussite tragedy and its relation to
   Christian education.
6. Give Dr. Trumbull's tribute to the Bible instruction of these persecuted sects.
7. Give a brief history of monasticism.
8. Describe the discipline of the monasteries.
9. What was the character of the monastic
   schools?
10. What important contribution did they make to
    manuscripts?

4

THE MOVEMENT TOWARD UNIVERSAL EDUCATION

ATTENTION has already been called to the woe-ful ignorance that existed in Christendom dur-ing the Dark Ages. Simple and pure Christianity was almost unknown in Europe. According to W. J. Hea-ton, in *The Bible of the Reformation*, priests of eighty years of age were ignorant of quotations from Paul, and teachers of long standing had never seen the New Testament. We are told that Archbishop Maintz said of the Bible, "In truth I do not know what this Book is, but I perceive that everything in it is against us." When Hooper was bishop of Glou-cester, he found that out of 311 of his clergy, 168 were unable to repeat the Ten Commandments. Thirty-one did not know where to find them. Forty could not tell where the Lord's Prayer is to be found and thirty-one did not know the Author.

Instead of advocating education, the popes were busy hunting and murdering the Waldensian believ-ers. John Huss and Jerome of Prague were martyred as by barbarians. The monasteries were filled with the timid, the lazy and the disappointed. The pulpit was largely given up to what was fanatical, ridicu-lous or political, and in many parts scarcely employed at all. The whole ecclesiastical system was used mainly either for money-getting or the gaining of secular power.

But the light of learning was destined to penetrate the darkness. Already a great movement was going on in the life of Europe which was to produce some of the energy needed for religious revolution. Great geographical discoveries, among them those of Columbus, were made in the East and the West, and thus the true form and size of the earth were determined. Even more wonderful was Copernicus' discovery of the solar system, revolutionizing men's ideas of the universe in which they lived. The geographical discoveries produced a swift expansion of commerce and industry, and roused in the nations of Europe colonizing ambitions. In the sphere of politics, the new life showed itself in the rapid development of national life. Three important contributions prepared the way for a revival of interest in Christian education.

I. The Renaissance

The fourteenth, fifteenth and sixteenth centuries were the period of the Renaissance, or the revival of learning. One of the principal causes of this awakening was the bringing of the mind of Europe into contact with the culture and civilization of Greece and Rome, of which it was ignorant during the Middle Ages. The fall of Constantinople before the Mohammedan army, in 1453, drove what was left of classical learning into northern and western Europe. The itinerant scholars carried with them the knowledge of Greek, which for a century had been an unknown tongue on the continent. Thus all the wonderful world of classical thought, literature, and art was suddenly opened. The sight of it thrilled men and aroused them to great achievements. The works of the Renaissance in art and literature, which included some of the world's most precious possessions, thus received their inspiration.

The Renaissance affected Italy and northern Europe differently. The Italian received his main inspiration largely from ancient Rome and Greece, while the German centered his interest on Palestine, the birthplace of Christianity. The former was interested in self-culture and self-development which lead toward an extreme individualism, while the latter was interested in education as a means to social and religious reformation. In the south the movement was pagan and aristocratic. In the north it was Christian and democratic.

The German Renaissance is most frequently referred to as a reformation, and it must be recognized as the most important step toward the Reformation, if not the Reformation itself. It was a reformation in that it brought its adherents back to the three great and original principles of Christianity: the Bible is the sole authority for faith and life; justification is by faith alone; and the priesthood is composed of all believers. This reformation became a revolution when the Catholic Church refused to be reformed according to the principles of the apostolic Church, and half of Europe broke away from the papacy and formed the Protestant Church.

The study of Greek meant that men could now read the New Testament in the original and were not dependent upon the priests—and many of them, we have noted, could not read — to interpret the Scriptures. With the jubilant enthusiasm which marked all their study of ancient literature, many of the humanists, as the leaders of the Renaissance were called, entered into the study of the New Testament. They saw face to face the Christian Church of the apostolic period, and as they compared this with the existing ecclesiastical system, many of the humanists became ardent reformers. This took place especially in Germany, and also in France and England.

These humanists of religious purpose greatly strengthened the spirit of reform in the Church. They also prepared the way for Bible study, the result of which opened the eyes of men to the authority of the Word of God rather than that of the Church. Finally, says Robert Hastings Nichols in the *Growth of the Christian Church,* "the whole Renaissance movement, by its influence in opening and rousing men's minds and accustoming them to cast off old ideas and strike out into new paths, was a powerful forerunner of the coming change in religious ideas. Without it the Protestant Reformation could not have occurred."

Erasmus, the most brilliant scholar of the Renaissance, was interested only in its religious aspect. Aside from his translation of the Greek New Testament, he edited numerous editions and translations of classical authors and the Church Fathers, the most valuable of which is that of Jerome. In these writings Erasmus was in many points a precursor of the Reformation. His satire against ecclesiastical abuses and corruption of the day was keen and bold. He also made the Scriptures the standard of doctrine and life in the Church. "I am resolved," Erasmus exclaimed, "to die in the study of the Scriptures. In them I find my joy and peace." And in regard to the new learning of the time, he said, "The highest object of the

revival of philosophical studies will be to learn to be
acquainted with the simple and pure Christianity of
the Bible."

II. The Rediscovery of the Bible

The revival of the study of Greek made it possible for those who had long remained illiterate to
have an entrance into the literary works of earlier
days. The fact that the New Testament, if not the
entire Bible, had been copied in its original language
more than any other literary production gave it the
largest circulation among students. Then, as today,
the Bible was the best seller, but the profound ignorance of both priest and people and the opposition
of the Church made it a hidden Book.

Despite the fact that the reading of the Bible was
prohibited to the laity, and even the priests discouraged from using it, the revival of learning found
many making a study of its contents. It was this circumstance that started the great Reformation. The
Bible was no longer looked upon as a volume unsafe
because of its obscurities, but as a treasure invaluable
because of its divine message.

It is not surprising that when men began to read
the Bible they began to appreciate it. The Bible itself,
both as a religious manual and a literary work, is
an instrument of culture. From a literary point of
view the Bible is a remarkable book. Nearly every
department of literature is represented in its pages.
It contains the most important of all history. It explains the universe. And no other book is half so
useful in leading men toward their goal as moral and
religious beings, for it ministers strength in weakness,
restrains evil tendencies, gives comfort in sorrow,

unites us to God. With the Scriptures as a guide, the reformers traversed the preceding centuries and sought out an evangelical Christianity.

The use of the Bible as the ultimate source of religious truth renders general education a necessity, a fact that was clearly and forcibly presented by a distinguished French scholar, Michel Breal. He said:

> In rendering man responsible for his faith and in placing the source of that faith in Holy Scripture, the Reformation contracted the obligation of placing every one in a condition to save himself by reading and study-ing the Bible.

In this connection Erasmus said:

> I totally dissent from those who are unwilling that the sacred Scriptures translated in the vulgar tongue should be read by private individuals; as if Christ had taught such subtle doctrines that they can with difficulty be understood by a very few theologians; or as if the strength of the Christian's religion lay in man's ignorance of it. The histories of kings it were perhaps better to conceal. But Christ wishes His histories to be published as widely as possible. I would wish even all women to read the Gospels and the epistles of Paul. And I wish they were translated into all languages of all people. I wish that the husbandman may sing parts of them at his plow; that the weaver may warble them at his shuttle; that the traveler may, with their narratives, beguile the weariness of the way.

III. The Invention of Printing

In the town of Harlem, Holland, in 1420, a man named Lawrence Koster was amusing himself by cut-ting some letters on the smooth bark of a tree. It occurred to him to transfer an impression of these letters on paper. He thus reproduced two or three lines as a specimen for the amusement of his children. Here was the beginning of the important art of printing. An apparently accidental circumstance provided Koster the needed hint of cutting whole pages of letters on blocks of wood and transferring them on paper.

Johannes Gutenberg, however, was the first to seize upon this discovery of Koster's and put it to practical use. He actually began printing in 1450 at Maintz. He expended nearly all of his means on the invention and was about to abandon it in despair, when through the advice and assistance of John Faust, a wealthy goldsmith, he was enabled to proceed. Faust was of a more practical turn and less of an enthusiast than his co-laborer, and the two could not agree. Gutenberg withdrew from the partnership and Faust took in his place Peter Schoeffer, who discovered a readier method of casting the type, and also succeeded in making a good ink.

The first book to appear with a printer's name and date was the best loved portion of the Bible, the Psalms in Latin. Four years later a Bible was printed, which was also in Latin. In 1463 the first German Bible appeared. Considering the difficulties to be overcome in what was at first so prodigious an undertaking, the mechanical and literary excellence of these earliest printed volumes was a marvel. It was evident from the first appearance of the printed book that the days of manuscripts were ended. Not only were the number of copies multiplied, but from the first the price of the printed volumes was only about one-tenth that of the manuscripts.

It was the purpose of the inventors to obtain the full advantage of their discovery by keeping their work a secret, and in this they were successful for a period of five years. John Faust took several copies of the first printed Bible to sell in Paris. The King purchased one of these for 750 crowns. The Bishop of Paris purchased another for 300 crowns. The latter was so proud of his possession that he took it to the King, and they were both astonished to discover that with the exception of the hand engraving of the initial letters, the two copies were identical. Comparison with other copies sold in Paris still further added to the amazement. Faust was arrested and thrown into prison on the charge of being a magician, but later was released when his secret was revealed.

In 1462 the city of Maintz was taken by enemy forces and the seal of the mystery of printing was broken by violence. The workmen were scattered and a knowledge of the invention was diffused, so that it was not long before the printing press was doing its beneficent work in Holland, Italy and England. Thus in the middle of the fifteenth century were the means provided for the emancipation of thought and the universal enlightenment of men.

IV. The Discovery of America

Fully as important as the means for furthering education was the discovery of a place where it could thrive unhindered and unrestricted. This was not possible in Europe. Despotism had so choked the rising germ of liberty that there was little hope that the plant of political and religious freedom would ever come to any considerable maturity. Ecclesiastical

domination had so monopolized and trampled down
the rights of the individual that it seemed vain to
expect that Christianity, pure and undefiled, should
ever flourish on such a soil. The discovery of America, coming just as the Reformation was about to
dawn, was one of those leading acts of Providence
for the propagation and establishment of the truth.
As Hollis Read says in *The Hand of God in History*:

> When God would enlarge the theater on which to
> display the riches of His grace, He caused a spirit of
> bold adventure to move upon the face of the stagnant
> waters of Europe, which found no rest until it brought
> forth a new world.

The discovery of America happened at the pre-
cise time when the Protestant Church required a
new and enlarged field for her better protection
and for the more glorious development of her excel-
lencies. When the Western Hemisphere had become
sufficiently known and prepared to receive the products of Protestantism, the Reformation had done its
work, and yet the Church was but partially liberated
from the bondage of papal corruption.

America seemed signalized from the first as the
asylum of freedom. Nothing else would thrive here.
Ecclesiastical domination and political despotism
were transplanted on more than one occasion, but
never thrived. A comparison of the records of the
first settlements in Massachusetts and Virginia
clearly show that only the colonies which were
founded upon the principles of toleration and freedom were successful. In this new territory was to
come into existence a nation equal in extent to that
of all Europe exclusive of Russia and more than six

times larger than Great Britain and France together, and as large as China and Hindustan united. To this fair land has come a constant stream of immigrants from every portion of the globe. While the population of the world doubles every 168 years, that of the United States has increased twofold every 25 years.

The Bible was first printed in Europe, but it was the American Bible Society which made it possible for more copies of the Scriptures to be published in the English language than all other tongues combined.

However, it was not so much the offering of an asylum to the exiles of Protestantism or the multiplication of copies of the printed Bible that have constituted America's greatest contribution to the movement of universal education. It was in this land that the public school system was to originate and to establish a standard in education for the common people which other nations would later appropriate.

And while the Sunday School was to originate in Europe, it was destined to thrive most successfully in America. The popularity and prestige of this institution was to encircle the globe, until the Sunday School would come to be known as the greatest international and interdenominational agency for Christian education in the world.

———————

1. Give several illustrations of the woeful ignorance existing during the Dark Ages.
2. What was the Renaissance?
3. In what different respects did it affect Italy and northern Europe?

4. Who was Erasmus?
5. How was the Renaissance responsible for the rediscovery of the Bible?
6. What effect did the invention of printing have upon the Bible?
7. How did the discovery of America affect Christian education?

THE REFORMERS' ATTITUDE TOWARD CHRISTIAN EDUCATION

THE RENAISSANCE in the North was distinguishable from the Reformation only in its spirit and its outcome. Its concern for social reform of morals and religion brought about a combination of mental enlightenment and religion which resulted in far-reaching changes. The Reformation leaders themselves recognized that the doctrines of Scripture contained inherently the right of liberty of conscience and the duty of interpreting the Scriptures according to one's own reason. The Reformation educators accepted the humanistic curriculum of the Renaissance, though they used it for a purpose different from that of the early humanistic educators. They heartily supported the revival of classical learning because study of Greek and Latin was essential to a knowledge of the Scriptures in the original language. Consequently this study became the immediate purpose of Protestant education and found a prominent place in Protestant schools. The curriculum received a profound religious bias in a variety of ways, but the Bible was used as a text, and the entire work of the school was directed to catechism, creeds, and expositions of Scripture.

One of the great educational influences of the Reformation was the establishment of a school system based upon the idea of universal education. The

basis for all such systems is found in the Protestant
doctrine that the material and spiritual welfare of
every individual depends upon the application of his
own reason to the revelation contained in the Bible.
Consequently the ability to read the Scriptures in
the vernacular, and the necessity for studying them
in the original, demanded not only elementary but
higher educational institutions for universal instruction.

This movement for the education of all classes only
succeeded in part. Owing to the tireless efforts of
Martin Luther, the public school became more of a
reality in Germany than in any of the other Protestant countries. Even then the failure of the reformers to prepare teachers limited the extent of the movement. The Catholics, who were quick to see this
weakness and to make adequate provision for the
teaching ministry, as we shall observe in another
chapter, were able to profit more in the general movement of restoring the apostolic methods of the first
century. Had the reformers concerned themselves
as much with training teachers as they did with preparing catechisms, universal education for religious
purposes would have been attained centuries earlier.

That the reformers believed in the importance of
reviving the neglected teaching ministry of the
Church is evident from the many references they
have made to this movement in their writings. The
Reformation and counter-Reformation movement
of the Catholics produced many great educators and
leaders. In fact, it was in consequence of the character of the later Renaissance movement that all the
religious leaders seized education as the chief instrument for bringing about the reforms which they de-

sired. On the Protestant side, the great leaders were Martin Luther and Philipp Melanchthon, and in a less important way, John Calvin, Ulrich Zwingli and John Knox.

I. Martin Luther

The ablest writers of modern times—historians, philosophers, theologians and poets—have eulogized the character and work of Martin Luther. His life kindles admiration. A man among men, yet towering above them, an epic hero who was unapproachable in greatness, holding the destiny of nations in his hands, he was strong and steadfast in God. In the words of Thomas Carlyle, "I will call this Luther a truly great man; great in intellect, in courage, affection and integrity. One of the most lovable and precious men."

As in almost everything else, Luther was great in industry. His writings fill twenty-four folio volumes. With his life filled with practical duties, it is almost incomprehensible how he could accomplish so much with his pen. The secret lies in his tireless industry that allowed no moment to escape unimproved. His interest in education is evident from the many references he made to it in his writings.

As early as 1524 Luther made an energetic appeal to the authorities of the German cities in behalf of popular education. According to Dr. F. V. N. Painter, in *Luther on Education,* "Education remained through Luther's whole life a cherished interest, and he has treated of it in many sermons and letters. There is scarcely any phase of the subject that he did not touch upon, and everywhere he exhibited masterly penetration and judgment."

1. Parental instruction

Luther recognized the responsibility that the Bible places upon parents for the instruction of their children. "Married people," he says, "should know that they can perform no better and no more useful work for God, Christianity, the world, and themselves, than by bringing up their children well. It is the big work of parents, and when they do not attend to it, there is a perversion of nature as when fire does not burn or water moisten."

Not content merely with reminding parents of their duty, the great reformer with intense earnestness urged them to its performance. In his *Large Catechism* he says:

> Think what deadly injury you are doing if you be negligent and fail to bring up your child to usefulness and piety, and how you bring upon yourself all sin and wrath meriting hell even, in your dealings with your own children, even though you be otherwise ever so pious and holy. And because this is disregarded, God fearfully punishes the world so that there is no discipline, government, or peace, of which we all complain. But do you not see that it is our fault, for as we train them, we have spoiled them and they became disobedient children and subjects.

Luther even went so far as to contend that persons should not marry until they were competent to instruct their children in the elements of religion. He says:

> No one should become a father unless he is able to instruct his children in the Ten Commandments and in the Gospels, so that he may bring up true Christians. But many enter the state of holy matrimony who cannot

say the Lord's Prayer; and knowing nothing themselves, they are utterly incompetent to instruct their children. Children should be brought up in the fear of God. If the kingdom of God is to come in power, we must begin with the children and teach them from the cradle. See to it that you first of all have your children instructed in spiritual things, giving them first to God and afterward to secular duties.

2. Public schools

Luther recognized that after the instruction of parents, that of the public school comes next in importance. His convictions in this matter may be judged from the following exclamation:

It is indeed a sin and shame that we must be aroused and incited to the duty of educating our children and of considering their highest interests, whereas nature itself should move us thereto, and the example of the heathen affords us varied instruction. In my judgment, there is no other outward offense that in the sight of God so heavily burdens the world and deserves such heavy chastisement as the neglect to educate children.

Luther also recognized that public schools were necessary for the success of the Church. By imparting Christian training to children, by training teachers and parents, and by fitting ministers to preach, educational institutions greatly forwarded the work of the Church. "When schools prosper," he said, "the Church remains righteous and her doctrines pure. Young pupils and students are the seed and source of the Church. If we were dead, whence would come our successor if not from the schools. For the sake of the Church we must have and maintain Christian schools."

The great reformer also recognized the importance
of religious education for the future of the State.
He said:

> There is nothing more necessary than to educate men
> who are to succeed us and govern. I maintain that the
> civil authorities are under obligation to compel the people
> to send their children to school, especially such as are
> promising. If the government can compel citizens to serve
> for military activities, how much more has it a right to
> compel the people to send their children to school.

From these statements it would seem that Luther
was the forerunner of compulsory education as we
have it today. He clearly realized that the fundamental principles of Protestantism could only be
maintained by popular education and thence it was
necessary for the State to make it compulsory if it
were to be universal.

Luther was gifted perhaps beyond any other man
of his time as an effective preacher. His wide range
of knowledge and experience made him exhaustless
in ideas, while his intense fervor and emotion set
forth his thoughts with tremendous force. But despite his ability and eloquence as a preacher, he
highly esteemed the office of teaching. He wrote:

> If I were to give up preaching and my other duties,
> there is no office I would rather have than that of school
> teacher, for I know that next to the ministry it is most
> useful, greatest and best. I am not sure which of the two
> is to be preferred. It is hard to make old dogs docile. Yet
> that is what the ministry works at, and must work at in
> great part in vain. Young trees, though some may break
> in the process, are more easily bent and trained. There-
> fore, let it be considered one of the highest virtues on
> earth faithfully to train the children of others, which duty
> but very few parents attend to themselves.

Perhaps Luther had in mind Paul's injunction to Timothy that the young preacher should be "apt to teach." At any rate he said:

I would I knew one chosen for a preacher who had previously been a school teacher. But at the present time our young men want to become preachers at once and to avoid the labor of school keeping. Yet the schoolmaster is as important to a city as a pastor. We can do without mayors, princes and noblemen, but not without schools, for these must rule the world.

II. Other Reformers

1. Philipp Melanchthon

Melanchthon is called the preceptor of Germany, since as a contemporary of Luther he was to educational reform what the great Protestant leader was to religious revolution. However, he was an outstanding Protestant leader, so that the educational reforms coincided closely with the work of Luther. The influence of the great German schoolmaster was widespread, and at his death there was scarcely a city in the entire country that had not modified its schools according to his program of learning, or that did not number some pupil of his among its teachers. For the last forty-two years of his life Melanchthon labored in the University of Wittenberg. Through his influence, this great school was soon remodeled along Protestant lines and became the model of many new universities of Germany. Thousands of students enrolled in Wittenberg, who in turn went out as teachers, carrying his ideals wherever they went.

This great educator's contact with the individual pupil was mainly through his many textbooks. The Greek grammar which he prepared when only a lad of sixteen years became the universal text for German schools, and his Latin grammar of later years was equally popular. Texts in rhetoric and ethics were similarly useful in the lower schools, while his theology became the study for Protestant universities and higher schools. His pedagogical writings consisted chiefly of inaugural addresses or lectures to students, and are of importance as indicating the content and spirit of the Protestant revival in education.

2. John Calvin

John Calvin shared Luther's view of the duty of the Church to instruct the young and the ignorant by interlocutory teaching. His greatest contribution was the catechetical lesson helps or lesson guides which he prepared, first in French and later in Latin. One of his tenets was that children must be carefully trained in the home by the parents and must attend the Sunday School noon catechetical classes. He also urged that the children be taught to sing the songs of the Church in order that they might lead in the congregational singing. He insisted that they should be trained not only in sound learning and doctrine, but also in manners, good morals, and common sense.

Like Luther, Calvin believed that the work of the Reformation could not be conserved unless 'there was a systematic program of reaching and teaching the young. Because of his emphasis upon education, Calvin is sometimes called the father of our public school system. His catechetical helps were widely used, and formed the basis of the *Heidelberg Catechism* prepared by Ursinus, and the *Westminster Catechism* of England.

3. John Knox

The leader of the Reformation in Scotland, when engaged with his constructive plans for the Protestant churches, clearly recognized the value of religious training for children and young people. In his *Book of Discipline* he says that the minister must take care of the children and the youth of the parish, instructing them in their first rudiments, and especially in the catechism.

Knox seems to have been the first to recognize the possibilities of religious education on Sunday, for he says that Sunday must "straightly be kept" in all places and attendance at morning worship shall be carefully observed. And then adds that in the "afternoon the young children must be publicly examined in their catechism in audience of the people, and in doing this the minister must take great diligence to cause the people to understand the questions propounded, as well as the answers, and the doctrine that may be collected thereof."

Like Luther, Knox also realized the importance of parental instruction. "Every master of a household," said he, "must be commanded either to instruct, or else cause to be instructed, his children, servants and family, in the principles of the Christian religion."

4. Ulrich Zwingli

The leader of the Reformation in Switzerland was also friendly to the indoctrinating of children. *The Christian Education of Youth,* which he prepared for publication, formed his main connection with education. He was not an iconoclast, but believed that when the truth entered the consciousness of the people, evil practices would fall into decay. His faith-fulness and courage and dependence upon the Scrip-tures for authority, led the people step by step in reform.

When it was evident that the Protestants would some day have to fight for their faith, efforts were made to unite the followers of Luther and Zwingli in a defensive league. An obstacle appeared in Luth-er's objection to certain of Zwingli's doctrines. In the hope of getting rid of this, a conference of the two leaders and some of their friends was arranged. The two reformers agreed on fourteen out of fifteen articles, stating the chief matters of the Christian faith, but differed on the doctrine of the Lord's Supper. Here began the Lutheran and Reformed Churches, the first of the many divisions of Prot-estantism.

Despite these denominational differences and vari-ances because of national peculiarities, however, it is important to observe that Luther in Germany, Calvin in France, Knox in England, and Zwingli in Switzerland were wholly united in their insistence upon the responsibility of the home, the school, and the Church for the Christian education of the children.

III. The Reformers' Catechisms

The reformers' greatest contribution to Christian education was their catechisms.

1. Lutheran

Moved by the great ignorance he discovered dur-ing his visits to Saxony churches, Luther prepared, in 1529, two manuals of doctrine, which in three or four decades reached a circulation of 100,000. The

Small Catechism grew out of his pastoral use of catechetical materials and was the result of thirteen years
of strenuous labor. At the recent four hundredth
anniversay of the appearance of this remarkable publication, it was announced that next to the Bible,
this is the most widely circulated and translated book
that has ever been published.

Luther was not alone in treasuring this little book,
for a great chorus of praise has been rendered in its
honor. The high estimate of this work has been well
expressed in the following:

> If Dr. Luther in the course of his life had accom-
> plished no other good than the introduction of his two
> catechisms into the homes, schools and pulpits, and the
> restoration of prayer before and after meals, when we
> lie down to sleep and when we rise again, the whole
> world could never sufficiently thank him or repay him.

In one of the prefaces to the *Small Catechism*
Luther says:

> This little work has been planned and undertaken in
> order to furnish a course of instruction for children and
> the simple-minded. The young should be thoroughly in-
> structed in the parts which belong to the catechism or
> instruction for children, and should diligently exercise
> themselves therein.

Luther did not contemplate a mere lifeless memorizing of the doctrines of the catechism, but a practical and intelligent instruction that would bear fruit
in every-day life. He seems to have been familiar
with the Socratic or question method as a means
of awakening the mind and impressing the truth,
and in this respect had a proper understanding of
the catechetical method that was so successfully em-

ployed in the early Church. This can be inferred
from his urging instruction for children not "simply
that they may learn and repeat words by heart, but
be questioned from article to article and show what
each signifies and how they understand it." He recommended that in the explanation of his catechism
many illustrations be drawn from the Scriptures.
This would also suggest that he did not intend that
the catechism should become a substitute for the
Bible, as unfortunately was the case in later years.

2. Anglican

This catechism was first published in 1549 as a
part of the first prayer book of Edward VI. The
Book of Prayer was prepared under the direction
of Archbishop Cranmer of the Church of England.

The outstanding characteristic of this catechism
is its simplicity. Unlike the one by Luther, which
begins with the Decalogue, this begins with the child
and moves outward. Its first question is, "What is
your name?" and the second, "Who gave you your
name?" In this simple manner, the child is led into
a comprehension of the Apostles' Creed, the Ten
Commandments, the Lord's Prayer, and the sacraments.

When compared with the other catechisms, the
Anglican is simple and meager, but a knowledge of
its contents was required as a prerequisite of full
church membership. Later, the Anglican Church prepared a larger work which was much more comprehensive.

3. Heidelberg

Even more elaborate than the Lutheran is the
Heidelberg Catechism, which appeared in 1563. It

has been widely used by the Reformed and Calvin-
istic Churches in many lands, having been translated
into almost every European language and into some
dialects of other continents. It is used by the German
Reformed and Dutch Reformed Churches of America, as well as by the Reformed Churches of Europe.
The first question is significant:

"What is thy only comfort in life and in death?"

The answer is:

> That I with body and soul, both in life and in death,
> am not my own, but belong to my faithful Saviour Jesus
> Christ, who, with His precious blood, has fully satisfied
> for all my sins, and redeemed me from all the power of
> the devil, and so preserves me that without the will of
> my Father in heaven not a hair can fall from my head;
> yea, that all things must work together for my salvation.
> Wherefore, by His Holy Spirit, He also assures me of
> eternal life, and makes me heartily willing and ready
> henceforth to live unto Him.

This question and answer suggests how personal
parts of this catechism are, and its individual warmth,
which is not found in the others. It is the most elaborate of the four catechisms and really serves as a
confession of faith.

4. Westminster

More than a century after Luther's catechism,
and nearly one hundred years after the preparation
of the Anglican and Heidelberg confessions, the
Westminster Catechism appeared (1643-1648).
While the earlier manuals of doctrine were more
directly the work of the reformers, this catechism
had the advantage of being prepared by a group

of able divines who drew largely from the doctrinal contributions of the earlier Protestant leaders.

Five years were spent on the work, and it is recognized as the ablest of all catechisms, being severely logical and theological. It lacks the personal warmth of the Anglican and the Heidelberg, but it begins with God and puts Him at the center, making the sovereignty of God and the authority of the Bible its great central theme.

The first question is, "What is man's chief end?" The answer is, "Man's chief end is to glorify God and to enjoy Him forever." The second question is, "What rule hath God given to direct us how we may glorify and enjoy Him?" The answer is, "The Word of God, which is contained in the Scriptures of the Old and New Testaments, is the only rule to direct us how we can glorify and enjoy Him."

The fourth question, "What is God?" proved the most difficult for the divines to answer. For days they deliberated. Then they decided to pray. One of their number began, "O God, Thou who art a spirit, infinite, eternal and unchangeable in Thy being, wisdom, power, holiness, justice, goodness and truth." "Stop," cried several of the assembly, "that is the definition." And so it became the answer to the fourth question.

Dr. Philip Schaff, in his church history, characterizes these four catechisms as follows:

> The *Lutheran Catechism* is the simplest, the most genial and childlike; the *Heidelberg Catechism*, the fullest and richest for a more mature age; the *Anglican Catechism*, the shortest and most churchly, though rather meager; the *Westminster*, the clearest, precisest, and most logical.

1. What was the general attitude of the reformers toward Christian education?

2. Quote from Martin Luther's writings to show his belief in the importance of parental instruction.

3. What were Luther's convictions regarding public schools?

4. How did he compare teaching with preaching?

5. What did Melanchthon contribute to Christian education?

6. Why is Calvin called "the father of our public school system"?

7. Quote from John Knox's *Book of Discipline* some educational principles.

8. Who was Ulrich Zwingli?

9. Give the outstanding facts regarding the *Lutheran Catechism*.

10. Compare the *Anglican Catechism* with the Lutheran.

11. What was the *Heidelberg Catechism*?

12. In what respect was the *Westminster Catechism* distinct from the others?

13. Give Philip Schaff's summary of the four catechisms.

6

THE CATHOLIC COUNTER REFORMATION

THE PROTESTANT Reformation grew by leaps and bounds. It spread with great rapidity in northern Europe and made great inroads into the southern countries, but by 1575 this tidal wave began slowly to subside. The Church of Rome was at last able to check the progress of Protestantism and win back parts of Europe which it had lost. This Catholic reaction is called the Counter Reformation. The success of the Catholic Church was largely due to a new organization which sprang up when the Church stood at its lowest ebb.

I. Society of Jesus

This epoch-making organization was founded by Ignatius Loyola. Born in Spain, he became a page in the court of Ferdinand and Isabella. Later he served in the Spanish army, where he was wounded and made a cripple for life. During the days of tedious recovery, his mind turned to religious matters. In the hope of saving his soul, he adopted for himself the hardest discipline of monasticism. He fasted, prayed, and scourged himself. In the midst of these spiritual exercises, he gathered a few followers and founded an organization which was called the Society of Jesus. Its members bound themselves by a vow of death to lead lives of chastity and poverty.

This brotherhood flourished. It planted its chapters first in France, Italy and Spain, and then in all civilized lands. It soon became recognized as the chief opposing force of Protestantism. The faith and the self-denying work of the Jesuits served as an inner spark that set the whole anti-Protestant machinery in motion. The Jesuits revived not only intense opposition to Protestantism, but also a spirit that was willing to suffer and fight for its faith.

In churches which they established the Jesuits provided able preachers and attractive services. They also put new life into the public worship of the Catholic Church. The three principal methods of counteracting Protestantism were:

1. The Inquisition

This was a Church tribunal whose objective was to discover and eradicate heresy by torture. Penalties usually consisted of confiscation of property, imprisonment, exile or death. The government executed these sentences of the Church.

This terrible institution, which prevented Protestantism from gaining any foothold in Spain, was first established in Italy in 1542. Its success in that country led the Pope to extend its use to other provinces. In time it became a world-wide institution. The Catholics justified the use of instruments for inflicting pain on the ground that there was no salvation outside of their Church. The physical tortures prescribed were claimed to be absolutely necessary in order that the body might be kept in a sound condition.

But popish persecutions in the long run were no more successful than the pagan cruelties of the first centuries. Again the blood of the martyrs became the seed of the Church, and the Inquisition wrought a real benefit to Protestantism in that it weeded out those who were only nominal believers. The real success of the Jesuit Society lay in their

2. Missions

The greatest of the Roman Catholic missionaries were Jesuits. Missionary work fitted exactly into their great purpose to extend the Church over the world, and they threw themselves into it with bound-less zeal and heroism. Protestants were so busy defending their doctrines that they failed to include the Great Commission in their program of reformation. Their leaders did not seem to realize that Christians had a world-wide responsibility. As a matter of fact, Protestantism did not get its missionary vision until the eighteenth century.

The Jesuits were quick to observe this neglected ministry which the early Church had furthered with such fervor. A great new field for Christianity to conquer was opened by the discoveries in North and South America, as well as the invasion of the Orient. One of Ignatius Loyola's first companions was Francis Xavier. In the year the society was founded he went to India, and from there to Japan. His methods were virtually those of medieval missionaries. He demonstrated an apostolic desire for the salvation of men and apostolic devotion in laboring for it. In going through the streets of India he would ring a bell and entreat parents to send their children to him to be instructed. Such a large place did the religious education of the children hold in his estimation, that he is credited with saying, "Give me the children until they are seven years old and anyone may take them afterward."

In the two and a half years that Xavier labored in Japan he founded more than two hundred churches and baptized 150,000 persons. So permanent was this work, that though an era of persecution and martyrdom extending over several centuries followed, descendants of these Catholic converts of Xavier were discovered when Western nations were once more permitted to enter Japan in 1854. From Japan Xavier started for China, but died before he could enter that country. Other Jesuits established Christianity in this part of the Orient, while large numbers went to North and South America.

In fidelity and courage and sacrifice no missionaries have ever surpassed the French Jesuits, who worked from the mouth of the St. Lawrence River, along the Great Lakes, and thence to the mouth of the Mississippi River. Many cities, rivers and lakes in the United States and Canada bear names of these Jesuit pioneers. While Roman Catholic historians admit that much of their work was not conserved, nevertheless the zeal and heroism of many of these men are a precious legacy to the whole Christian Church.

3. Education

The Jesuits' most successful method of counteracting Protestantism was their educational work. Jesuit leaders evidently recognized the large place the Christian schools of the early centuries had in breaking down the pagan religions of Rome. At any rate, they gave much attention to educational work.

Schools for children were opened, which were

soon crowded because good teaching was given free. They provided not only religious but also the most thorough secular education of the times. So successful did they become that they drew pupils even from Protestant communions. The pupils were primarily trained to be devout Roman Catholics, and through the children the Jesuit teachers worked on the parents. By this means large districts in Germany were won back from Protestantism.

The superiority of the Jesuit schools lay in the fact that they all maintained a high standard and at the same time were a unit in the subject matter of their teaching. Much was made of the principle of apperception, each day's session beginning with a review of the previous one. Each week closed with a review, and each year with a review of the year's work. Each class was divided into groups presided over by decurions, to whom the boys recited under the general supervision of the master. Another division placed one boy over against another as a rival, to be a corrective and an incentive to his companion. The larger division of the class devoted itself to discussion concerning points of the lesson. The entire program was based upon the principle that it is much better to give a small amount in a thorough manner, than to give an indefinite impression of a large quantity of information. While from a modern view this instruction was not broad, it was very thorough and very effective; and since the purpose of the Jesuits was primarily to indoctrinate with a love and devotion to the Church, the curriculum was not necessarily extensive. According to Monroe:

> While the Jesuit teachers wrote many textbooks and texts even yet used to a considerable extent, the charac-

teristic method for all classes was the oral one. Herein lay one other explanation of their success, for it put the teacher and pupil in such close personal contact that it gave to their schools a molding power beyond most others. Next to this personal interest and oral method was the principle of thoroughness underlying all their work. Each day's work for the lower classes was practically one recitation—but three or four lines were given for the day's work for these lower classes. Then frequent reviews were given.

Another important feature of the Jesuit schools was the education that they gave to the preparation of the teachers. The faculties were made up for the most part of those who had passed through the rigid course of the lower and usually of the superior college, while the permanent teachers who directed the work of the student instructors were trained through a long university and normal career. Those best adapted for teaching were selected for this permanent service. Jesuit teachers thus were far superior to any of their contemporaries, and they not only commanded the Catholic universities, but also found their way into such schools as received State support. Not until the rise of the normal school in the nineteenth century did either the State or the Church give such careful attention to the preparation of teachers.

Thus it was through superior teaching that the Jesuits in a single generation, according to the testimony of one of their chief historians, "became masters of the present by the men whom they trained, and directors of the future through the children who were young in their hands, realizing a dream which no one until the time of Ignatius Loyola had dared to conceive."

II. The Council of Trent

The Council of Trent went into session in 1545 and continued its conferences for eighteen years. It not only gave the Church a complete statement of its doctrine, which it had never possessed in the Middle Ages, but it also reorganized its church system of government to make it more efficient, and removed some of its worst evils. But its greatest work was the program of education that was adopted. The clergy, whose illiteracy and ignorance had been notorious, were henceforth to be educated. There was to be stricter discipline, more pastoral care of the laity, and more constant and helpful oversight of the clergy by the bishop. An official statement of faith, constituting the *Catholic Catechism,* was published in 1566. The liturgy was revised and arrangements were made for a new edition of the Latin Bible.

The Council of Trent recognized the peril to the Church of Rome through the Protestant use of catechetical teaching. "The heretics have chiefly made use of catechisms to corrupt the minds of the Christians," was the declaration of that council. To counteract this educational effort all priests were specifically charged by the Council of Trent with the duty of instructing the young in the primary elements of the Christian faith.

In consequence of this ruling, we find that many outstanding prelates zealously devoted their energies to the apostolic method of child-reaching and child-teaching. Bishop Carlo Borromeo of Milan, who presided over a diocese of 1,220 churches and 170 monasteries, gave himself largely to gathering and teaching children in his great cathedral. At his death, in

1584, 743 schools with more than three thousand teachers and forty thousand pupils had come into existence as a result of his vision of apostolic success.

In a similar manner Cardinal Bellarmine, while Archbishop of Capua, not only distinguished himself by his writings, but set an example to his under-pastors by going personally into the parishes and gathering the children about him for instruction. Not only his works on theology, but his simple catechisms have continued in use as the approved textbook of the Church of Rome down to the present century.

III. The Catholic Gains

At a time when it seemed that the triumph of Protestantism would sweep Romanism from the face of Europe, the counter Catholic movement not only checked the advance, but systematized and consolidated the efforts of the Church of Rome, so that it has ever since continued to be numerically superior to those who have taken only the Bible as their authority.

When the Jesuits entered Belgium in 1542, it was only half Protestant. A century later it was exclusively Roman Catholic. While the Protestant Church pushed its outposts farther into the Netherlands, in Germany the counter Catholic movement succeeded in producing a reaction which actually turned back the current of the Reformation. The influence of the Jesuit teachers was so successful in the Catholic universities that it counteracted the prestige of the Protestant universities of Wittenberg and Geneva, and other schools were greatly admired on account of the consistent method of the teachers and the sure progress of the pupils. As mentioned above, even Prot-

estants sent their children there, and through his
pupils the Catholic teacher noiselessly penetrated into
the Protestant family with fasts, rosaries and ritual-
istic worship dear to the heart of Rome. Austria,
Syria, Carinthia, Bavaria, into which the Reformation had made large inroads, were made solidly Catholic. In Poland the same thing occurred. In fact, the
Catholics regained whole countries that seemed to
have been lost.

Noah Porter, in his *Educational Systems,* declares
that Catholic and Protestant historians are agreed
that it was the religious school machinery of the Jesuits that arrested the Reformation in its onward and
apparently triumphant advances, and fixed the dividing line between Protestant and Catholic Europe, so
that it remains today almost exactly where it was
thirty years after Luther had broken with Rome.
As H. Clay Trumbull says, "It was particularly by
the Sunday School agency that the Protestant reformers hoped to make permanent the results of the
Reformation, but it was by a more adroit and efficient use of the Sunday School agency in its improved forms that the Church of Rome stayed the
progress of the Reformation. That is the plain lesson
of history."

To this day, the emphasis the Church of Rome
places upon the parochial school is evidence that she
has never forgotten the lesson learned in that crisis
hour of her history. According to statistics released
by this the greatest of all Christian denominations,
19 per cent of the world's religious population today
is Catholic, 16 per cent Confucianist, 13 per cent
Mohammedan, 12 per cent Hindu, 11 per cent Budd-
hist, 9 per cent Protestant. The Church of Rome has

proclaimed a corrupt apostolic message, but it has practiced a correct apostolic method.

---

1. What was the Society of Jesus?
2. Show why the Inquisition was an effective instrument.
3. Compare the Catholic and Protestant attitude toward the Great Commission.
4. Describe some of the activities of Francis Xavier.
5. What evidences are there of Jesuit trails in America?
6. Wherein lay the superiority of the Jesuit schools?
7. To what does Monroe attribute their success?
8. What was accomplished at the Council of Trent?
9. Enumerate some of the Catholic gains through Jesuit schools.
10. Give quotations from Porter and Trumbull as to the far-reaching effect of the Catholic Counter Reformation.

EARLY EDUCATION IN AMERICA

I T HAS already been observed in preceding chapters that the history of education during the Christian era is largely the history of the Church, and that while there were periods of profound ignorance and prevailing indifference to intellectual enlightenment, still what educational agencies there were, or those that were instituted, were sponsored by the Church.

The first schools in America were clearly echoes of the Protestant Reformation in Europe. The reformers had insisted upon a knowledge of the Bible and an individual interpretation of its content as a means of personal salvation. This required that children should be taught to read, so that they might become acquainted with the commandments of God and learn what was demanded of them.

We err when we say that the Pilgrims came to America seeking religious freedom. To a certain extent they enjoyed that liberty in Holland. It would be more accurate to say that they came to America seeking an opportunity to give to their children the kind of religious education that was impossible either in England or Holland. From the landing of the Pilgrims in 1620 until the birth of the American Republic in 1787, there was scarcely any difference in secular and religious education. Nearly all the early settlers of America came from those lands which had embraced some form of Protestant faith, and most of them sought religious liberty that would give them larger political freedom than they had enjoyed in Europe.

I. Education in the Colonies

1. The first schools

The first settlers of America were almost entirely English-speaking people, and the vast majority of them were Protestants. Nevertheless, it is interesting to note that the beginning of education in America followed along three lines:

a. The apprentice plan

Since Virginia and the southern colonies were settled by the upper class of English society, it was natural that the wealthy should provide education through private tutors for their own children, and afford no better preparation than that of apprentice for the poor. Seventeenth century legislation in the southern colonies, as well as in England, required compulsory apprenticeship of the children of the poor. All were expected to be trained in a trade, and public authorities were delegated to provide opportunities for this type of education.

To show the indifference of these colonists from the upper class of England to the mental development of the masses, there is the recorded statement of Governor Berkeley, of Virginia, in 1671. When questioned concerning what action should be taken by the government in public education, he said:

The same course that is now taken in England out of town; every man according to his ability instructing his children. . . But I thank God there are no free

schools nor printing, and I hope we shall not have these
hundred years; for learning has brought disobedience
and heresy and sects into the world, and printing has
divulged them and libels against the best government.
God keep us from both!

William and Mary College, established in 1616,
was opened only to the limited few financially able
to pay tutors to prepare them for entrance examinations.

b. *The parochial plan*

The middle colonies were settled by such a variety
of nationalities that there was no common point of
contact for education. The parochial school concep-
tion of the Hollanders, Moravians, Mennonites, German Lutherans, Quakers, Presbyterians, Baptists and
Catholics was the only institution known, and of
course in these churches it received marked attention.
It carried over the idea of continental Europe, that
all educational effort should be controlled by the
Church. It resented State interference and was carried on only for Church purposes. Clergymen were
usually the teachers, and the instruction was limited
to reading, writing and catechism, rather than any
form of higher learning. The chief objection to the
parochial school then, as well as now, was that religious education was emphasized to the neglect of
intellectual development.

c. *The Puritan plan*

The longer the world stands the more profoundly
will it revere the character of the founders of this
nation. The principles so boldly proclaimed by
Luther and so logically and judiciously sustained by
Calvin became the standards of the Puritans. Puri-

tanism was the Reformation reformed. The principles which led to the settlement of New England were but the principles of the Reformation matured and advanced. Europe was sifted and her finest wheat was sowed in American soil. The American vine was the choicest slip of the Puritan flower that was already blossoming in England. The Puritans were few in number, but their influence was so powerful that it was destined to shape the educational policies of the new world.

Early New England was intensely religious as well as democratic. The people believed that education was essential to religion and that religion was the end of man. Their community was a small state under religious control. Hence a parochial school and a community school were identical. Dexter points out that "never since in the history of our country has the population as a class been so highly educated as during the first half century of the Massachusetts Settlement."

(1) *Massachusetts Bay school*

Fifteen years after the Puritans landed in the new world the Massachusetts Bay Colony in their town meeting took official action authorizing the first public school. The support of this school was at first voluntary, but a law passed in 1642 was the first American act toward State support of public schools. By this legislation, officials of each town were directed to ascertain from time to time if parents and teachers were attending to their educational duties, and if children were being taught to read and understand the principles of religion and the capital laws of the country. The officers were empowered to im

pose fines on those who failed to give proper instruction.

This ordinance, however, did not establish schools
nor direct the employment of teachers. It was the
legislation of 1647 which completely made the school
a tax supported institution. The preamble and decrees of this ordinance are interesting:

> It has been one of the chief projects of that old de-
> luder, Satan, to keep men from a knowledge of the
> Scriptures, as in former times, by keeping them in an
> unknown tongue, so that in these later times by persuad-
> ing from the use of tongues, so that at least the true
> sense and meaning of the original might be clouded by
> false gloss is of Saint-Seeming deceivers that learning
> may not be buried in the graves of our fathers in the
> church and commonwealth. The Lord assisting our en-
> deavors it is therefore ordered:
>
> First, that every township in this jurisdiction, after
> the Lord hath increased them to the number of fifty
> householders, shall forthwith appoint one within their
> town to teach all such children as shall resort to him
> to write and read; whose wages shall be paid either by
> the parents or masters of such children, or by the inhabi-
> tants in general.
>
> Second, it is further ordered that where any town
> shall increase to one hundred families or householders,
> they shall set up a grammar school, the master being
> able to instruct youth so far as they may be fitted for the
> university.
>
> If any town neglect the performance of the above
> one year, that every such town shall pay five pounds to
> the next school until they shall perform this order.

These laws reveal not only the large place that
religion occupied in the minds and plans of the Puritans, but also their fervent belief that the State had
a right to require communities to furnish schools un-

der penalty of a fine for neglect. The underlying purpose of this legislation was patriotic as well as religious. The child was educated not to advance his personal interests, but because the State would suffer
if he was not educated. The State did not assume the
responsibility for schools to relieve the parents, or
even because it was better equipped for this task
than the parents, but because it could thereby better enforce the obligation which it imposed.

(2) The dame school

The dame school was distinctly for beginners.
Some women who had obtained the rudiments of
education in youth earned a livelihood by imparting
to the children of the neighborhood the letters of the
alphabet and the simplest elements of reading and
writing, to prepare pupils for the school of the
three R's.

(3) The school of the three R's

As the Massachusetts Bay school was copied in
other parts of New England as the common school
of the community, it came to be known as the school
of the three R's, since reading, writing and 'rithmetic
composed the curriculum.

(4) Latin grammar school

In large communities provision was made for advanced students. The school took the boy from the
school of the three R's and prepared him for entrance
to college. Latin was given a large place in the curriculum, but other cultural subjects were included.
The large use of Latin was employed since this language was still recognized as the sacred dialect of
religious learning. In these schools the great teachers

of early time were found. These schools became the basis of that most typical American institution, the high school, and for a long period furnished the teachers in elementary schools.

(5) *The college*

The Puritans brought over their own pastors from England, but in order that their high ideals of an educated ministry might be continued, the first college was established within twenty years after the landing of the Pilgrims at Plymouth. In 1638, John Harvard, a young minister, died in Charleston, Massachusetts. Seven hundred fifty pounds and his entire library of three hundred volumes were given to found a school of advance study to qualify men for the Christian ministry. The first American college was immediately opened and named for its benefactor.

Not only was Harvard College the product of the Church, but likewise Yale in 1716, Princeton in 1747, King's College in 1754, and Rutgers in 1764. Their purpose, as the Yale charter expresses it, was to "fit young men for public employment in Church and State." An advertisement published in the New York papers announcing the opening of King's College plainly indicated the religious purpose for which these higher educational institutions were brought into existence:

> The chief thing that is arrived at in this college is to teach and engage children to know God in Christ Jesus, and to love and serve Him in all sobriety, godliness, and richness of life with a pure heart and willing mind, and to train them up in all virtuous habits and all such useful knowledge as may render them creditable

to their families and friends, ornaments to their country, and useful to the public weal in our generation.

All of these early institutions of higher learning adhered to the one purpose of training leaders to serve the Church. Half of the graduates of Harvard for the first hundred years entered the ministry, and the majority of the others became master teachers. The rules of government adopted at Harvard in 1642 give a clear understanding of the ideals of that day.

> Let every student be plainly instructed and earnestly pressed to consider that the main end of his life and studies is to know God and Jesus Christ . . . and seeing the Lord only gives wisdom, let every one seriously set himself by prayer in secret to seek it of Him.

While on the campus, students were obliged to converse in Latin, and all recitations were carried on in that tongue. Daily prayers were conducted at 6:00 A. M. and 5:00 P. M. and all students were required to attend.

2. The first textbooks

Textbooks were scarce and in the first schools it was necessary to make use of whatever books had been brought over by the colonists from England. Nearly all of these were religious in their general nature. The Catechism, Psalter, Testament and Bible were the only books that were to be found in the majority of New England homes, so that these constituted the main sources of instruction. In addition there were:

a. *The Hornbook*

This name was not derived from the nature of the contents, but from the form of the study material.

It was not a book at all in the modern sense of the word, but rather a piece of wood shaped like a paddle, bearing on the upper smooth side a printed sheet covered by transparent horn, from which the object derived its name. The printing consisted of the alphabet in large and small letters, the apostolic benediction, and the Lord's Prayer. The purpose of the *Hornbook* was to teach children the rudiments of reading in order that they might take up the Catechism and the Bible.

b. *The New England Primer*

The *Hornbook* was superseded in 1690 by a wonderful little volume known as the *New England Primer*. In the foreword of the twentieth century reprint by the publishers Ginn and Company is the statement that the *New England Primer* was one of the greatest books ever published. It went through innumerable editions, and reflected in a remarkable way the spirit of the age that produced it. It contributed perhaps more than any other book, except the Bible, to the molding of those sturdy generations that gave to America its liberty and its institutions. Its total sales have been estimated at three million copies.

Every home possessed copies of the *New England Primer,* and it was used both in the school and in the church, since the school masters drilled the children in the reading matter and catechism in the schools, and the people recited the catechism yearly in the church. Compared with the primers and first readers of today, its contents were limited and its illustrations crude, but no modern textbook will ever exercise the influence for good over children and adults as did this little religious reader of eighty-eight pages. It has been said that "it taught millions to read and not one to sin."

The contents of the primer included the alphabet, vowels and consonants, capitals and small letters, easy syllables for children, the Lord's Prayer, the Apostles' Creed, the Shorter Catechism, an account of the martyrdom of John Rogers, and a dialogue between Christ, youth and the devil. Eighty-seven per cent of the wonderful book was made up of selections from the Bible.

3. The first teachers

Attention has already been called to the fact that the best teachers in the early colonial days were employed in the Latin grammar schools. They were capable men, who had secured their education in England. Among these was Ezekiel Cheever, who prepared *Cheever's Accidence,* used as the principal textbook in the Latin grammar school for more than a century.

The meager pay in the elementary schools did not attract the comparatively few competent teachers of the day. The instructors therefore were largely graduates of the Latin grammar school, or college students and itinerant school masters. Academic qualifications were not considered nearly as important as religious faith, and before teachers could be licensed they were carefully examined as to their Christian experience. This was generally done by the minister, and every teacher was required to adhere closely to the tenets of his particular church and attend regularly all of its services. This illustrates what a large place religion occupied in determining the qualifications of a school teacher.

II. Education Under the Constitution

Up to the time of the Revolutionary War there was but one motive for maintaining schools—the religious motive. When the Constitution was adopted in 1777 no mention was made of public education, as it was still largely a private matter and generally under the control of the Church, in both Europe and America. The New England colonies were a notable exception to the common practice. However, the framers of the Constitution did take action upon the religious question, which had a far-reaching effect upon education.

The *First Amendment* forbade the establishment by Congress of any national religion, and thus guaranteed freedom of worship to all. The Tenth Amendment provided that the powers not delegated to the nation by the Constitution should be assumed by the respective states. The failure of the Constitution to make provision for education through this amendment passed on the responsibility to the jurisdiction of the states. This action was not only wise, but far-reaching, since the new Republic recognized the religious freedom of the individual as well as the sovereignty of each state.

Congress early showed its concern for public education by donating the sixteenth section of land in every township for the maintenance of schools within that township. That religious interest motivated this action is evident from the reading of the Ordinance of 1787, for the government of the territory north of the Ohio. In this significant document Congress stated: "Religion, morality and knowledge being necessary to good government and happiness of mankind, schools and the means of education should be forever encouraged." Since the beginning of the nation, more than one hundred million acres have been given by the national government for school purposes, which at its lowest value is equal to $125,-000,000. These gifts of uncultivated lands helped greatly in the early days to create a sentiment in the new states for tax-supported schools, instead of the parochial and apprentice schools that prevailed in the middle and southern colonies.

1. The rise of district schools

While the Constitution left the problem of education to the states, of the sixteen states forming the Union in 1800, nine made no mention of the subject in their Constitutions. Delaware and Georgia merely directed the establishment of schools. North Carolina and Pennsylvania recommended schools where tuition would be cheap. Pennsylvania favored the maintenance of the pauper school system. Only Massachusetts, New Hampshire, Vermont, Connecticut and New York made provision for carrying on the state-supported institutions that had been so successful in the New England States.

The history of education in the new territory west of the Atlantic seaboard was determined largely by the settlers that crossed the mountains from their first homes in the colonies. Those coming from the southern colonies carried with them their idea of the apprentice school. Those from the middle colonies were prejudiced in favor of the parochial schools. Only the settlers from New England could be de-

pended upon to advocate tax-supported district
schools.

Immediately after the close of the Revolutionary
War a great movement of New England people began to pour into central New York and northern
Pennsylvania, and from then until 1810, when the
pioneers pushed still farther west, the character of
the people of these states strongly reflected that of
the early New England settlers. Their influence
largely helped to bring New York and, later, Pennsylvania, to advocate tax-supported schools.

The new Republic had not yet reached the first
quarter of a century of its existence when the strong
tide of emigration of New England people flowed
into large portions of the Northwest Territory. The
history of these settlements is a repetition of the
Puritan invasion of New England. Wherever the
Puritan went he took his New England institutions
with him, and of course this included the tax-supported school. Where the New England people were
in the ascendancy, the zeal for education, religion
and local government control was most marked.
Eventually their ideals of education prevailed.

a. *Change in character of schools*

Not only were the earliest schools controlled by
the Church and dominated by the religious motive,
but the right of the Church to determine instruction was clearly recognized. Moreover, the State
looked to the Church to make the necessary provision, and assisted it by donations of land and money.
The minister, as we have seen, examined the teachers
and the instruction. Even under the Constitution
this relationship continued. The Church recognized

the importance of education and remained one of the warmest advocates of the establishment of public schools.

But there was a gradual and almost imperceptible movement in secularization of American education. This was brought about not through any lack of religious interest on the part of the government or the people themselves, but rather from a trend of circumstances which militated a g a i n s t religious schools. [Emigration broke up communities which strongly favored tax-supported schools. Foreign immigration played its part, contributing diversified religious faiths. Denominational loyalty made it increasingly evident that education would have to be non-sectarian in character. In a country into which flocked members of every creed and also those who had no interest in religion, the unity of Church and State was doomed, and with it the joint control and fostering of education.

The school question was brought into politics. Party candidates, on the lookout for issues that might attract public attention, pledged themselves against sectarian teachings in public schools. The Whigs, in 1841, opposed all Church schools. The American Party, in 1842, denounced union between Church and State, although demanding the retention of the Bible in the public schools. The Know-Nothing Party of 1855 declared itself in favor of public schools rather than religious schools, but compromised by recommending the use of the Bible in all schools.

Probably the greatest difficulty that the advocates of the district school experienced was the necessity of having it supported by taxes. For the first time direct taxation for schools was felt by the taxpayer, and in many localities half of his tax was required for this purpose. The progress of the struggle to se- cure taxation for the maintenance of public schools differed in various parts of the country. Where the influence of the New England settlers predominated, success was easily attained. In other localities, cam- paigns of education had to be prepared and carried out. Many thought that tax-supported schools would be dangerous for the State. Many did not see the need for schools at all. Some felt that a partial con- fiscation of one man's property to educate another man's child was depriving the American citizen of his liberty. Other factors also, such as the Sunday School, helped to turn the tide in favor of tax-sup- ported schools.

b. *Change in curriculum of schools*

We have already observed that up to the time of the Revolutionary War the curriculum of the schools was predominantly of a religious character. The popular *New England Primer* could have served as effectively as a textbook in the Sunday School as in the public school.

(1) *Dillsworth's Guide to the English Tongue*

This volume, published in England and introduced into the colonies in 1750, was so superior to the Bible as a general textbook that it gradually displaced it. The reading material as well as the word lists showed gradation. There were easy sentences for the beginners and longer paragraphs for the more ad- vanced pupils. The reading material was less religious than that of the *New England Primer,* but it retained a decidedly religious tone. The easy reading sen- tences were taken from the Psalter and some editions included the catechism. Nevertheless, the admission of extra-biblical material at this time proved to be the entering wedge that was destined eventually to displace all selections of Scripture from public school textbooks.

(2) *Webster's American Spelling Book*

Webster's *American Spelling Book* appeared in 1783 and was fashioned after the *Guide to the English Tongue,* except that it was more secular and more thoroughly American in character. It was an immediate success.

Noah Webster entered Yale College when he was sixteen years of age, his father mortgaging the farm to get money for the education of his son. In the midst of his studies, the Revolutionary War broke out and Noah joined with his two brothers under the command of his father. Noah wanted to study law, but in order to earn money to support himself, he taught school. He was displeased with such texts as were used in the schools of his day, and decided to prepare something himself. He went to work on a text that would combine a spelling book, reader and grammar, although he was so poor he did not know how he would get it published. This is the background of the most famous American textbook.

Because it was clearer in its explanations, better reading and more interesting than the usual school book, Webster's publication filled a great need. It became the outstanding authority for spelling matches, which were a favorite social amusement of both old and young, especially in rural districts. Storekeepers carried this book as a staple along with rum, molasses, needles and cheese. So great was its

sale that the author was able to support his family
during the twenty years he was at work on his famous *Dictionary of the English Language.* By 1861,
eighteen years after Webster's death, his "blue-back
edition speller" was selling at the rate of one million
copies a year. By 1890, the total was more than
seventy million—the best seller of all time with the
lone exception of the Bible.

Besides a list of words, this famous speller contained fables, with a few pictures and many short
sentences of advice, instruction and description. Examples drawn from all parts of the book express deep
religious sentiments which tended to inculcate right
conduct.

(3) *Other early textbooks*

Following Webster's famous contribution, there
appeared *Little Reader's Assistant* (1790) by the
same author; the *Columbian Primer* (1802), a mod-
ernized, secularized imitation of the old *New England Primer;* Caleb Bingham's *American Preceptor*
(1794) and *Columbian Orator* (1806). The *Preceptor* was a graded reader, which soon replaced the
Bible as an advance reading book, while the *Orator*
contained selections for declamation.

2. The displacement of the Bible

All of the above mentioned books contained some
biblical selections and were well saturated with moral
and religious truths, so that it is not difficult to understand why the Bible was quite rapidly displaced
as a reading book in the American schools. But even
this partial substitution was not without protest. As
early as the beginning of the nineteenth century Rev.
Thomas Thatcher, of Dedham, Massachusetts, de-

clared in an ordination sermon that "the reading of Scripture in schools is either wholly neglected or reduced to an inferior and disgusting part of puerile duty."

Horace Mann, who was one of the greatest advocates for tax-supported schools and probably one who contributed more than any other single man toward their popularity and improvement, admitted that the Bible was an invaluable book for forming the character of children, and should be read without comment in schools, but that it was not necessary to teach it there. He contended that any attempt to decide what creed or doctrine should be taught would mean the ruin of public education.

The parochial schools played a large part in preserving the Bible as the textbook of public instruction. Their founders possessed strong religious convictions, and not only were concerned about the intellectual development of their children, but recognized that their moral and religious character could be improved only through religious instruction, and that the Bible was an important factor in improving manners and morals. In these parochial schools, therefore, the religious element was more strongly emphasized than in the public schools which were gradually becoming the standard of education in the United States. As the parochial schools continued to be well attended and supported for several decades, a large proportion of the American children in the early part of the nineteenth century received adequate religious instruction.

1. What was the real purpose of the Pilgrims' settling in America?

2. Describe the apprentice plan of education.
3. Discuss and criticize the parochial plan of education.
4. What was the Puritan plan of education?
5. What provision was made for supporting the Massachusetts Bay School?
6. What was the dame school? The Latin grammar school?
7. Describe the beginning of Harvard College.
8. What was the purpose of these early colleges?
9. What was the *Hornbook*?
10. Why was the *New England Primer* so influential in shaping American character?
11. What qualifications were required of the early teachers?
12. Does the Constitution of the United States concern itself with public education?
13. How did Congress show its early concern for public education?
14. Discuss the rise of the district schools.
15. What changes took place in the character of the schools?
16. What was their greatest problem?
17. Describe Webster's *American Spelling Book*.
18. Show how the new textbooks gradually displaced the Bible.

8

EARLY HISTORY OF THE SUNDAY SCHOOL

AMERICAN religious education, or, as it might be more accurately stated, the American revival of the Bible school program of the first century, dates from the rise of the Sunday School movement. However, to say that the religious school of the nineteenth and twentieth centuries was the same as that of the first century would not be true. There has never been a complete restoration of the apostolic teaching program. Only in the sense in which there was new interest and emphasis upon reaching and teaching children can we say that the modern school compares with the ancient. In fact, modern religious education differs from ancient and medieval methods in three respects: (1) It is a laymen's movement. (2) It is a Sunday enterprise. (3) It is organized.

Up to this period all religious education, as well as secular education, had been in the hands of the Church and was largely conducted by Church teachers. The Sunday School started apart from the Church, and in many instances has carried on its work successfully independent of the Church. Religious instruction heretofore had been merged with secular instruction, but it remained for the Sunday School to make the former distinctive, and to set aside a day which had hitherto been considered sacred for worship purposes, as the most suitable time for religious instruction.

The large place laymen have taken in the advancement of the Sunday School has brought into the movement the genius of the businessman for organization, and enabled the Christian forces to carry out the Great Commission for reaching and teaching in a far more systematic effort than has been known since apostolic days. Utilizing the talents of these laymen for organizing has made it possible to extend the field of Sunday School activities and to improve its forces more rapidly than any other world movement.

I. The English Movement

It would not be true to state that the Sunday School started in Britain and that Robert Raikes was the originator of the movement. Schools of a similar character and apparently with all the features of his agency were organized in upper Egypt, in Armenia, and elsewhere in the East more than fourteen centuries before 1780. All the way along the intervening centuries there were repeated revivals of this agency of religious instruction with more or less success. But there were peculiar circumstances which magnified the work of Robert Raikes and contributed to making it a world-wide movement rather than the effort of an individual.

1. Robert Raikes

A reformer and a philanthropist, Robert Raikes had a large place in his heart for children. When a resident of the slum district of Gloucester, England, complained to him of the bedlam created by the rough and rowdy children, he refused to condemn the reprehensible laxity of the parents through his newspaper, or demand additional policemen from the authorities. Instead, he rented a room in the most congested district and gathered a group of these "miserable little wretches" for secular instruction as well as a knowledge of God and the Bible.

At that time there were no public schools in Europe, and as we have already seen, only in the New England colonies in America. Education was claimed only by the privileged classes. Children, for the most part, were as ignorant of the fundamentals of education as of the Bible. Working long hours as apprentices during the week, and being deprived of any intellectual or moral interest, when Sunday came they ran riot upon the streets.

Looking out at the world in his day, Robert Raikes saw that some drastic measures were needed to stem the tide of evil and conserve the basic elements of Christian society. With his conviction that wickedness was the result of idleness caused by ignorance, he first tried to give instruction to the prisoners at Gloucester. But these efforts were so frequently shown to be fruitless by a speedy return of the recipient to the prison for a new debt or a fresh crime, that gradually Raikes was led to see his endeavors to teach and reform the adult were largely a waste of time and labor. Thus his thoughts turned toward the neglected children. "The world marches forward on the feet of little children."

Raikes' plan for educating the "savages," however, was considered a wild and fruitless enterprise. No one could be found to give support or encouragement. The Church considered all such efforts as hopeless, and such a use of the Sabbath day as sacrilegious. His friends dubbed him and his school "Bobby Wild Goose and his ragged regiment." Nev-

ertheless, he persisted in his plan. He rewarded with
pennies the faithful few who came regularly, and imposed no other requirements but that they should
have clean hands and faces and hair combed. Out of
his own pocket he provided four teachers to instruct
in reading, writing, good morals and religion, from
ten to twelve o'clock in the morning and from two
until five in the afternoon. The remuneration which
these teachers received was only twenty-five cents a
Sunday, but in those days that amount of money
had greater purchasing value than the dollar of today.

There were many difficulties and discouragements,
but eventually Robert Raikes proved that "the little
vermins could be made to learn." Order improved
and numbers increased. The first rooms soon became
inadequate, and school after school was established
to accommodate those who sought admission.

As the publisher of a weekly periodical, Raikes
had a peculiar advantage in giving publicity to his
enterprise. Yet it was not until his experiment had
had a successful trial of more than three years that
he ventured to make his first announcement, in No-
vember, 1783. Other papers republished his article,
and the accounts of the origin and progress of the
first Sunday School were reproduced in various forms
in the metropolitan and provincial press of Great
Britain. This did much to call public attention to
the importance and possibilities of the new undertaking. It is said that through the means of the press,
the knowledge and nature of Sunday Schools were
"diffused with the rapidity of lightning throughout
the world."

At first the Church opposed the movement. Many
thought that it was sacrilegious to spend the Sabbath

day for this purpose. But despite ecclesiastical opposition the Sunday School had the support of many influential individuals. The Earls of Ducie and Salisbury gave it their approval. John Newton, William Cowper and Thomas Scott were hearty in its support. Ladies of fashion undertook the work of Sunday School teaching. The Queen herself gave fresh impetus to the new movement by placing on it the stamp of royal favor. Sending for Robert Raikes she learned from his own lips the story of his work and his progress. And so Sunday School teaching came not only to be reputable, but fashionable among the better classes of English people.

Robert Raikes lived to see the success of his "ragged school," and when he died in 1811, Sunday Schools were widely established in England, their combined attendance amounting to 400,000 pupils. As a proof of his love for children, each child who attended his funeral was presented with a plum cake and a shilling, in accordance with his will. During more than thirty years of his life this man had given freely of his time, talents and money to a movement destined to transform moral conditions in England and to shape the destiny of America.

2. William Fox

The year 1736 will ever be memorable in the history of Christianity because it gave birth to two most noble philanthropists, Robert Raikes and William Fox. They were born not only in the same year, but on the same day of the month, and while they were not acquainted with each other in their early life, their two great educational projects eventually blended in one united movement. It is doubtful, even with the advantage of his publication, whether Robert Raikes would have been so successful if it had not been for the organization and co-operation of the influential Sunday School Society which William Fox founded.

Mr. Fox was a prosperous London merchant who had a vision of a great moral and religious transformation that might take place if every poor person in Great Britain was able to read the Bible. In his business journeys throughout England, he often found hamlets and even villages where the poor were entirely without the Bible. Even when presented with a copy, he discovered that not one in twenty persons could read. The friends with whom he consulted gave him little encouragement. They thought that nothing short of legislation by Parliament could effect anything worthwhile. The magnitude of the undertaking seemed too great, and there was no one willing to take the lead. Consequently Mr. Fox himself gathered together a group of influential Christian men and presented the urgent need of an organization that would provide the common people with sufficient education to enable them to read the Bible. About this time the success of Robert Raikes' Sunday Schools attracted the attention of Mr. Fox, and he saw immediately that this plan of using Sunday rather than weekdays for instruction could best accomplish his purpose.

On September 7, 1785, William Fox launched the Sunday School Society for the express purpose of organizing and supporting Sunday Schools. A donation of ten guineas a year constituted a life membership, and Mr. Fox succeeded in interesting a considerable number of philanthropists in his project.

The society furnished Bibles, Testaments and spelling books for the use of the schools, and also paid the salary of the teachers. The latter was the most important item of expense, for although the salaries were small, in fourteen years, $17,000 was paid out for this purpose. Within two years after it was organized, the society had assisted 282 schools, consisting of 16,000 pupils, and supplied 20,295 spelling books, 6,217 Testaments, and 1,141 Bibles. Within twenty years 2,542 schools, enrolling 226,-945 pupils, had been established, and altogether 219,410 spelling books, 50,126 copies of the New Testament and 7,213 copies of the Bible had been distributed.

The movement for volunteer teachers championed by John Wesley not only increased the growth of the Sunday School by greatly reducing the expense, but also enabled the Sunday School Society to concentrate its efforts on the distribution of teaching materials.

3. John Wesley

Next to the large assistance of the Sunday School Society, the educational movement launched by Robert Raikes owes its marvelous success to the active support of John Wesley. The founder of the Methodist Church was closely identified with the Sunday School movement from the beginning. While most of the clergymen in Great Britain and America were either hostile or indifferent to the movement, he took an active interest and friendly attitude. He is attributed with saying that the Sunday School is "one of the noblest specimens of charity which has been set on foot in England since the days of William the Conqueror" and it seems that "it will be one great means of reviving religion throughout the nation."

Wesley directed his preachers to form societies for the children within the larger Methodist congregations whenever there were ten or more children, and to guide Methodist parents, in their areas, in the training of their households in religion. He reminded the itinerants that the least part of their office was preaching; they should teach and engage in pastoral work in its various phases. "What avails public preaching alone," he asked them, "though we could preach like angels? Spend an hour a week with the children in every large town, whether you like it or not. Talk with them any time you see any of them at home. Pray in earnest for them." His chief reason for this solicitude was in the relation these children bore to the revival then under way. He asked, "If religion is not extended to the children, what will be the outcome? If family religion be neglected—if care be not taken with the rising generation—will not the present revival of religion in a short time die away?"

To the Sunday School the Methodist Church owes a large measure of its success, if indeed it is not indebted to it for its continuous as well as its steady growth. This is particularly true in North America. W. E. H. Leckey, in his review of the methods and influence of the Wesleyan movement, says, "The Methodists appear to have preached especially to children."

4. The Sunday School Union

Under Raikes and Fox the Sunday School had been largely a charity movement. There was no standardizing of the schools and, consequently, some proved to be much better than others. William Brodie Gurney asked, "Why not get Sunday School teachers together and improve the methods of instruction?" The answer to this question, largely through the efforts of Mr. Gurney, resulted in the London Sunday School Union, July 13, 1803. Its chief purpose was to improve Sunday Schools, and thus to promote some system in religious education.

In every way this organization proved successful. It held quarterly meetings in its four London auxiliaries, for devotional exercises and the discussion of practical questions. It appropriated considerable sums for establishing schools, as well as publishing books, periodicals and papers. About 1805 it reported four publications: *A Plan for Forming Sunday Schools, A Guide to Teachers, A Catechism in Verse,* and *A Reading Primer.*

In London and throughout England local unions were formed as auxiliaries. Each of these was represented by a secretary and three members, who with twenty other members chosen on a committee at an annual meeting directed the affairs of the London Sunday School Union. The formation of new schools and aid in housing and equipping them were a large part of its activities. The union also rendered important service in loaning money or granting financial aid to schools making improvements. The abandonment of paid teachers, which had constituted such a large portion of the expense of the Sunday School Society, enabled the London Sunday School Union to devote its means almost entirely to the preparation and publication of periodicals.

5. Summary of results

It is impossible to overestimate the political and religious results of the Sunday School movement. One historian goes so far as to state that it was the Sunday School, together with the revival of Wesley and Whitefield, that spared England from the horrors of the French Revolution. Green says specifically, "The Sunday Schools established by Mr. Raikes of Gloucester were the beginning of popular education." Leckey also refers to "the establishment of Sunday Schools" as "an important step" in the line of "a revived interest in education."

At the centenary celebration of the origin of the Sunday School in 1880, Rev. J. F. Kitto said:

> One hundred years ago it was a rare thing for a child of a laboring hand to be able even to read, but today we can point to the gratifying fact that among all the twenty thousand pupils who are assembled here today, there is probably not one who is in a similar condition of ignorance. Nor is this the only or chief result of the Sunday School. The seed of Christian faith and Christian enterprise which was sown by Robert Raikes and his associates has now borne fruit in almost every parish of our land, and its influence has spread far beyond the confines of our country. Wherever our Christianity extends, the importance of the Sunday School is recognized as the nursery and training school of the Church, and the zeal and activity of thousands of volunteer teachers have been enlisted in its behalf.

Not only was the Sunday School the beginning of the English system of public school education, but indirectly it was responsible for the formation of the

British and Foreign Bible Society and the Religious
Tract Society. The ability of the common people
of England to read multiplied the demands for Bibles
and religious literature, which was the direct occasion for the organization of these two societies whose
activities have now become world-wide.

The Sunday School also was the indirect cause
of the larger interest in the world's religious needs,
which led to the modern missionary movement for
the evangelization of the globe less than twenty years
after the beginning of the first Sunday School.

H. Clay Trumbull fittingly sums up the far-reaching results of the Sunday School in *Yale Lectures:*

> It is evident that the great religious decline of the
> eighteenth century was consequent on a lack of a di-
> vinely designated church school agency for the winning
> and training of the young; and that the direct religious
> advance of the nineteenth century is consequent upon
> a revival and expansion of that agency, with its legiti-
> mate influence and outcome.

II. The American Movement

While the Sunday School originated in Great
Britain, it achieved its greatest growth and development in America. In 1785, two years after Great
Britain had declared the thirteen original colonies a
free and independent nation, the first Sunday School
was started on this side of the Atlantic; and from
that time, which was almost simultaneous with the
adoption of the Constitution (September 17, 1787),
the Sunday School has been organically a part of
this great Republic. While it is true that the Sunday
School owes its marvelous development to this country in whose soil it has so signally flourished, it is
equally true that this nation is as fully indebted to

the Sunday School for its extraordinary era of progress and prosperity. Indeed, as we shall see, the Sunday School has made America just as much as America has made the Sunday School.

Perhaps more than anything else, the Sunday
School has contributed to the unique public school
system, which has been one of the important factors
in the preservation of this great Republic. History
does not record many successful republics; other
forms of government have proved more permanent.
But none of the republics of the past have been
blessed with such a popular form of education as
the one that has thrived so well on the Western
Hemisphere.

The hearty reception given to the Sunday School
of America soon convinced educators that here was
the solution to the problem of the separation of
Church and State in public instruction. Religion
could be taught independent of secular instruction.
Parochial schools were no longer necessary, and the
State could give its full support and encouragement
to secular instruction. The people soon became so
enthusiastic over the new plan of teaching religion
that they began to ignore the early efforts to make
religion the principal purpose and subject of the public school. There is much truth in the statement that
religion has been omitted from the public school curriculum because the church people did not care to
keep it there.

1. The first Sunday Schools

a. *In the South*

Perhaps the absence of education for the common
people in the South was the occasion for the first

recognition of the value of the Sunday School. No other instruction was afforded the poor people except that for the apprentice, while Negro slaves were neglected entirely. The state-supported schools of New England and the parochial schools of the central colonies had not penetrated into the Southern States.

(1) *Virginia, 1785*

Oak Grove Sunday School in Accomac County, Virginia, is the oldest Sunday School in America. William Elliott, in 1785, set aside each Sunday evening for the purpose of instructing his own children and the servants on his plantation. Neighboring children were invited and attended. Both whites and Negroes were taught, but at separate hours. As rapidly as possible the pupils were prepared to read the Bible, which was the object of this school. The Scripture was read, explained, and much of it memorized by teacher and pupil.

The Sunday School was continued in the home of its founder until 1801, when it was transferred to_the church building. William Elliott remained its superintendent until he was too feeble to attend to the duties. The first documentary mention of the affiliation of the Sunday School with the church was in 1818, and as the founder did not die until 1836, he lived more than eighteen years after his Sunday School had become an agency of the church. Though it has an enrollment of less than one hundred, it is interesting to note that the Oak Grove Sunday School still continues its sessions. During its century and a half of existence, there have been just ten superintendents, one of whom became a preacher, and another, a representative to the Eighth World's Sunday School Convention in Japan.

The second Sunday School was established by Francis Asbury, in 1786, in the home of Thomas Crenshaw, of Hanover County, Virginia. It was expressly provided for the instruction of the slaves.

Asbury, who later was made bishop of the Methodist Church, was a great admirer of John Wesley, and being in constant communication with him, learned from him the success of the Sunday Schools in England.

(2) *South Carolina, 1790*

The Methodist Conference in Charleston, South Carolina, gave official recognition to the Sunday School as the best means for instructing poor children who were unable to read, by the following resolution, adopted in 1790:

> Let us labor as the heart and soul of one man to establish Sunday Schools in or near the places of public worship. Let persons be appointed by the bishops, elders, deacons, or preachers to teach all that will attend and have capacity to learn, from six o'clock in the morning until ten, and from two o'clock in the afternoon until six, where it does not interfere with public worship. Be it further resolved that the council should compile a proper school book to teach them learning and piety.

These early efforts seem not to have been attended at first with very great success, but the rapid spread of the movement in the North tended to revive the institution until Sunday Schools were popular in this portion of the country.

(3) Maryland, 1804

A Sunday School was opened in the Broadway Baptist Church of Baltimore, which is the oldest and first denominational school of the United States. Two years later Rev. S. Wilmer commenced a school at Kent, Maryland.

b. In the North

(1) Rhode Island, 1791

Mr. Collier, of Brown University, opened a Sunday School in Pawtucket, Rhode Island, in 1791. He was assisted by Samuel Slater, who first introduced machinery into this country for the manufacture of cotton.

(2) New York, 1792

The first Sunday School in the state of New York was organized at Stockbridge in the house of an Indian woman, a sister of the Rev. Samson Occom. Mr. Occom was a distinguished Indian preacher.

(3) New Jersey, 1794

A cotton manufacturing company in Passaic County employed a teacher in 1794, to instruct gratuitously on Sunday the children employed in the factory.

(4) Pennsylvania, 1809

Pittsburgh was only a village in 1809, but it was large enough for the formation of a society whose purpose was "the suppression of vice, reformation of manners, and the propagation of useful knowledge." For carrying out this program, a school for religious instruction on the Sabbath was recommended, and the first school of the state was organized August 22,

1809. Two hundred forty children and adults attended the first session.

(5) *Massachusetts, 1809*

The success of the tax-supported schools in Massachusetts prevented earlier recognition of the value of the Sunday School, but in the summer of 1809 Hannah Hill and Joanna B. Prince organized a Sunday School at Beverley after hearing of the success of Raikes' school in England.

(6) *Delaware, 1814*

As the result of a visit of Dr. Sharpe's wife, of Wilmington, Delaware, to the Charles Street Baptist Sunday School, Boston, the first Sunday School was commenced in Delaware.

2. The first Sunday School Society

Philadelphia was the largest city in the new Republic, and it is not surprising to learn that the first movement for Sunday School organization had its start in this place. Even though surpassed in population today by Chicago and New York, Philadelphia still has the distinction of having the largest number of Sunday Schools of any city in the United States.

Preparatory to the formation of the First-Day or Sabbath School Society, a meeting was called by some of the most distinguished citizens of Philadelphia. Among these may be mentioned Rev. William White, D.D., the Episcopal bishop of Pennsylvania; Dr. Benjamin Rush, whose reputation as a physician was world-wide. The preamble of the constitution adopted by this society January 11, 1791, declared:

> That the first day of the week called Sunday, a day which ought to be devoted to religious improvements,

being employed to the worst of purposes, depravity of morals and manners, it is therefore the opinion of sundry persons that the establishment of first-day or Sunday Schools in this city would be of essential advantage to the rising generation.

Although it is not stated that the men who projected this society were acquainted with what had been done in England, the similarity of plans would so indicate. Both recognized the importance of secular instruction in order to read the Bible, and both employed paid teachers.

From March, 1791, to January, 1800, the sum of $3,968 was expended by the Sabbath School Society for the support of its schools. During these nine years 2,127 pupils were admitted for instruction, the average attendance being about 180; the average expense, $403, about $2.25 a year for each pupil. This was more than the expenses of the Sunday Schools that employed volunteer teachers, and 40 cents more than the public schools that operated on the Lancaster plan, even though the latter were in session five days of the week.

Bishop White was chosen president of the society at its first session, and continued to direct its activities for forty-six years. In the first twenty-three years, the benevolent receipts were $9,186.49 and its expenditures $9,133.01. Early in the nineteenth century volunteer teachers were used so extensively by the Sunday School that the society decided to discontinue its paid instructors and expend its funds for aiding institutions in other ways. As in England, the expense of paid teachers was too great to be continued, and voluntary teachers were absolutely necessary for any large extension of the Sunday School movement.

It must be remembered that all the money raised was contributed by individuals rather than churches. Nearly a generation passed before the Church appreciated and in some instances even tolerated the Sunday School movement. The organized Church either opposed the scheme, or believed that to make it an integral part of the church would debase the divine plan by a mere man-made appendage. Thus Sunday Schools were of necessity partly or totally independent of Church control, although often held in churches. Even when the Church "came to itself and realized the value of the Sunday School for perpetuating its existence and improving its ministry, the school was permitted to pay its own expenses."

3. American Sunday School Union

The Revolutionary War left the colonies a heavy debt. The country had few industries and its foreign trade was badly hampered by European nations. France threatened war, and later, England declared war on the new Republic so that the first quarter of a century was largely spent in ways and means of holding the Union together. Other limitations interfered with the promotion of schools of any character, and their development was a slow process. The success of the Sunday School was largely due to its provision of secular as well as religious instruction by means of volunteer teachers.

The achievements of the first Sunday School Society in Philadelphia led to similar organizations in other cities. Unions for the promotion of Sunday

School work were organized in such cities as New York and Boston, in 1816.

Notwithstanding these new societies, the wants of the Sunday Schools were not fully supplied until the organization of the Philadelphia Sunday and Adult School Union in 1817. As soon as this society was inaugurated, it entered vigorously upon its work. Its first annual report in 1818 showed that it had taken care of 43 schools, 565 teachers and 5,970 pupils. By 1824 the number of teachers and pupils it assisted amounted to 57,000, and were distributed in seventeen of the twenty-four states of the Union. Meanwhile the most cordial relations existed between this organization and the Sunday School Society of 1791, but as the aim of the former was to merge everything in the United States to a common center, its purpose proved more popular, and many of the existing unions dissolved their organizations and merged with the Philadelphia institution.

The idea of a society still more national in its character so impressed itself upon the men of vision that at the seventh anniversary of the Sunday and Adult School Union a constitution was prepared, presented and adopted, inaugurating the American Sunday School Union. All the property of the Sunday and Adult School Union, amounting to upward of $5,000, was transferred by unanimous vote to the new organization. The General Assembly of the Presbyterian Church was in session at the time, and its members participated in the exercises. This, however, was the nearest relationship that the churches were to take toward sharing responsibilities that the American Sunday School Union assumed as the purpose of its institution.

The objects of this organization as stated in its constitution were "to concentrate the efforts of Sabbath School societies in the different sections of our country; to strengthen the hands of friends of religious instruction on the Lord's Day; to disseminate useful information, circulate moral and religious publications in every part of the land, and to endeavor to plan a Sunday School wherever there is a population." The members declared "that the society is composed of citizens of several denominations, embracing within its plans and objects all ranks, sects and ages in our country."

Thus was started a movement which was destined to play a very large part not only in the nation-wide promotion of the Sunday School, but in laying the moral and religious foundations of the sparsely settled portions of the new Republic. In a subsequent chapter additional information will be given concerning the remarkable work of the Union, which has placed the nation eternally in its debt by its support of Sunday School missionaries, the preparation of lesson materials, and the circulation of inexpensive library books long before the denominations took up the work in any large way.

---

1. How does modern religious education differ from ancient and medieval methods ?
2. Describe the beginnings of Robert Raikes' Sunday School.
3. What was the attitude of the Church toward the new movement?
4. Who was William Fox and what did his society accomplish for the Sunday School?

5. Quote some of John Wesley's statements regarding the Sunday School.

6. Name some accomplishments of the London Sunday School Union.

7. Quote Green, Leckey and Trumbull on the far-reaching results of the Sunday School.

8. How did the Sunday School further the public school system in America?

9. Describe the first Sunday School in America.

10. What official recognition was given by the Methodist Conference in Charleston, S. C.?

11. Give the dates for the first Sunday Schools in Rhode Island, New York, New Jersey, Pennsylvania, Massachusetts and Delaware.

12. Describe the work of the first Sunday School society.

13. What was the relation of the early American Sunday School to the Church?

14. How did the American Sunday School Union come into existence?

15. How was the purpose of the Union stated in its constitution?

9

PROGRESS OF THE PUBLIC SCHOOLS

IN THE preceding chapters we have traced the development of the early schools in America, and observed that for many years religious instruction was the main purpose of their existence and the principal content of their curriculum. We have also observed the rise of the Sunday School and its success both in England and America. In addition we have seen how, under the Constitution, which called for a separation of Church and State, the Sunday School fitted the more perfectly into a program of education which was calculated not to show favor to any religious sect. It now remains for us to trace the comparative progress of the secular education of the State with that of the religious instruction of the Church. The fact that at the beginning of the century the public school still included religious instruction and required religious teachers, and the Sunday School taught secular subjects, will arouse our interest to see how the purposes of these two institutions became gradually more distinctive. It is also to be observed that while both institutions were to expand greatly, one was to improve far more than the other.

I. The Lancaster System

Probably no movement, with the possible exception of the Sunday School, did more to turn the tide in the long struggle for free state schools than the

Lancaster monitorial system of instruction. In 1797, Andrew Bell published in England an account of an experiment in education he had made in an orphan asylum in India. His plan was to use monitors to assist the teacher. About the same time Joseph Lancaster, an English school master, independently announced a similar discovery. The fact that teachers were scarce and pay was poor, suggested the employment of student help for extending if not improving the instruction. The idea attracted attention and spread rapidly over England and later to America.

Once introduced into the United States, in 1806, the movement proved very popular, and it quickly spread from Massachusetts to Georgia, and as far west as Cincinnati and Louisville and Detroit. In 1818, Lancaster himself came to America and spent most of the remaining twenty years of his life in organizing and directing schools in various parts of the United States.

With Lancaster, the idea was for one teacher to control a school of a thousand boys. This was accomplished by means of monitors. The brightest pupils were selected as monitors, and each was held responsible for a group of ten pupils. The teacher first taught these monitors a lesson from a printed card, and then each monitor took his group in hand and proceeded to teach them what he had just learned. Sometimes the master teacher gave instruction to the entire assembly, leaving the monitors to drill and examine the individual pupils. At first the monitors heard only lessons in reading and catechism, but later they took charge of lessons in spelling, writing, and arithmetic.

The system was very popular from 1810 to 1830. Some even believed that a new era in education had been established. But by 1840 its popularity had waned.

The Lancaster system of instruction came at the most opportune time to awaken a public interest in and a sentiment for free schools. One of the main difficulties up to that time had been the cost of education and the unwillingness of the people to be taxed for this purpose. College graduates went into the ministry or were employed by the State, and few were willing to accept the small remuneration that teaching afforded. Moreover, the time-honored method of instruction limited the number of pupils that could be placed under the instruction of a single teacher. The Lancaster system not only improved but greatly reduced educational expenses. In 1822 the annual expense per pupil in New York City was only $1.22 compared with $12.00 in private and church schools.

There is no doubt that this movement materially hastened the adoption of the free school system by gradually accustoming the people to bearing the necessary taxation. Had memory work and drilling been all of education, the Lancaster system might have become a permanent institution, but the rise of normal schools and the multiplication of trained teachers put an end to the popularity of this system of education. The growing material prosperity of the people and their increased willingness to contribute more liberally to the cause of education led them to demand better training for the monitors who centered so conspicuously in the Lancaster movement. This was the real origin of normal training in the United States.

The Lancastrian schools made religious instruction secondary, although the Bible content of the textbooks and the Christian requirements of the teacher created a distinctly religious atmosphere. The Massachusetts Act of 1827, which declared that school books should not favor the tenets of any particular sect of Christians, was the nearest measure to expressing any disapproval at that time of the teaching of religion in the public schools.

II. Infant Schools

The district schools made no provision for beginners. They were expected to learn the alphabet and the elements of reading at home or in the dame schools. In many cities no children were admitted until they had learned to read and write, and the common age of entrance was eight years.

Meanwhile in Scotland, Robert Owen, a manufacturer, had established a school for the factory children in his town. Parents who had no one to care for their little children while they were employed could send them to this new school, which instructed boys and girls of five, six and seven years of age. The success of this and other schools started an agitation for primary schools in America.

In 1818, the city of Boston appropriated $5,000 to organize such schools to supplement the public school system. The plan was to admit children at four years of age, to employ women teachers, and prepare the younger boys and girls for admission to the city schools. Separate buildings were erected for this purpose. This practically put an end to the dame school instruction and added the primary grades to the previously existing school.

The new school was most timely, as the limitations of Lancastrian instruction were becoming evident and the popularity of that movement was beginning to wane. It established a preference for
women teachers in primary work, giving them a
larger consideration and place in the teaching profession, which up to this time was carried on mostly
by men. It also had the value of making the instruction of little children distinctive and laying the foundation for a new psychological basis in teaching.

The course of study began with the alphabet, and
as soon as it was mastered, easy reading material
was given, until the pupil could be promoted to
the New Testament. In fact, the New Testament as
reading material was stressed above all other, which
not only indicates the religious emphasis in public
instruction, but the purpose of these schools "to operate upon the will and affections as well as the understanding and its thoughts." The supreme purpose of
education in that day was to make good men rather
than learned men—men of society rather than men
of knowledge. A study of the manual entitled *Infant
Education,* published in 1828, makes it plain that
moral and religious themes made up a fair proportion of the course of study.

As these schools became widespread, it came to be
readily seen that the younger children had the benefit
of a great deal of moral and religious instruction
through the use of biblical material. The management of the infant school remained separate from
that of the district school until the middle of the
century, when they were combined under one school,
and eventually united in one building.

III. Secondary Schools

1. The academy

We have already seen how the Puritans provided a Latin grammar school for their advanced students. Latin was the language of the classroom and even attempted for the playground as well. English grammar was introduced and soon rose to a place of great importance, as did also oratory and declamation. However, with the shifting of the population after the Revolutionary War, these Latin grammar schools lost their supporters, especially in the rural districts—and it is estimated that more than three-fourths of the population in the early days of our national history lived outside the cities.

But a new institution—the academy—arose to meet the needs for secondary education. Like the common school and the college, it also had its origin in the Church. In earlier days, colleges and seminaries had arisen from humble beginnings in some wide-awake ministers' homes, where students were tutored in advanced courses. In this way pastors prepared some of the most promising of their young men for college entrance examination. In time, through the tireless efforts on the part of a few enthusiasts and the meager financial support of half-interested churches whose sons and daughters received large benefits, all the states east of the Mississippi were dotted with these Christian secondary schools.

Like the Latin grammar school, the academy was found to be a valuable means of supplying teachers for the district schools. This, in addition to preparing men for college and seminary, made the movement very popular. It spread with great rapidity during the first half of the nineteenth century. In 1850, there

were more than one thousand academies in New
England; 1,636 in the middle Atlantic States; 2,640
in the Southern States. Altogether in the United
States there were 6,085 schools, 12,260 teachers,
and 263,096 students. The zenith was reached in
1880 when more than half the nation's middle
schools were academies.

2. The high school

Others besides ministers came to appreciate the
importance of secondary institutions in preparation
for college, so that the high school movement eventually eclipsed and ended the reign of Christian
academies.

The first high school in the United States was
established in Boston, in 1821. Students were required to have the prerequisite of reading, writing,
English grammar and arithmetic as far as it was
taught in the district school. No other language than
English was taught, and in this respect the school
differed widely from the academy and the Latin grammar school. Its aim, as restated in the regulations of
the school committee in 1833, reads as follows:

> It was instituted in 1821 with the design of furnish-
> ing the young men of the city who were not intended for
> a collegiate course of study and who have enjoyed the
> usual advantages of their public schools, with the means
> of completing a good English education to fit them for
> active life or qualify them for eminence in private or
> public station.

Thus it can be seen that its aim was intensely practical.

The American high school did not prove popular
immediately. The public had to be educated to its

importance, as it did the tax-supported schools for elementary instruction. The added expense was now used as an argument against public instruction. In some states private citizens brought suit to prevent the collection of additional taxes, and it was not until several important court decisions had been rendered that the friends of higher education felt sufficiently supported by government action to press their claims. Gradually the high school came to be accepted as part of the state common school system, and the funds and taxation provided for the district schools were extended to cover the high school as well.

In 1890, high schools contained two-thirds of the students that were taking secondary instruction. To-day they have almost entirely supplanted Christian academies. The latter served a lofty purpose, but the Church found financial competition with the State too arduous a task.

Nevertheless, it is well to note that the high school was purely a non-religious movement and its students have never received the Bible instruction that occupied such a large part of the academy curriculum. Nearly all the academies charged tuition; and while many became semi-state institutions through the public aid they received, usually they were constituted as private schools with a self-perpetuating board of trustees. The demand for an upward extension of the public school that would provide free instruction constituted a call for a higher institution of public instruction.

IV. Improving Teachers

The success of educating monitors as teachers in the Lancastrian system prepared the way for institutional training of public instructors. As early as 1826 Governor Clinton of New York recommended a state seminary for the education of teachers in a monitorial system of instruction, and the following year, the creation of "a central school in each county for the education of teachers."

Up to this time the state was entirely dependent upon the academies for the training of teachers, and in some instances state aid was provided for this purpose. The training was almost entirely academic. There was no organization and little methodology of instruction. Principles of teaching and school management taught from personal experience was all that was afforded, in addition to a better knowledge of the materials to be taught.

Meanwhile the news of the success of teacher-training seminaries in Europe had crossed the ocean. Several enthusiastic educators led the campaign for similar institutions in this country. Notable among these agitators was Horace Mann, a young lawyer, who gave up a promising career in law and politics to devote his entire life to educating public opinion to the importance and improvement of education. Mr. Mann had traveled in Europe and studied the success of normal institutions in Prussia and other countries. He returned to this country with a firm conviction that normal schools were essential to the completion of the educational program.

On July 3, 1839, the first state normal school in the United States was opened in the town hall at Lexington, Massachusetts. The course of instruction was only one year in length, and the entire student body consisted of three students. Only the enthusiasm of a few leaders like Mr. Mann could have permeated an institution which started out so humbly. Many teachers regarded its creation as a criticism of their work. Academies did not welcome its competition. State aid was already being provided the academies for the training of teachers, so that it seemed an unnecessary institution.

But despite all opposition and indifference, the movement grew. More and more people caught the vision of Horace Mann and realized the truth of his word that "normal schools are a new instrumentality in the advancement of the race and without them free schools will be shorn of their strength." A second school was started in Massachusetts the same year, and a third, the year following. By 1860 there were twelve state normal schools in nine states of the Union, and at the close of the Civil War no less than twenty. No achievement in general education was more influential for improving the public schools, and today the State is more dependent upon these normal schools for instructors of elementary education than upon the colleges.

V. Improving the Methods

The Lancastrian schools not only provided a valuable contribution in reducing the expense of public education, but also improved the methods. Mechanical as they now seem, they were a great improvement over the individual method of instruction upon which the colonial teachers wasted so much of their energy and effort. In place of idleness, inattention and disorder, the military discipline of the Lancastrian system greatly improved the efficiency. Teaching methods were to be further improved by:

1. Graded instruction

The one-room school of the colonists, and even the larger assembly room of the Lancastrian system, did not lend themselves for the separation of the pupils into departments and classes for segregated instruction. The rise of the primary and secondary schools with the district school completed a three-fold division of instruction; but as the schools increased in size, it became apparent that further divisions would be necessary.

The first step in the development of a graded system was the division of the school into departments, known as primary, secondary, intermediate, grammar and high. This was accomplished generally in the cities by 1845.

The next step in the development of a graded system was a division of each department into classes. This began by the employment of assistant teachers, known as ushers, and the addition of recitation rooms, where the classes could be segregated and instructed by the extra teachers.

The final step in the development of a graded system called for schools built with smaller classrooms or subdivision of the larger rooms, and arrangement of the instruction by years. These changes were largely accomplished in the cities by 1850, though a good many years passed before the plan was adopted in the rural communities. As new buildings were erected with smaller classrooms, the number in the classes was reduced and the recitation rooms were eliminated. The primary classes gradually ceased to take pupils under five and, later, under six years of age. This made it easy to dispense with separate buildings for the infant schools and to unite all elementary instruction under one roof.

2. Child-centered instruction

We have already observed how the idea of normal schools was taken from the successful training institutions in Europe, but there were other innovations taking place on the other side of the water which also attracted the attention of American educators. A young German Swiss by the name of Johann Heinrich Pestalozzi opened a school on his farm, in 1774, and took in fifty abandoned children, to whom he taught reading, writing and arithmetic, and gave them oral discourses while he trained them in gardening and farming. At the end of two years he had spent all his money and the school was obliged to close. But as the result of Pestalozzi's experience in this experiment, he launched a new era in teaching methods. From that time on he interested himself in working out a teaching method based on the natural development of the child, and in training others to teach.

Up to this time most instruction had been material-centered. Pestalozzi's great contribution lay in his rejection of the teaching of mere words and facts, and reducing the educational process to truths based on natural and orderly development of the instincts, capacities and powers of the growing child. Formal instruction for its disciplinary value gave place to an effort to teach only knowledge that was worth while. The public school pupil was beginning to study reading, arithmetic and geography in terms of his own immediate interest and problems.

American schools made no great haste to accept the newer educational methods. As early as 1848, Pestalozzian methods were introduced into a few private institutions in Massachusetts, a state always in advance of all others in educational movements; but there was no great influence among schools elsewhere until after the Civil War. Not until the curriculum of the normal schools was changed and a larger place was given to the study of child psychology and pedagogy did the new methods eventually find their way into the public schools.

VI. Improving the Curriculum

The final chapter of the story of the gradual change from religious to secular material in the textbooks of the public schools would not be complete without mention of McGuffey's famous contribution, *First Electric Reader.*

William Holmes McGuffey was ordained a Presbyterian minister in 1828. But he soon discovered that his talents lay in teaching, and he won a great reputation as an inspirer of his pupils. In 1836 he published his famous first reader, with older grades following in due course. The books were immensely popular, and their sales amounted to more than one hundred twenty-two million copies.

The success of these readers was due to McGuffey's understanding of children and his production of a style that was all his own. "His familiarity with the Bible," says R. J. McGinnis, "might lead one to believe that his diction would follow closely that of the Bible, but a curious stroke of genius led him to evolve his own style, which was as much that of the frontier as the log cabin and the hoe-cake." Indeed a large part of these readers could be used in church school classes to illustrate and apply lessons from the Bible.

Copies of the McGuffey's readers make a fascinating study. There is not a dull page in them anywhere. They carry detailed lessons on articulation, pronunciation, spelling, defining and use of words, and on accent and inflection. The moral quality and uplifting power of material chosen for the readers was the first great characteristic. These textbooks gave a permanent picture of the universal ideal in patriotism, politeness, honesty, courage, kindness, and thrift of our first century and a half as a nation.

1. What was the Lancaster system?
2. How did it support the sentiment for free schools?
3. Why did it not become a permanent institution?
4. Describe the infant schools.
5. How much religious instruction appeared in early infant education?
6. How did the academy originate and what were its contributions?
7. Compare the academy with the high school and explain why the latter finally supplanted the former.
8. Describe the rise of the normal school
9. What progress was made in graded instruction?
10. What was Pestalozzi's great contribution to better schools?
11. What were the McGuffey's readers and what large contribution did they make to character building?

PROGRESS OF THE SUNDAY SCHOOL

THE POPULATION of the United States in 1824 was between ten and twelve million. Of these about three million were between four and sixteen years of age. Not more than one hundred thousand of these children were in Sunday School and the number of unreached was constantly increased by the heavy tide of immigration. As it was evident that the population of the new world would double in a quarter of a century, the number receiving religious instruction should have been ten times as great as it was. At that time the number of Sunday School pupils in Great Britain was approximately nine hundred thousand, so that the Sunday School enrollment, though destined to outstrip that of all other nations, was still comparatively small.

The American Sunday School Union, which we have already noted came into existence at this time, entered upon a nation-wide work with vision and system and enthusiasm hardly surpassed in the present century. They sought men qualified to introduce better principles and methods of instruction, with sufficient magnetism and force of address to inspire a deeper and wider interest in the cause at the very centers of population. Some of the leading educators gave their services. Others were paid a nominal salary for devoting their time to this work.

A system for gathering information was introduced, which disclosed the weakness as well as the strength of the schools. Knowledge was obtained of neighborhoods without S u n d a y Schools or churches—how many and where they were. Also information regarding education in general was secured, that the Sunday School leaders might ascertain the progress of secular education, especially in rural and remote districts. Considering the poor facilities for transportation, for this was before the introduction of railroads or steamboats, telephones or telegraph, and the mails were slow and costly, it is a marvel that so much valuable information was obtained from the twenty-four states then composing the Union.

Democracy was on trial in the new world. There were many who believed that sooner or later some form of monarchy would be established. But those who recognized that the permanence of a republic depends upon the character of its citizens were fully persuaded of the importance of the Sunday School. They realized that only through religious education could the nation be preserved from "that ruin with which it will be overwhelmed, should vice and infidelity loosen the restraints of virtue and make our population a turbulent mass of moral pollution."

As a result of its survey of existing conditions, the American Sunday School Union proposed to make definite advances along three related lines:

(1) Educational: by providing a system of lessons, a decidedly religious juvenile literature, a complete equipment for the schools, and definite information upon principles and methods of teaching.

(2) Organization: by promoting teachers' meetings in the local school; by forming county and state unions among schools and teachers, for inspiration, counsel, and mutual improvement.

(3) Extension of Sunday Schools: by employing general agents and missionaries, and providing a medium of communication for and between all Sunday School workers.

The enthusiasm created for organization was so great that within eighteen months from its founding, the American Sunday School Union had nearly four hundred branches in twenty-two of the twenty-four states, nine of these being state unions. The demand for juvenile literature which it created, exceeded all expectations. In 1825 it was necessary to print ninety thousand pages of reading material each day. The same year nine hundred thousand copies of different publications were issued, besides periodicals. In 1827 there were 1,616,796 copies, making a total in three years of 3,741,849 copies of publications.

But it was in its missionary work that the union accomplished its greatest success and made its largest contribution to the permanence and prosperity of the nation.

I. Missionary Achievement

The leaders of the American Sunday School Union might have been recognized as members of the apostolic Church, because of their zeal for carrying out the Great Commission. Not only were they impressed with the necessity of instructing all the children of America in the Word of God, but of making extensive plans for reaching as well as teaching them.

1. Mississippi Valley enterprise

As a result of the information gained from their systematic surveys, the Sunday School leaders were convinced that the Christian public was ready to support a movement, the magnitude of which would have appalled less courageous souls. In May, 1830, Arthur Tappan proposed that an effort be made to form a Sabbath school within two years, in every town in the Mississippi valley. The boldness and magnitude of the proposition amazed the public and won friends immediately for its support. So great was the interest that the annual meeting of the union was attended by more than two thousand people, who adopted by unanimous vote the following action:

> Resolved that the American Sunday School Union, in reliance upon divine aid, will, within two years, establish a Sunday School in every destitute place where it is practicable throughout the valley of the Mississippi.

It was a "stupendous missionary enterprise" and seemed presumptuous for an organization whose annual funds were less than a thousand dollars to propose to cover a territory now occupied by more than twenty states. The valley of the Mississippi meant all of the country west of the Alleghenies to the Rocky Mountains, and from Michigan to Louisiana. It comprised an area then estimated at one million three hundred thousand square miles with a population of approximately four million, one-tenth of which was believed to be children and youth. It was estimated that not less than thirty thousand dollars would be required to start the enterprise, and if measurably successful, ten thousand dollars the second year.

The assembly of two thousand that unanimously voted to accomplish the seemingly impossible were men of great faith. They attempted great things for

God because they fully expected great things from Him. Their enthusiasm spread. Three successive times meetings were held in Philadelphia. Subscriptions amounting to seventeen thousand dollars were received, besides offers to be responsible for the organization of various numbers of schools. Similar meetings were held in New York, where the enthusiasm was so great that hundreds could not even gain admission to the building. Vigorous speeches were made, and $15,229 more was pledged.

There were large gatherings in Boston, Washington and Charleston, but perhaps the most momentous meeting was held in Washington. It was remarkable because of its national character. A United States senator was the presiding officer. The clerk of the House of Representatives acted as secretary. Among those who addressed the meeting in behalf of the enterprise were seven senators and congressmen, including Daniel Webster and Francis Scott Key. The magnitude of the proposition appealed to the patriotism of these statesmen, and they commended it in the strongest terms as an important movement to promote the stability of the Republic. The meeting was reported in the newspapers as "one of the most important ever held in the country."

Sustained by public interest and supported by generous contributions, the Sunday School leaders divided their vast field into districts. Agents and missionaries were first assigned to those sections where immigration was forming the largest number of new settlements. That these were increasing with amazing rapidity is indicated by the state census of Illinois, which in 1825 showed a population of seventy-five thousand, but by 1830 a population of one hundred fifty-six thousand. In a short time, from sixty to seventy-five thousand dollars were actually contributed and expended in this unparalleled scheme of Sunday School extension, and it was estimated that half of the ten thousand new settlements in the great valley were supplied with Sunday Schools. Eighty to one hundred missionaries were employed.

A library, costing at least ten dollars, was furnished to every school that raised five dollars or more for this purpose. Probably more than a million volumes were thus put into circulation through these Sunday School libraries.

2. The Southern enterprise

The marvelous success of the Mississippi Valley program called for a similar effort to be made in the neglected regions of the South. In May, 1834, the American Sunday School Union launched a campaign to provide religious instruction in a vast field computed at three thousand square miles with a population of four million, of which eight hundred thousand were children and youth, five hundred thousand of these being white and three hundred thousand colored. The school funds of the Southern states were comparatively small, and at this time there had been little provision for the instruction of the poor. Hence the Sunday School was needed for the encouragement, if not the provision, of secular as well as religious instruction. A careful survey discloses the fact that there were less than seventy-five thousand members in all the Sunday Schools in the South, which left a total of seven hundred twenty-five thousand growing up without moral and

religious training and only such rudiments of general
education as they might receive in the home.

The southern people entered with alacrity upon
this campaign. It created an enthusiasm which swept
over the country, second only in magnitude to that
aroused by the larger Mississippi enterprise. Well-
known ministers and educators of the South were
present at the meeting in Philadelphia when the enterprise was proposed, and more than forty men rose
in succession and gave pledges of what they would
do in support of this campaign. Similar enthusiastic
meetings were held in the cities of both the North
and the South; liberal subscriptions were made and
strong pledges given for carrying forward this movement. A few liberal men in Boston subscribed more
than one thousand dollars and one thousand two
hundred dollars was pledged in a similar meeting
in Hartford. Difficulties were experienced in the
South which were not met in the West. Yet in the
face of these obstacles a great work was accomplished.
In addition to the organization of many Sunday
Schools, churches were strengthened, Bible study
was widely increased and one thousand libraries of
120 volumes each were especially prepared and contributed to the public schools of the Southern states.

3. Summary of results

It would be difficult to estimate fully the far-
reaching results of this vast missionary effort in the
West and the South of the new Republic. In some
places changes were almost immediate. In one year
seventeen thousand were reported to have made public confession of their faith in Christ, and foundations were laid for a multitude of new churches.

One minister and missionary of the society for twenty years gave a list of fifty churches that had grown out of the Sunday Schools organized by himself or his associates. Another reported forty churches following the new Sunday Schools in his field. A third, well qualified to speak from his records, gave as his opinion that "eight-tenths of the churches in the valley of the Mississippi organized in the previous fifteen years, had grown out of the Sunday Schools."

Even where a church was not founded as the result of a Sunday School, children were brought under Christian instruction and entire neighborhoods led to religious belief and practices. From 1824 to 1874, there were 61,299 organizations with 407,-242 teachers and 2,650,784 pupils. In addition, a vast work was accomplished in reviving and aiding 87,291 schools with literature. The amount expended in missionary operations from 1824 to 1874 was $2,133,364.13, of which about $517,000 was for literature to needy schools and families. The total value of the American Sunday School Union's literature circulated by sale and donation in this half century was computed at approximately six million dollars.

Another important contribution of the Sunday School was its encouragement to general education. It is doubtful whether the excellent public school system would have grown into favor so soon in the great Middle West had it not been for large donations of Sunday School literature. This created a taste for good reading and increased the desire for an education among the young. The enthusiasm thus aroused in education is believed to have stimulated legislation in the Western states to make early and munificent provision for free public instructors and to give public schools better equipment and support. As we have already seen, it was the wholehearted support of the New England settlers in the Western states to tax-supported schools that eventually won them a place in the thinking of the entire nation.

II. A Great Missionary

Volumes might be written on the thrilling experiences and marvelous accomplishments of the Sunday School missionaries that the American Sunday School Union sent out into the frontiers, to organize and establish Sunday Schools. These heroic men braved hardship and privation and even peril in the country that was yet a wilderness and still infested with Indians that were often hostile. There were no roads, and traveling had to be done almost entirely on horseback. Difficulties of communication often kept these men out of touch with civilization for weeks and months at a time, but a spirit of consecration to their task and full realization of its importance urged them forward.

When the work of Sunday School expansion began, Chicago was only a mud hamlet and most of Illinois was a wild prairie, but the missionaries were warmly welcomed in the lowly communities on the plains or in the mountains of the Middle West. Schools provided meeting places for the scattered inhabitants of rural communities, and Sunday School literature often afforded the only reading matter for many of these pioneer homes.

If a hall of fame should ever be built for the world's great missionaries, one niche would surely be preserved for Stephen Paxson. He lived in the small village of Winchester, Illinois, where through missionary enterprise a Sunday School had been established. His little daughter attended this school and one morning asked her father to go with her, as the superintendent had asked every one to bring a new pupil. Mr. Paxson, to oblige his daughter, complied. He enjoyed the school and especially the library books which they permitted him to take home to read. He became a regular attendant, was converted and joined the church that grew out of that little frontier Sunday School.

But happily it did not end there. He became so interested in Sunday School work that he gave up his trade as a hatter and offered his services to the American Sunday School Union. This organization assured him a salary of only a dollar a day, considerably less than he had made at his trade. Unable longer to afford the upkeep of his home in the village, the Paxson family climbed into a covered wagon and went out into the wilderness of Pike County, where a rude log cabin became the headquarters from which the Sunday School missionary set out on what proved to be his life work.

Few men have been as handicapped as Mr. Paxson. He had a crippled ankle which gave him considerable pain. In addition, he stammered so badly that as a boy he had been nicknamed Stuttering Steve. His school teacher had not had the patience to instruct him, and he had been obliged to get his education without an instructor. He had learned how to read by spelling out the letters on the sign boards. Despite these handicaps Paxson accomplished great things.

He first traveled over the state of Illinois. He was away from home for long periods, sometimes weeks and even months. He visited pioneer homes, talked to the people about the need of a Sunday School, and urged them to organize one. He was never daunted by bad weather. A favorite expression with him was, "A Sunday School born in a snow-storm will never be scared by a white frost." In pleading his cause among backwoodsmen of the prairie or giving his experiences before cultured audiences in the East, he would say, "Facts are God's arguments."

Because of the impassable roads at times, Mr. Paxson traveled by horseback. His first horse became disabled after traveling for several years and a new one was needed, but no funds were available. At the close of an address in the Congregational Church of Pittsfield, Illinois, the pastor suggested that an offering be taken to buy "a missionary horse." The new mount was named Robert Raikes and soon became one of the best known animals in the country. In twenty-five years he carried his master more than one hundred thousand miles. So well did the horse learn the habits of Stephen Paxson that he would never pass a child on the road without stopping, and would always turn in when he came to a church or school house. When the horse was worn out, Robert Wells, of New York, sent one hundred dollars to purchase Robert Raikes, Junior.

In twenty years this tireless missionary organized 1,314 new Sunday Schools with more than 83,000 members, and encouraged and aided 1,747 other schools. It is said that no one ever equalled his record of organizing forty-seven Sunday Schools in forty consecutive days. Like the apostle Paul, this American missionary was highly successful in interesting others in his work. "His intensity of manner, homeliness of speech, and graphic sketches fascinated his audiences." A city daily in New York reported: "Stephen Paxson made an address in which his aristocratic auditors were so deeply interested that they wept and smiled alternately, never heeding mistakes in grammar or rhetorical discrepancies."

The ability of this missionary as an organizer was recognized by business concerns and he received several flattering offers. On one occasion a friend proposed to invest fifty thousand dollars in the purchase of land if Paxson would promote the enterprise, the two to share equally in the profits. Years later the two compared notes. His friend had doubled his fifty thousand dollars. Paxson from his memorandum pointed to a record of fifty thousand pupils gathered into Sunday Schools up to that time and said, "I would not alter the record nor change the investment."

III. The Early Conventions

"The convention idea," said W. C. Pearce, "was born in a desire for and the need of mutual helpfulness." The Sunday School convention constituency is international and interdenominational. The Sunday School convention platform is the only one upon which all evangelical denominations can meet to discuss the evangelization of the world. The Reformation slogan of Chillingworth, "The Bible and the Bible alone is the religion of Protestants," is one basis upon which all Protestant churches can unite. The carrying out of the Great Commission to teach the Bible to every creature is common to every branch of the Christian faith.

But not only is the Sunday School convention an important agency for unifying the many branches of Protestantism, but it also affords a place where the entire international field can be reported and studied. In denominational gatherings interest is narrowed to local spheres, but in the international conventions, national and world-wide work can be studied.

Above all, however, the convention movement, with its vast numbers gathered from all parts of the hemisphere, not only promotes new interest and enthusiasm, but is a source of cheer and encouragement to many discouraged workers. The coming of thousands engaged in a common task to report their trials and triumphs is one of the strongest factors for the remarkable advance of the Sunday School movement. "Despite the weakness of the early gatherings," says E. Morris Fergusson, "the convention movement was destined to prove a mighty factor not only in Sunday School advancement, but in reshaping the life and ideals of North American Protestant Christianity."

1. First National Convention

The convention movement had its birth at a conference of friends of the Sunday School held in Philadelphia during the anniversary of the American Sunday School Union and the General Assembly of the Presbyterian Church, May 23, 1832. A resolution was adopted recommending that superintendents and teachers of the entire country convene to consider the duties and obligations of Sunday School workers and the best plans of organizing, strengthening and managing their sessions.

As a result of this Philadelphia conference, the First National Convention was held in New York, October 3, 1832. It was attended by 220 delegates, among whom were leading laymen and clergymen representing Sunday Schools in fourteen states and territories out of the twenty-four that then composed the Union. There were only three hundred miles of railway in the country and the scourge of Asiatic cholera was devastating the land, so that under the circumstances this attendance was exceptionally large.

Hon. Theodore Frelinghuysen was elected president. Among the topics considered were infant Sunday School organizations, qualifying pupils to become teachers, organization of county unions, and a Sunday School of two sessions. The discussion developed so much interest, and the conference in general was valued so highly, that it was decided to hold another convention the following year.

2. Second National Convention

The Second National Convention was held in Philadelphia, May 22, 1833. The Hon. Willard Hall, an eminent Delaware jurist, was chosen president. Looking back over the years, it would seem now to have been unwise to call a second convention within eight months after the first, especially in view of the limitations of communication and transportation. The results of the first convention had not yet been fully transmitted to the outlying districts, nor plans fully formulated for a program that would be representative. But the pressure was strong to continue the discussions of questions which had been raised at the first meeting and placed in the hands of special and regular committees.

This convention was not so largely attended as the earlier gathering. There were delegates from nine states, among them "some of the most distinguished and enlightened friends of Sunday School which our country furnishes." One profitable discussion was private Sunday Schools, meaning schools or classes taught in private homes for those who were not willing on account of poverty or sectarian prejudice to attend Sunday Schools in other neighborhoods. This was a prophetic foreshadowing of the home department movement.

3. State unions and conventions

These two national conventions threshed out most thoroughly and much in advance of their time, fundamental questions relating to the organization and conduct of the Sunday School. This fact, together with smaller attendance and accompanying lessening of enthusiasm at the second convention, postponed any national effort for a third convention for twenty-six years.

Meanwhile smaller conventions were being held in the various states. These were largely promoted by the American Sunday School Union, and generally for the purpose of promoting the extension of the Sunday School and the general improvement of the work. These smaller meetings, which had no relation to each other, suggested to leaders the possibility of state gatherings. In 1846 a Sunday School convention met in the territory of Wisconsin largely through the influence of J. W. Vail, an agent of the American Sunday School Union, supported by William

H. Byron, a member of the First National Convention.

The same year the first wholly self-managed, self-perpetuating county Sunday School convention was organized in Scott County, Illinois, by Stephen Paxson. Through the efforts of H. Clay Trumbull, another pioneer in organization, Hartford County, Connecticut, held its first convention in 1856, and in 1858 New Jersey held its first state convention.

4. Third National Convention

The nation-wide religious revival of 1857 aroused new interest in a national convention. Sunday School leaders were encouraged to call for such an assembly to be held in Philadelphia, February 22, 1859. Seventeen states and the District of Columbia were represented by delegates, and there was one representative from Great Britain. Dr. John S. Hart, editor of *The Sunday School Times,* then published by the American Sunday School Union, was temporary chairman of the convention. Former governor Joseph Pollock, of Pennsylvania, was chosen president, and H. Clay Trumbull, of Connecticut, and George Baughman, of Virginia, secretaries. Among the representatives were several who had been prominent in the conventions a quarter of a century earlier

The list of speakers was a notable one, though no topic of far-reaching significance appears to have been on the program. A committee of which George H. Stuart was chairman was appointed to arrange for "a similar assemblage of the evangelical Sunday Schools of America." This convention marked the beginning of a central leadership for the Sunday School cause other than that of the American Sunday

School Union. The union which had been instrumental in bringing about the earlier gatherings, cor-
dially endorsed this convention enterprise, and in its
new weekly, *The Sunday School Times,* printed a
verbatim report of the entire proceedings.

5. Fourth National Convention

The plans of Mr. Stuart's committee were frus-
trated by the outbreak of the Civil War. Not only
during that turbulent period, but in the years that
immediately followed, a national gathering of Sunday School workers was impractical if not impossible. In June, 1868, at the International Convention
of the Young Men's Christian Association in Detroit, an informal meeting of Sunday School workers was held, advocating another national convention. They soon learned that a committee appointed
by the convention ten years previously was in existence, and representatives of both groups finally
got together and issued a call for the Fourth National Convention. This was held in Newark, New
Jersey, April 28, 1869.

Twenty-eight states and one territory were represented by 526 delegates, and there were visitors from
Canada, England, Ireland, Scotland, Egypt, and
South Africa. George H. Stuart, of Pennsylvania,
was elected president, and H. Clay Trumbull, John
H. Vincent, and B. F. Jacobs served as secretaries.
The chairman of the executive committee was Edward Eggleston. This was the first national introduction of four leaders who were destined to render
outstanding and far-reaching accomplishments for
the Sunday School movement.

The convention was international in character as well as in name, and its sessions were characterized by extraordinary spiritual power. Much enthusiasm was created by the crowded sessions and stirring speeches. The chief subject was the promotion of teacher training through institutes and normal classes. The convention made far-reaching decisions in disapproving of the idea that the Sunday School was in any sense a substitute for family or pulpit instruction, or that it was to be regarded as independent of the church. According to *The Sunday School Times,* "never before had so many Sunday School leaders of the land been brought face to face. Taken as a whole, it was the most memorable Sunday School gathering ever assembled in the United States, if not in the world."

IV. Developing a Curriculum

In the earliest days of the Sunday School, especially in the South where a part of the program was instruction in the rudiments of learning, the *New England Primer* was adopted for this purpose and constituted the curriculum. As the public school grew in favor, the Sunday School was able to confine itself distinctly to religious materials.

1. Catechism

From 1790 to 1815 the catechism, with a few exceptions, was the curriculum. This was largely because there was no other course of Bible study in print, and catechisms were inexpensive and could be readily procured. Moreover, they lent themselves easily to divisions, sections and lessons for the purpose of instruction, and for this reason were better than the Bible even if copies had been available. But as all printing of the Bible had to be done in Great Britain, volumes were expensive and it was impossible for every pupil to be supplied. Naturally, therefore, the teachers turned to the catechism as the more economical textbook.

Attention has already been called to the three great catechisms—Lutheran, Heidelberg and Westminster—which were available at this time. These splendid compendiums of doctrine, however, were framed and worded for adult instruction, while a child should be taught about redemption, regeneration, the meaning of the cross and the significance of the sacraments in terms sufficiently simple for him to understand. Although graded lessons in the religious curriculum are the product of the twentieth century, an examination of the catechetical materials of this early period leads one to conclude that there was a decided attempt to adapt this doctrinal instruction to the capacities of the child. Isaac Watts' *Catechism for Children and Youth* is a good illustration of the effort to adapt the Bible to the child.

a. *The first catechism*

This was intended for young children, beginning at the age of three or four years. The teacher was expected to see that the child understood every word of each question, and the child was required to memorize the answers before learning to read them for himself. The opening questions of this catechism illustrate the principles of grading as they were understood at that time.

Q. Can you tell me, child, who made you?
A. The great God who made heaven and earth.

Q. What doth God do for you?
A. He keeps me from harm by night and by day, and is always doing me good.

Q. And what must you do for the great God who is so good to you?
A. I must learn to know Him first, and then do everything to please Him.

b. *The second catechism*

Watts extended this catechism for children who were beginning to read. Seventy-eight questions and answers comprised its contents. The nature of its material may be ascertained from the following excerpts:

Q. Dear child, do you know what you are?
A. I am a creature of God, for He made me both body and soul. "Thus saith the Lord . . . I have made the earth, and created man upon it" (Isa. 45:11, 12). "Thou hast clothed me with skin and flesh, and hast fenced me with bones and sinews" (Job 10:11). "The Lord . . . formeth the spirit of man within him" (Zech. 12:1).

Q. How do you know you have a soul?
A. Because I find something within me that can think and know, can wish and desire, can rejoice and be sorry, which my body cannot do. "There is a spirit in man" (Job 32:8). "Who teacheth us more than the beasts of the earth, and maketh us wiser than the fowls of heaven?" (Job 35:11). "Knowledge is pleasant unto thy soul" (Prov. 2:10). "The desire of our soul is to thy name" (Isa. 26:8). "My soul shall be joyful in the Lord" (Ps. 35:9). "My soul is exceeding sorrowful" (Matt. 26:38).

c. *The third catechism*

This was arranged for youth between the ages of twelve and fourteen. The pupil at this age was thought to be sufficiently mature to take up the original catechism.

d. *Advanced catechism*

Watts' catechism on the sins and follies of youth concluded the series. Its purpose was to make a practical application of doctrinal instruction. This catechism was divided into four parts: sins against God; sins against others; sins against ourselves; follies and frailties of children and youth. The following examples illustrate the content:

> Q. What is the first mark of ungodliness?
> A. If I never know nor praise God for His own greatness and glory.
>
> Q. What are the ill consequences of sinful anger?
> A. These five.
>
> Q. What is the first?
> A. Railing and calling ill names.
> *Reason against this sin*. Because railers are not fit for sober company, and are very displeasing to God.

In one way the catechism had many things in its favor. It emphasized doctrine, and it was systematic and logical in its arrangement. But even with the attempt to grade the material there was failure to grasp the idea that the child was not a miniature adult, and that there were better avenues of approach. Moreover, the catechism set forth only the doctrines of the Bible and neglected the vast portions that were devoted to narrative, poetry and prophecy.

2. Memory period

With the formation of the American Bible Society in 1816, it was possible to procure copies of the

Scriptures at greatly reduced prices. The fact that volumes were now to be found in homes enabled the Bible to make a stronger bid for popularity and to be moved nearer to the center of the curriculum. It was argued that if the children could memorize the catechism, they could also memorize portions of Scripture; and thus the use of lesson material directly from the Bible for memory work rapidly crowded out the catechism from its long-established place.

There were two reasons why the memory method of Bible study was used and the Bible was given a prominent place in the religious curriculum. The Bible is not a graded book and it was not the purpose of its writers to prepare their material for immediate teaching use. Again, the commonly accepted method of learning in the schools of that period was memorizing.

These two considerations explain why Sunday School children for a quarter of a century had for their lessons Bible passages for memory work, which, in the absence of definite assignments, were largely determined by whim and personal preference. No restrictions or suggestions were made; the child selected verses as he pleased from the entire Bible. But the plan proved popular, especially after it was stimulated by a system of prizes and rewards. Pupils memorized an almost unbelievable number of verses. There were schools that reported an average of five thousand verses of Scripture committed to memory in a quarter. The fourth annual report of the New York Sunday School Union says:

> In many schools individuals ten or twelve years of age have committed to memory in a single quarter from

800 to 1,350 verses. An amount of 18,859 verses has been recited in one school during the past year. In another instance a boy of seven years has recited 1,003 verses in eight weeks, and a boy of eleven years, 400 verses in six weeks.

Even the adults memorized Scripture. One school reported that the enrollment ranged in age from seventeen to seventy-eight, and that they recited Scripture every Sunday and "repeated at a time from one to eight chapters in the New Testament."

A social occasion which greatly encouraged memory work for both old and young was the Sunday School concert. This was a very popular service in which the program consisted of prayer, a brief address, and the reciting of Scripture verses. Contests were even staged to determine which one in the community could recite the largest amount of Bible content. The last named feature may have accounted considerably for the popularity of the Sunday School concert. At any rate, these meetings drew crowded houses and appealed to Sunday School interest in the same way that the spelling bees attracted the community to the public school.

3. Babel period

The period from 1840 to 1872 in the history of the American Sunday School curriculum is generally referred to as the babel period. This seemed to have been a time of great confusion, for there was no unity of teaching material or systematic plan of its presentation. A great variety of instruction prevailed. Both the catechism and the Bible memory work gave way to other teaching material.

a. *Selected Scripture lessons*

Shortly after its organization, the American Sunday School Union launched a plan for substituting the unprofitable committing of large portions of Scripture to memory without religious instruction by a system of lesson study of from ten to twenty Bible verses each week. A list of lessons with the dates on which they were to be studied was provided, so that the absent pupils might also learn the lesson in the course. The same Scripture was used in the entire school, with the possible exception of the children in the infant school, who were unable to read. To facilitate the use of these uniform lessons, teachers' helps were issued, adapted to the main school and to several grades. This was the first step toward uniformity of instruction.

b. *A verse a day plan*

About this time the memorizing of promiscuous verses gave way to the study of a verse a day, a plan which had long been practiced by the Moravians and which for a brief period became popular. The Sunday School Teachers' Association of Oswego County, New York, adopted this plan and recommended it to the American Sunday School Union and other Sunday School societies. In 1831, the *American Sunday School* magazine endorsed the plan, while the *Sunday School Journal* published the verses each week. The purpose was for the pupils to commit to memory each day consecutive verses, the total comprising the Sunday School lesson. This had in it the element of preparation by the pupil and explanation by the teacher.

c. *Denominational lessons*

The denominations now began to awake to their responsibilities in furthering and providing for the Sunday School; but their injection of denominational teaching was to lead to a multiplication of courses. Private publishers competed with the Sunday School Union and the denominational publishing houses in placing on the market their rival schemes. Thus various systems sprang up, resulting in confusion and lack of unity.

d. *The question book*

In the babel period the question book was the representative type of Sunday School material. Whether the system of lessons covered one year or more, or whether issued by the Sunday School unions, denominational presses, or private individuals, all teaching material throughout almost the entire period took the form of a question book. While superior to the catechism in that its biblical content was greatly enlarged and arranged in more logical order, nevertheless the question book was of a mechanical order. The questions were not prepared for the purpose of making the pupil master the context, and the child was naturally completely ignored in the adaptation of the lessons.

The most serious defect of the entire period was a neglect of a psychological approach. The words and concepts used were for the most part too difficult for a child. The individual lessons did not have definite aims, and the one purpose appears to have been to cover so much material and master so much factual knowledge. Something was greatly needed to systematize and unify the instruction of the Sunday School

V. Typical Schools

What was a Sunday School of this period like? Of course, as we have noticed in the public schools, there was considerable difference between the organizations in the city and those on the frontier. The former secured the best teachers, and generally received the support of the pastor and the churches in which they were held. The independent organizations out on the frontier, apart from what aid they received from the American Sunday School Union, were obliged to shift for themselves.

There were, however, a few elements which were found in all schools. Most of them recognized at least two departments, infant and main, and the larger schools had many classes in each. Although the Sunday School was a children's institution, adults seem to have taken a great interest in it from the beginning, and their attendance and support to a large extent counteracted the early indifference of the Church.

Few pastors of this period appreciated the importance of the Sunday School. Seminaries had no courses in Christian education and most ministers were unprepared to deal effectively with the children of their congregation. A marked exception was Dr. Stephen H. Tyng, an Episcopal clergyman, who held successful pastorates in Philadelphia and New York. Dr. Tyng recorded his accomplishments in *Forty Years' Experience in Sunday Schools,* and from these pages we are able to gain a good impression of the typical school of that day.

1. St. Paul's Sunday School

Dr. Tyng's first experiences were in St. Paul's Church at Philadelphia, to which he was called in 1829. Of this school he writes:

> The large, well-organized Sunday School of this church made it the field of labor for which I had longed and which I ardently and instantly embraced. I organized a weekly lecture on the lesson for the teachers, besides a weekly Bible class for women. I spent every Sunday morning in a personal visitation of all the classes, and every Sunday afternoon I devoted to a personal address to the assembled pupils.

2. Epiphany Sunday School

The five years' ministry at St. Paul's prepared Dr. Tyng with a knowledge and experience which he brought into operation in the successful founding and establishment of the Church of the Epiphany in the same city. That church was founded upon the Sunday School. "Previously," he says, "the school had been considered an appendage to the church, and by some ministers and members a troublesome appendage. We founded this church with a distinct understanding and plan that the Sunday School should be the main and prominent object of record."

Starting in 1834 with nine teachers and twenty-five pupils, when Dr. Tyng removed to New York in 1845 there were eighty teachers and 804 pupils enrolled. Two distinct schools were maintained, one for boys and one for girls, and in these Dr. Tyng continued his weekly habits of lectures to teachers and weekly Bible classes for women, as well as a monthly address and the devotion of every Sunday morning to a supervision of the work. In addition, he established an anniversary occasion, at the exercises of which every pupil received a book as a token of the interest and affection of the church.

3. St. George Sunday School

Dr. Tyng's culminating work was in the St. George Sunday School of New York. He commenced his school here in 1847, and when the first anniversary exercises were held, it had grown from 30 to 505. At the third anniversary there was a total of 1,002.

Meanwhile the rapid development of this school had encouraged other churches to build up their Sunday Schools, and more than ten different schools were established in the neighborhood. A mission school was also operated under the direction of the St. George Church, and this was the beginning of branch Sunday Schools, which many churches have since carried on so successfully. The description of the eleventh anniversary is of special interest as throwing light upon this important annual gathering:

> Galleries, which were given to the congregation, were crowded long before our exercises began. The schools assembled in their rooms and moved from thence to the church. They came in perfect order and occupied the pews designated for them, each teacher preceding the class and having a card indicating the location. The first to enter was the main school headed by the two women's Bible classes of 88 members. Then the men's class of 28 members followed. After the adult classes came the infant department with 459 pupils. The third division was the intermediate school, consisting of 253 girls and 189 boys.
>
> After the main school of 63 teachers and officers and 1,017 pupils had been seated, the English mission school entered with its 35 teachers and 382 pupils, and occupied

the reserved seats. The third group to be seated were the
members of the German mission school, which totaled 9
teachers and 131 pupils. Altogether 107 teachers and
1,530 pupils were present.

The exercises were simple. The children united in
familiar hymns and the pastor delivered a prepared sermon. After the address a missionary offering totaling
$4,224 was presented by messengers from successive
classes. The exercises were concluded by the distribution
of 1,600 books, the annual gift to teachers and pupils.

"Two hours," says Dr. Tyng, "were occupied in
all these exercises, and the unwearied crowd seemed
unwilling even then to depart. The whole result was
to create a deeper attachment in St. George to our
Sunday School work."

———————

1. How many American children were in Sunday
   School in 1824?
2. Why was the Sunday School needed to preserve the Republic?
3. Along what three lines did the American Sunday School Union plan its work?
4. What was the Mississippi Valley enterprise?
5. What support was given to it in eastern cities?
6. How were the contributions expended?
7. Describe the Southern enterprise of the American Sunday School Union.
8. What were some of the far-reaching results of
   these missionary efforts?
9. Write a biography of five hundred words on
   Stephen Paxson.
10. What are some of the values of the Sunday
    School convention?

11. When and where was the First National Convention held and what did it accomplish?
12. Describe the Second National Convention.
13. What progress was made in state unions and conventions?
14. Give the outstanding features of the Third National Convention.
15. What took place at the Fourth National Convention?
16. Why was the catechism so largely used in the early years of the Sunday School?
17. Compare the first and second catechisms of Isaac Watts.
18. What was the nature of the advanced catechism?
19. Describe the memory period of Sunday School curriculum.
20. Give four types of lessons used during the babel period.
21. What was a Sunday School of this period like?
22. Write an account of two hundred words on the three Sunday Schools of Dr. Stephen H. Tyng.

11

FORTY YEARS OF ADVANCE

THE LAST forty years of the nineteenth century were epoch-making in the progress of the Sunday School, being eclipsed only by the even greater advance of the first forty years of the twentieth century. The period following the Civil War was one of national peace and prosperity. The Sunday School grew and improved with the nation. The revival of 1857, which grew out of a prayer meeting held on Fulton Street, New York City, swept the nation and created a new interest in the Sunday School in the same manner as the revival of Wesley and Whitefield in the days of Robert Raikes.

The national convention of 1859 indicated that the growth of the Sunday School movement had been rapid and widespread. The recognition and establishment of the tax-supported state schools and their elimination of the Bible from the curriculum made the nation turn its attention to the Sunday School as the best agency for religious instruction.

The place that the Sunday School occupied in national thought is best illustrated by the report of the commission sent over by the French government to study the educational agencies in America. Dr. H. C. Trumbull declared that no department of primary education impressed the president of that commission as more important and more noteworthy than

that of the Sunday School. From its voluminous report we read:

> The Sunday School is not an accessory agency in the
> normal economy of American education; it does not add
> a superfluity; it is an absolute necessity for the complete
> instruction of the child. Its aim is to fill by itself the
> complex mission which elsewhere is in large measure
> assigned to the family, the school, and the church. All
> things unite to assign to this institution a grand part in
> the American life.

The first great accomplishment of the last forty
years of the nineteenth century was the adoption of

I. International Uniform Lesson

It has already been observed that the Sunday
School curriculum was in a state of chaos between
1840 and 1872. While selected lessons had fully displaced the catechism and the memorization of Bible
verses, as yet there was no consensus regarding the
portions of the Bible that should be used, and the
multiplication of efforts to prepare courses only
added to the confusion. We have already seen the
popularity of the question book, which sold as low as
six and one-half cents a volume. Within fourteen
years from the first issue in 1827, nearly two million copies were sold, and their wide use was a factor in preparing for the yet far away national and international uniformity.

It was in 1869 that the first explanatory book was
added to the series, giving answers to the questions
of the other books. Then the *American Horticultur-
ist* supplemented prior schemes of lesson study by
adding to each selected lesson its "connecting history" and "analysis."

However, it was left for John H. Vincent and
B. F. Jacobs to take the last steps toward unifying
a lesson system. These men were Sunday School leaders of Chicago, but their accomplishments were far-
reaching.

Mr. Vincent was a Methodist minister who, called
into exclusive service as a Sunday School specialist
by the Sunday School Union, began publishing in
1866 *The Sunday School Teacher.* The first issue
contained a newly conceived lesson series entitled
"A New System of Sunday School Study." The Vincent system was the first in the world with analytical
and illustrative helps for the teacher and lesson helps
for the pupil. It was at once widely adopted by Western schools. When Rev. Edward Eggleston became
editor of the *Chicago Teacher,* he elaborated and
extended the lessons. While his paper was leading
the way rapidly toward national uniformity, Eggleston himself singularly and strenuously combatted the
idea as inconsistent with the graded principle.

Meanwhile the Fourth National Convention met,
in 1869, in Newark, New Jersey, and B. F. Jacobs,
who was an enthusiast for having the same lesson for
the whole school, was made chairman of the superintendents' section of the convention. As such he
secured the endorsement of his plan of uniformity
by three-fourths of the superintendents.

Mr. Jacobs next appeared before the National Executive Committee that was preparing a program for
the Fifth National Convention in Indianapolis. He
urged instant action upon the question of uniformity.
The committee decided to call a meeting of all lesson publishers and writers, and by a vote of twenty-
six to three, a committee was selected to prepare a

list of lessons for the following year. The lessons selected comprised two quarters of Eggleston's outlines, one quarter from Vincent's lessons, and the
other quarter prepared by the committee itself.

The climax came at the Fifth National Convention
at Indianapolis in 1872, where a vote was taken on
Jacobs' plan of uniformity. Jacobs led the memorable
discussion with five clean-cut points that such uniformity would be better for teachers, pupils, parents,
pastors, and lesson writers. Dr. Eggleston opposed
the resolution, declaring that it was a move back-
ward. It was Dr. Vincent who turned the tide. When
called to the platform, he said, "A year ago I opposed the scheme of national uniformity. Today I am
thoroughly converted to the other side." With a mi-
nority of only ten votes, the resolution of Mr. Jacobs'
was adopted, the convention with great enthusiasm
joining in the singing of the Doxology. The dream
was realized and Vincent's lesson idea and Jacobs'
world-wide plan of uniformity became a reality.

The newly formed system of lessons found instant
favor at home and in foreign lands. One by one
the denominations swung into line. The religious
weeklies gave large space to critical study of the
current lessons. Many secular papers also began to
furnish expositions. Interest and progress were
equally great in Canada, and the plan was adopted
shortly after in Britain. Within three years the lessons had gone into nineteen nations.

The resolution of Mr. Jacobs' fixed the number
of the first Lesson Committee at ten, five clergymen
and five laymen. This was later enlarged to fifteen.
So intelligently and thoroughly were the selections
of the first committee made that they have been the

landmarks of succeeding committees. At first the chosen lesson text was brief, the intention being that the entire lesson should be well studied and committed to memory. The "golden text" was not selected by the committee until two years after the system of lessons began.

The adoption of the International Uniform Lessons is recognized as one of the greatest accomplishments in the history of the Sunday School. The old question book was set aside and the new lessons were gladly accepted by the Sunday Schools everywhere.

Their greatest value lay in unifying and standardizing the school. Not only were old and young studying the same lesson throughout the school, but the identical lesson was being used in every part of the country. This permitted the use of prepared Bible readings in the home, since every member of the family would have a common interest in the lesson. It also multiplied lesson helps and expositions of the selected Scripture in religious and secular papers. The use of a single lesson provided an enormous constituency for the use of lesson helps which would be common to all. As the public schools were now standardizing their curriculum in order that there would be similarity of instruction in every city, so the Sunday School took its place in this advance of instruction by having the same lesson for every locality.

II. International Sunday School Convention

Attention has already been directed to the beginning of the Sunday School convention movement and a brief description given of the first four national conventions. The last forty years of the nineteenth century produced a new interest in these gatherings. Not only were the state and district conventions held faithfully and enthusiastically year after year, but the Sunday School movement assumed such world-wide proportions that international assemblies became necessary.

The convention movement probably did more than anything else to promote the growth and improvement of the Sunday School. Those who attended these gatherings often here received their first vision of the greatness of their task and returned to their work with new energy and enthusiasm. Sunday School leaders recognized the importance of these conventions and took an active part in promoting them.

Perhaps the greatest achievement along these lines was the work of B. F. Jacobs, William Reynolds and D. L. Moody. Despite the fact that the Civil War was raging, these three eminent Sunday School leaders set out to organize every county in the state of Illinois so that each would have a secretary and an annual convention. In less than one year they had one hundred and two counties successfully organized and the entire state Sunday School-minded. This marvelous accomplishment not only gave this state in the Middle West a large voice in such far-reaching movements as the International Uniform Lessons, but also made its leaders commanding figures at international conventions.

The adoption of the International Uniform Lessons overshadowed everything else at the Fifth National Convention in Indianapolis. B. F. Jacobs, through whose indomitable energy and effort the convention adopted this far-reaching measure, had more in mind than to bring order out of chaos in the field of curriculum. A uniform lesson meant "a functioning Bible-centered Protestant community; religion exercised in the field of Sunday School instruction without violence to any denominational ties."

There were two other forward steps in the pathway that led toward a centralization, which was to produce thirty years later the International Sunday School Association. The first of these was the appointment of E. Payson Porter as statistical secretary to serve without salary. He thus became in effect the first staff worker. The second was the recognition of the Canadian representatives as delegates from another country and the change of the nomenclature of the convention from national to international.

1. First International Convention

The First International Convention was held in Baltimore, in 1875. Rev. George A. Pelz, of New Jersey, was elected president, and 463 delegates were in attendance. Twenty Canadian representatives participated in the convention proceedings.

The convention appears to have been mainly a jubilation over what had been accomplished at Indianapolis. The report of the Lesson Committee was inspiring in that it showed how extensively the uniform lessons had been adopted by the Sunday Schools of many denominations. Mr. Porter, the statistical secretary, reported a total Sunday School membership for United States and Canada of 6,850,834 in 74,272 schools.

2. Second International Convention

Nothing particularly new was done in the way of progress at the Second International Convention in Atlanta, Georgia, April 17-19, 1878. Governor Colquitt, of Georgia, presided, and the most important matter for discussion was the International Lesson system. The delegates seem to have had but one feeling, that of warm approval.

But the main feature of this convention was the fellowship which it brought about between the North and the South. Nothing since the Civil War had done so much to promote good feeling between the sections as this convention. Governor Colquitt melted all hearts with his farewell words. The union of hearts there was inexpressibly delightful.

3. Third International Convention

The Third International Convention met in Toronto, Canada, June 22-24, 1881, and Hon. S. H. Blake, of Toronto, presided. The special feature of this convention was the inauguration of the interdenominational work undertaken by the International Executive Committee. This, again, was the suggestion of the fertile brain of B. F. Jacobs, and at this convention he began his long service as chairman of the International Executive Committee, to continue until his death, twenty-one years later. President Garfield sent a message of interest and congratulation. It was at this convention that the home class work was first mentioned.

4. Fourth International Convention

Hon. Thomas W. Bicknell, of Massachusetts, presided at the Fourth International Convention in

Louisville, Kentucky, June 11-12, 1884. The program was an alliterative one—the Work, the Word, and the Workers. That suggests the character of the gathering.

The discussions were of special value to the delegates who had come long distances to obtain new ideas and inspiration. Pastor John Paul Cooke, of Paris, France, gave an interesting and instructive address on "Sunday School Work in Europe." The third Lesson Committee was appointed, and five persons were added as corresponding members, four from Great Britain and one from France.

5. Fifth International Convention

Chicago entertained the convention of 1887, June 1-3, which elected William Reynolds, of Illinois, as president, and later appointed him field superintendent, the first official organizer for the international field. It was the first gathering of the kind at which the Home Department was presented. The plan of home classes had been so far tried and perfected that here it was set forth as a movement meriting and demanding attention. Mr. and Mrs. W. N. Hartshorn, of Massachusetts, came into prominence among the international workers at this convention, by reason of their leadership in the primary work of the convention.

6. Sixth International Convention

The Sixth International Convention, at Pittsburgh, Pennsylvania, June 24-27, 1890, was instructive and inspiring, but without special characteristics. Hon J. G. Harris, of Alabama, presided, and the convention, by resolution, placed its endorsement on the Home Department. Action was taken regarding

the erection of a Sunday School building in connection with the World's Fair at Chicago in 1893, a
structure which was put up and in which many a
memorable meeting was held while the exposition
was in progress. After a prolonged discussion, the
plan of having a quarterly temperance lesson on a
Sunday of its own was approved by the convention.

7. Seventh International Convention

The Seventh International and the Second World
Convention were held jointly in St. Louis, Mis-
souri, August 30 to September 5, 1893. During
this time the field workers held their first conference.
The emphasis of the convention was laid upon state,
county, and township work, and great impulse was
given to systematized effort, with the aim to leave no
part of the field overlooked.

The chief discussion was on the International Lessons, and the system was approved in the heartiest
kind of an endorsement. Uniformity in study had
bound the Sunday School workers of the different
denominations together in a tie of brotherhood which
to them was very precious. Other topics discussed
were: "The Sunday School and Its Influence among
the Negroes in the South," "The Training of Teachers," "Summer Schools," "Training Schools for
Christian Workers." Hon. Lewis Miller. of Ohio,
was the presiding officer.

8. Eighth International Convention

The Eighth International Convention, at Boston,
Massachusetts, June 23-26, 1896, was notable in
many directions. There were 1,063 delegates present, the largest number in the history of international
conventions. The devotional leadership of D. L.

Moody, who conducted the opening hour each day,
was a great inspiration. Bishop Vincent, who had
been chairman of the Lesson Committee from the
beginning in 1872, resigned, and Dr. John Potts,
of Toronto, Canada, was appointed. All debts of
the convention were reported paid and $35,203 was
pledged for the work of the next triennium. The
addresses of the convention were of an unusually
high order, and under the presidency of Samuel
B. Capen, of Boston, the convention reached a very
high standard. The "field" of the convention was extended to include Mexico, Central America, and the
West Indies.

At this convention William Reynolds made his
last report as field superintendent. He stated that
he had attended one hundred and fifty-four conventions and visited every state, province and territory
in the international field, except Alaska, Alberta and
Newfoundland. Mr. Reynolds had the assistance of
Professor H. M. Hamill for the whole field, Hugh
Cork for the Northwest, and Rev. L. B. Maxwell
among the colored people of the South.

The fifth Lesson Committee of fifteen, together
with five corresponding members in Great Britain,
were chosen to select the lessons for 1900-1905.

9. Ninth International Convention

Atlanta, Georgia, welcomed the convention for
the second time. At this Ninth International Convention, held April 26-30, 1899, Hon. Hoke Smith,
of Georgia, was chosen president. The convention
was called to mourn the death of William Reynolds
(1897), the first field superintendent. The work was

broadened by the election of Marion Lawrance, of Ohio, as general secretary; Professor H. M. Hamill, of Illinois, as field secretary; and L. B. Maxwell and Silas X. Floyd, both of Georgia, as workers among the colored people. Mr. Jacobs, asking retirement from active service as chairman of the Executive Committee, was made honorary chairman for life, and Hon. John Wanamaker, of Pennsylvania, was elected to succeed him. Mr. Wanamaker afterward declined the honor, and Mr. Jacobs continued in service.

III. The Teacher Training Tragedy

One hundred years ago there was little difference between the ability of the public school teacher and that of the Sunday School instructor. It is true that the teaching material of the former was superior to the catechism and memory verses of the Sunday School, and there was also the distinct advantage of more hours in the week for secular instruction. But in either case a teacher's qualification was largely his knowledge of a subject and his ability as a drill master. However, the normal school changed all of this. With the acceptance of this new agency for the training of teachers, the improvement of the public school was rapid, and the Sunday School sadly suffered in comparison.

1. Early efforts of educators

The success of institutional training for public school teachers profoundly impressed Sunday School leaders, and as early as 1847 Dr. D. P. Kidder, corresponding secretary of the Methodist Sunday School Union, made an earnest plea for similar preparation of Sunday School instructors. In his annual report he said:

> We think it time to ask whether a system of normal Sunday School instruction may not be established. Schools thus designated have been founded by several states of the Republic for the express purpose of training and qualifying teachers for common schools.

The lack of response to the suggestion of this far-sighted educator led him to sound a discouraging note, which reveals the existing apathy of the Church in improving its schools.

> The proposal of normal instruction for Sunday School teachers was suggested in our last report. We confess, however, that we fear the day is distant when the Church will take as high ground on this subject as that assumed by several states of the Union, viz., that in order to promote general education most effectually institutions must be provided for the special instruction of teachers.

In 1860 Dr. John H. Vincent, who was just beginning his notable career of recognized leadership in Sunday School circles, issued this challenge: "Why cannot we have a teachers' institute, similar to that of the public schools, in every district?" Two years later at a London convention he said, "We cannot have normal colleges yet in every community, so I recommend that we do the best we can with opportunities now within our reach." With this in mind, Dr. Vincent recommended a normal or training department in every Sunday School, to provide its own supply of teachers. He also was one of the first to suggest that short term institutes be conducted in various parts of the country.

Dr. John S. Hart, an eminent educator and the first editor of *The Sunday School Times,* in 1866 published *The Sunday School Teachers' Institute.* In the introduction he said:

> It is time that some general movement was made in the matter of teacher training. Of the 300,000 teachers who are guiding and sustaining the great work of instruction, probably less than one-tenth have ever had any regular professional training for the business of teaching. Why should not our theological seminaries make some provision on this subject? A young man goes to a theological seminary for the purpose of being fitted and trained for the pastoral office. In the providence of God, and the practical working of Christian institutions at this time, a large portion of the pastor's work—that part of his work which is most productive of results—lies among the young of his flock.
>
> Let the plain, painful truth be spoken. Our Sunday Schools are taught by those who know not how to teach. Our schools will never accomplish what they must do until our teachers know better how to teach and what to teach. Our teachers must themselves be taught. Whoever shall devise the means of doing this effectually will help forward the great cause as much as if they were to put a hundred missionaries in the field.

2. Teachers' institutes

Perhaps Dr. Hart had in mind that the institutes Dr. Vincent was furthering would parallel the work of the state normal schools. At any rate, by 1866 Dr. Vincent had elaborate plans for teacher training in which he recommended a course that would include:

(1) Five lectures by a professional and experienced teacher on the principles and art of teaching.

(2) Ten lectures on the Bible, its history, writers, inspiration, original languages, style, evidences, and biblical criticism.

(3) Ten specimen lessons for infant, advanced and adult classes.

(4) Ten exegetical exercises from the Old and New Testament history, the Psalms, prophecies and epistles.

(5) Ten catechetical lessons for concert recitation on Bible history, geography, chronology, ancient manners and customs covering in comprehensive lessons the field of biblical archaeology.

(6) Five lectures on the organization, objects, history, management, church relations, and development of the Sunday School work.

Although lacking in psychological and pedagogical studies, this curriculum provided a remarkably comprehensive content of teaching material—far better than the later courses were to offer—and had it been possible for the teachers of that period to receive this instruction, even more would have been accomplished for the Sunday School than the achievement of launching a uniform lesson. The real problem was to find the time and the place for the teachers to secure this training.

In response to Dr. Vincent's challenge, teachers' institutes were started in different parts of the country. In the East they were promoted by such leaders as Dr. Hart, Dr. Kidder, Dr. Trumbull, R. G. Pardee and Ralph Wells. In the West the movement was supported by Mr. Jacobs and Dr. Eggleston. The institutes did not hold continuous sessions. They were flexible also in size and the field represented. Sometimes teachers in a small district or an entire county seat or state would gather for such training. The primary purpose was instruction, while the convention continued for promotion and inspiration. The growth and permanence of this agency for better teaching was hindered and finally arrested by the Chautauqua movement, as well as the adoption of the Uniform Lesson.

3. The Chautauqua movement

The difficulty of finding a time and a place where a teachers' institute could be held long enough to complete Dr. Vincent's normal program led this enthusiastic educator, together with Lewis Miller, in 1874, to start a summer school for teachers on the shores of Lake Chautauqua, New York. It was thought that by combining study with vacation the teacher training problem would be solved. For the first three years this promising movement confined itself to the purpose for which it was organized; then unfortunately, some well-meaning leaders proposed to broaden the program to include general culture and make the gatherings more popular by introducing lectures on secular themes.

The success of this change in the program exceeded the fondest anticipations. Little Chautauquas sprang up all over the country, attended by thousands, few of whom were interested in securing a teacher's diploma. While the broader curriculum and larger outreach undoubtedly proved to be a national blessing, nevertheless the abandonment of teacher training was tragic. Sunday School teachers were to suffer more than ever in comparison with the graduates of state normal schools.

4. Weekly teachers' meeting

The Uniform Lesson, which was so extensively and enthusiastically adopted, also played its part in discouraging teacher training. Instead of attending institutes, teachers now gathered in classes for the study of the next Sunday's lesson. The multiplication of lesson helps provided more accessible, if not more popular, reading material than that of the training manuals, and many came to believe that these were a more practical way by which to make themselves competent.

Hundreds and even thousands attended these weekly teachers' meetings, and it was thought, as with the Lancaster movement, that a new era for the improvement of Sunday School teaching had dawned. But with the advent of the graded lessons interest in a collective study of the lesson waned. Teachers prepared their lessons hastily, if at all, and the asking of questions from a printed page became in many places as routine a performance as the hearing of the catechism a half century earlier.

After the noble efforts of so many far-sighted leaders and the launching of so many ill-fated movements, it is tragic to record that at the close of the nineteenth century the progress of training the Sunday School teacher in no way compared with the great strides taken to improve the public school teacher.

Dr. Vincent's dream of normal training for religious instructors was never realized. He had expected the colleges and seminaries of the Church to establish chairs in Christian education, but the dawning of that day was postponed until another century. He had hoped the teachers' institutes would become popular, and that a normal department would be added to every Sunday School. But these promising agencies deteriorated into a weekly meeting for the study of the next Sunday's lesson, and the teachers continued to be woefully ignorant of the principles of psychology and pedagogy, as well as vast portions of the Bible which were never included in the International Uniform Lesson.

IV. Improved Grading and Housing

The evolution of the graded system in the public schools and the gradual recognition of the value of segregating pupils in groups for instruction year by year have already been observed. The success of this plan impressed religious leaders and early efforts were made to have a modified form of the graded principle adopted in the Sunday School.

1. Four general divisions

In the early Sunday Schools both in Britain and America where reading and writing were included in the curriculum, pupils were classified into four general divisions:

Infant	Scripture
Elementary	Senior

Pupils in the first division were taught the alphabet and words of one syllable. Those in the second division, while unable to read, would be able to spell out words of two or more syllables. The third division contained pupils who could read, but with considerable difficulty; and only the highest division included those who could readily read in the New Testament. These four tests for proficiency in reading continued to be used for the classification of pupils

even after the growth of the public school movement no longer made it necessary to teach the rudiments of learning in the Sunday School.

2. Dr. Vincent's classification

In addition to the four recognized divisions Dr.
Vincent recommended units for the older pupils:

Normal   Inquirers
Archaeological

The normal division, we have already seen, was
for the training of teachers. Archaeology was in reality a class in Bible geography which generally met
during the week. The inquirers division also was
frequently conducted as an independent organization by the pastor. The last two divisions, because
their curricula were not connected or correlated with
the Uniform Lesson studied by the entire school,
never became a permanent part of Sunday School
organization and, as we have observed, the normal
division degenerated into a teachers' meeting for
the study of the lesson.

3. Later classification

The complete distinction of the function of the
public school from the Sunday School and the entire
separation of their work gave the latter liberty to
establish its own nomenclature, and before the end
of the century the divisions were known by different
terms:

Infant—Beginners
Elementary—Primary
Scripture—Junior
Senior—Adolescent and Adult

The introduction of the junior high school in public instruction called for a department in the Sunday School to represent its constituency. The rapid growth of high schools and colleges later suggested independent divisions for these groups also, so that the present department plan eventually became the recognized divisions of the Sunday School:

> Beginners—Pre-school age
> Primary—Grades I, II, III
> Junior—Grades IV, V, VI
> Intermediate—Junior high school
> Senior—Senior high school
> Young People—College
> Adult—From 24 years up

The value of grading the Sunday School to conform with the divisions to which the pupils are accustomed in public schools is obvious. The failure of so many schools for decades to parallel this superior plan of organization and the contentment of these schools with nothing better than a main school and a primary department, can be attributed in large measure to the wide use of the International Uniform Lessons. The fact that both old and young were studying the same lesson created a situation which had no parallel in the public school and made it all the more difficult to adopt its program of grading.

4. The Akron plan of architecture

The housing of the Sunday School was very closely related to its grading. The absence of grading made it difficult for many to see the need of any improvement in housing. In the early days, sessions were held in private houses. When the churches somewhat reluctantly took over the Sunday School they provided for it nothing better than the main auditorium of worship. Before 1860 most schools were held in one room church buildings, or sometimes in the basement of larger buildings. Fortunately, the absence of a church never prevented the organization of a Sunday School, and in thousands of cases homes, schoolhouses, and even village halls housed the beginning of a new enterprise.

The Akron plan, so named because it originated in Akron, Ohio, was the result of the co-operative work of Dr. Vincent and Lewis Miller. Their plan provided for separate divisions and for classrooms within the division, all opening to a common auditorium when the partitions were pushed out of the way. The first building was designed in 1867, and the adoption of a uniform lesson in 1872 tended to increase the popularty of the plan, since all the classrooms opened to the superintendent's platform. It provided admirably for a unified program of opening and closing exercises, and particularly the summing up of a uniform lesson.

The majority of Sunday School buildings before 1910 used the Akron plan in some form, but the adoption of the principle of graded lessons and their widespread use called for the substitution of the department building of modern church architecture.

V. Christian Endeavor Movement

Christian education is not merely the acquisition, but the use of knowledge. In fact, the educational program involves the four steps of acquisition, assimilation, appropriation, and application of knowledge. But the Sunday School, largely because of the absence of trained teachers, had contented itself with instructing and drilling its pupils. No provision was made for expressional activities which would appropriate and apply the instruction.

Dr. Trumbull recognized this outstanding omission in the Sunday School program, for he wrote in *Yale Lectures on the Sunday School,* in 1888:

> Our Lord in training His band of apostles first enlisted them as His followers; then He instructed them in the principles and methods of the service to which they were called; after this He sent them out to practice in the line of His instructions to them. This was and is the one true method in right training, and of course, it was adopted by our Lord in His work.
>
> The threefold work of winning, of informing, and of exercising—of enlistment, of instruction, and of drill—must proceed, wherever the training process is made practical, to the completion of the religious life of young disciples of Christ, today. The first factor in this work, we may say, is represented by the pulpit; the second, by the Sunday School; the third, by those auxiliary agencies which for lack of a better name may be counted as the "gymnasia" of the church in which the young membership is to have practice in moral and spiritual athletics.

Dr. Trumbull, in speaking of an auxiliary agency to supply the *training* that completes religious education, undoubtedly had in mind the Christian Endeavor movement, which had been launched by Francis E. Clark six years earlier. It was usual in Sunday Schools, for most of the older boys and girls to get "too big to attend." While a few were held by an unusual instructor and others remained to serve as teachers and officers, the majority dropped out, and there was nothing for their interest and activity apart from the regular services of worship.

Dr. Clark proposed a simple plan of a self-managed organization for young people that would provide instruction and worship, but above all, opportunity for expression.

His idea was no sooner tested out in the Williston Congregational Church of Portland, Maine, February 2, 1882, than it grew by leaps and bounds. Four months after the date of organization six societies held their first convention in Portland, but by 1889 there were 6,500 delegates in attendance at the convention in Philadelphia, while 14,000 gathered in Minneapolis in 1891.

During the first decade societies were organized successively in China, India, Africa, England, Australia, Turkey, Japan, Spain and France, and eventually the constitution was printed in more than forty languages. All evangelical churches were represented in the movement, although the ties of international Christian fellowship were weakened by the promotion of several denominational organizations. The second decade was signalized by a growth even more wonderful than the first. The international conventions surpassed all previous religious gatherings in the world's history in their vast proportions, their unbounded enthusiasm, and their deep spiritual results. Fully 35,000 delegates attended the convention in New York in 1892, while Boston registered the immense number of 56,435 in 1895.

The Christian Endeavor Society must be recognized as the greatest movement in religious education of the past century. As there were few if any of its constituents who were not enrolled at some time in the Sunday School, it is doubtful if it could ever have attained such signal success without the existence of the older agency. Dr. Clark only added an essential superstructure to the foundational work of Robert Raikes. In providing opportunity for expressional activities the Christian Endeavor Society proved a most valuable supplement to the Sunday School, and constituted the first serious effort of the modern church to put training on any large scale into its educational ministry.

The weakness of the Christian Endeavor movement lay in the failure to correlate its work with the Sunday School. As attendance of the former has always been optional, the majority of Sunday School pupils have failed to enroll, largely because the Christian Endeavor program is poorly correlated with the instruction it should supplement. In the public school, a pupil first studies his lesson and then recites it, but in the average church the pupil receives instruction in one lesson in the Sunday School, and attempts to speak in a Christian Endeavor meeting on a subject of which he has not been previously informed.

---

1. What was the report of the French Commission regarding the Sunday School?
2. What were the contributions of John H. Vincent and B. F. Jacobs to the International Uniform Lessons?
3. What action on the lessons was taken at the Fourth and Fifth National Conventions?
4. Describe the far-reaching results of the Uniform Lessons.
5. What outstanding Sunday School achievement was accomplished by B. F. Jacobs, William Reynolds and D. L. Moody?

6. What other forward steps besides the adoption of the Uniform Lessons marked the Fifth National Convention?

7. When and where was the First International Convention held?

8. What was gained principally at the Second International Convention?

9. Give the special features of the Third and Fourth International Conventions.

10. When and where were the Fifth and Sixth International Conventions held?

11. What topics were discussed at the Seventh International Convention?

12. What was accomplished at the Eighth International Convention?

13. What outstanding men figured in the Ninth International Convention?

14. Compare the ability of the early Sunday School and public school teacher.

15. What early efforts were made to secure institutional training for Sunday School teachers?

16. Outline the curriculum of the first teachers' institutes.

17. Wherein was the Chautauqua movement a tragedy?

18. How did the Uniform Lesson undesignedly militate against teacher training?

19. What were the four general divisions of the early S u n d a y School? What distinguished them?

20. What additions to these divisions did Dr. Vincent recommend?

21. Why did Sunday Schools for so many years fail to parallel the public school plan of organization?

22. Describe the Akron plan of architecture.

23. Quote from *Yale Lectures* the recognized importance of expressional activities in the Sunday School program.

24. Write a paragraph of one hundred words on the Christian Endeavor movement.

12

THE STRUGGLE FOR GRADED LESSONS

THE INTERNATIONAL Uniform Lesson system, launched in 1872 on a wave of tremendous enthusiasm, became so popular that within three years they had gone into nineteen nations, while in six years two million were reported studying them in Great Britain. Secretary Warren Randolph, of the Lesson Committee, reported to the International Convention at Atlanta:

> These lessons are largely used throughout our own land by a mighty host, to be enumerated only by millions, and they have found their way to the Sunday Schools along the shores of the Atlantic, down the slopes of the Pacific, and through all the region which lies between. East and West and North and South have come to love and to use them.

By 1890 there were no less than eleven million committed to these lessons, and this number was increased to fifteen million at the opening of the century and to seventeen million five years later. Unquestionably the inauguration of the uniform lesson plan was one of the most significant events in the history of the Sunday School. In unifying and standardizing the Sunday School and multiplying its literature, the new lessons made possible an era of great progress; and we have already seen their influence in shaping the architectural plans of the day, as well as creating the popular teachers' meeting.

I. Dissatisfaction with the Uniform Lessons

Despite their popularity, the Uniform Lessons did not provide comprehensive, consecutive and complete knowledge of the Bible, and constituted a brief outline study rather than a complete curriculum. It is not surprising, then, to discover a growing wave of dissatisfaction, especially as the Sunday School became less a supplementary agency in Christian education and carried more and more the exclusive responsibility for removing the spiritual illiteracy of the nation.

As early as 1878 there were four very definite objections to the Uniform Lessons. They were declared to be "scrappy and fragmentary"; no attention was given to denominational doctrines; temperance, missions and reform movements were given insufficient consideration; and the lessons were not arranged to coincide with the Church year. But the objection which was eventually to lead to "one of the greatest developments in religious education" was the neglect of the graded principle, already recognized as an absolute essential to public instruction. The need for lessons more suitable to young children was obvious, especially to normal school graduates, and as early as 1880 members of the Newark Association of Infant Sunday School Teachers were creating their own lesson material.

II. First Graded Courses

Opposition to the Uniform Lessons found concrete expression in two distinct movements. One group

sought to attain their end in the creation of new
courses independent of the International Lesson Committee. The other group believed that more could be
accomplished by working with those who had been
authorized to prepare lessons that would have both
international and interdenominational use.

1. Denominational courses

In Catholic schools, in which catechisms are
largely used, the principle of grading the subject
matter has had recognition from the beginning to
the present time. The Lutherans and the Protestant
Episcopal Churches, which have retained to some
extent the Catholic emphasis upon the Church year
and the imparting of instruction appropriate to the
festive days of the Church calendar, did not find the
Uniform Lessons suitable to their needs. These denominations were the first to prepare a system of
lessons for their own Sunday Schools.

a. *Lutheran Graded Series*

In 1886 the Lutheran Convention instructed its
Educational Committee to report on a graded system of instruction for the Sunday Schools. The report was made in 1888, but it was not until 1893
that the movement for graded material was sufficiently advanced to demand the publication of a lesson system. Theodore E. Schmauk was chosen editor
of the new series, and subsequently took such an
active part in its development as to secure for himself
the title of "Father of the Lutheran Graded Series."

These denominational lessons emphasized loyalty
to the doctrines of the Church and made special
effort to create a distinct sectarian consciousness.
Each text began with New Testament material, and

concluded the latter half of the year with lessons from the Old Testament. While Bible narrative was largely employed as material for the children's texts, selections from the poetic, prophetic and doctrinal portions of Scripture were chosen for adolescent studies. Cloth bound textbooks for the older pupils gave prestige and permanence to the course.

b. *Christian Nurture Series*

The Uniform Lessons had not long been in use before the leaders of the Protestant Episcopal Church felt the need of a course that not only would correlate instructions with the holy days of the year, but would more adequately stress certain teachings concerning the Church which they desired their children to receive. It was not until 1912, however, that Dr. Lester Bradner, associated with Dr. William E. Gardner, began the preparation of what became known as the Christian Nurture Series. Coming at this late date when supplemental materials were appreciated, the writers made much of correlated readings, drills, and notebook work in connection with the teacher's textbook. The series was graded on a one-year basis, beginning in the kindergarten with the age of four, and providing a separate course for each grade to the end of the high school period.

2. Independent courses

Even before the denominations had begun to break into the solid flanks of Sunday Schools that protected and preserved the Uniform Lessons, there were pioneer educators who had sufficient courage to voice their convictions in the production of a better series.

a. *Constructive studies in religion*

One of these pioneers was Dr. William R. Harper, a distinguished biblical scholar and a leader in modern methods of Bible study, who, while president of the University of Chicago, took the initiative in planning a new course. Having been elected superintendent of a large Sunday School near the university, he accepted the office with the understanding that he be allowed a free hand in experimenting and demonstrating with graded materials. His first step was to reorganize the Sunday School along public school lines. All existing curriculum materials were discarded, and with the aid of the faculty of the divinity school of the university new lessons were created for the various grades as rapidly as possible. These materials were first mimeographed, to be tried out in the classes and published only after a year's experiment. The difficulty of getting those who were able to create courses of study to test out their lessons in classes, limited the original experimental work at first to a few grades, but eventually the work was completed and widely used by schools of many denominations.

b. *Completely Graded Series*

Rev. Erastus Blakeslee, who had served as an army officer in the Civil War, was impressed with Dr. Harper's experiments, and began about the same time a series of lessons which covered the Bible in three-year cycles, making much of a work book for the pupil's written answers to printed questions. The Blakeslee six-year course, which was created as a protest against the Uniform Lessons, quickly sprang into prominence. It found its way into the schools of nearly all denominations, and was popular not only in the United States, but in foreign countries as well. The success of his first lessons inspired Blakeslee to prepare a complete graded series. In 1910 this pioneer lesson writer died, but Charles Scribner's Sons took over the publication of his materials, which then became known as the Completely Graded Series.

The Biblical World of October, 1908, called the Blakeslee lesson system a new plan of Bible study. It pointed out five distinctively new principles not observed in the Uniform Lesson:

> A connected study of biblical history
> The use of more biblical material
> The division of the Bible into large sections
> An orderly arrangement of the entire course
> The use of questions for written answers.

The Completely Graded Series was really semi-uniform, since the Gospels, the apostolic history and the Old Testament formed the three-year-cycle on which the system revolved, and the predominance of New Testament material subjected it to the same criticism as the Uniform Lessons. However, its distinctively new principles won for it such popularity that not only did the Uniform system borrow from its rival several improvements, but the International Graded Lessons also adopted some of its characteristics.

III. International Graded Lessons

While denominational and independent series were beginning to compete with the Uniform Lesson outside of the organized Sunday School movement, an even more formidable opponent challenged its supremacy from within.

In 1894 Miss Bertha F. Vella, secretary of the International Primary Union, through a questionnaire, secured the views of three hundred Primary teachers concerning lesson materials. These were tabulated and submitted to the International Lesson Committee with a request for a separate series of lessons for the Primary department. As a result the Lesson Committee prepared a list of "optional Primary lessons," somewhat reluctantly, however, since they went on record saying that "the committee still believes in the wisdom of one uniform lesson for all." The course was printed in the fall of 1895 by *The Sunday School Times,* but no helps were prepared by denominational publishing houses, and it was supposed that the matter had ended.

1. Graded supplemental lessons

But the agitation for better lessons was not to be easily suppressed. It became the particular object of discussion at the New Jersey School of Methods, which was organized by E. Morris Fergusson in 1894 for experimenting with better teaching materials and methods. In 1896 Mrs. J. Woodbridge Barnes, an outstanding Primary leader, proposed at this summer school the following question, "What do we wish our children to know about the Bible before they are twelve years of age?" Together this group of children's specialists worked out on the blackboard an outline which became the basis of the Graded Supplemental Lessons of the Elementary Division of the Sunday School, that were finally approved by the International Convention in 1902.

Meanwhile, Miss Margaret Cushman, an experienced kindergartner, had presented to the Newark teachers a new and constructive ideal of Bible teaching for little children. So impressed were the leaders with this plan that Miss Cushman was asked to prepare a two-year course for children of pre-school age. In 1898, these lessons were printed with helps, and scores of teachers began using them. Their success led Fleming H. Revell Company to issue them in book form and thus gain for them recognition from a publisher. The sales were gratifying and the movement made its desired impression in influencing the International Convention at Denver, in 1902, to grant graded supplemental lessons for the Elementary Department of the Sunday School.

2. Demand for an independent course

Thus far the graded lesson movement was not considered of much consequence. "The International Sunday School Association was so suspicious of the graded lesson idea," says George Herbert Betts, in *The Curriculum of Religious Education,* "that it would not allow the name 'International Lessons' to be attached to the Primary materials and would not approve of a plan for advanced lessons at all."

Nevertheless, the friends of the graded curriculum refused to be discouraged. Mrs. J. Woodbridge Barnes, to whom the Sunday School owes a greater debt than it can ever pay, in her patient, persistent manner, accomplished what no one else seemed able to do. At the Eleventh International Convention at Toronto, in 1905, she succeeded in getting Professor Edward P. St. John on the program. In six lectures, with large charts depicting childhood and adolescence, he taught the delegates the principles underlying the demand for lessons adapted to childhood's graded needs. This created a favorable sentiment which enabled Mrs. Barnes the following year to gain the permission of the International Executive Committee "to co-operate with the Lesson Committee, the Editorial Association and denominational bodies, as well as others, who may be planning graded lessons for the Primary and Junior departments."

Mrs. Barnes next organized the Graded Lesson Conference for the purpose of selecting lesson material for the Primary and Junior departments, and revising the Beginner's course which was already in use. The proceedings of this conference were forwarded to the Lesson Committee through Mrs. Barnes, and sufficient interest was created to call an informal meeting of the Executive Committee of the International Sunday School Association in 1908, to' debate the question of graded lessons. The following resolutions were drawn to be presented at the next International Convention:

> That the system of a general lesson for the whole school, which has been in successful use for thirty-five years, is still the most practical and effective system for the great majority of Sunday Schools of North America. Because of its past accomplishments, its present usefulness, and its future possibilities, we recommend its continuance and its fullest development.
>
> That the need for a graded system of lessons is expressed by so many Sunday Schools and workers that it should be adequately met by the International Sunday School Association and that the Lesson Committee should be instructed by the next International Convention, to be held in Louisville, Kentucky, June 18-23, 1908, to continue the preparation of a thoroughly graded course covering the entire range of the Sunday School.

3. A partial course approved and published

These resolutions were passed without one un-friendly speech or vote at the Louisville convention, and the Lesson Committee, which up to this time had given its attention entirely to preparing outlines for the Uniform Lessons, was now directed to pre-pare a second system to be known as the Interna-tional Graded Series.

These lessons were built on the closely graded plan, and patterned after the public schools, having a separate unit of study material for each grade or year. Four leading denominational houses, Congre-gational, Methodist Episcopal North, Methodist Episcopal South, and Presbyterian, organized a syn-dicate for the joint publication of the lessons. Frances Weld Danielson prepared the Beginners; Marian Thomas, the Primary; and Josephine L. Baldwin, the Junior. Using the same outlines, the Baptists pre-pared independent lesson helps, which were known as the Keystone Series.

The first lessons were ready for the Sunday Schools in 1910, and by 1914 the series was com-pleted. Once available, the Graded Lessons won their way rapidly, competing with the Uniform Lessons as well as the denominational and independent series that were already in the field. The success of graded material in the elementary division of the Sunday School soon created a demand for a full graded se-ries, and lessons for adolescents were under way even before all the material for the younger children had been written.

IV. Modification in the Graded Series

The battle for graded lessons had hardly been won

when new difficulties arose, dividing the forces and
making it impossible for a uniform graded series to
be acceptable to all who believed in the principle
of adapting biblical material to the capacity and
comprehension of the child.

1. Extra-biblical material

The Uniform Lesson had always been based upon
Bible passages, but in the preparation of the outlines
for the Graded Lessons some had ventured to introduce the lives of modern missionaries and other extra-
biblical material for study themes. The following became objects of study under the caption "Later Christian Heroes": John Eliot, Roger Williams, William
Penn, John B. Goff, and Frances Willard.

This led a brilliant Sunday School writer to oppose
the plan with ridicule by publishing a suggested series to parallel this for the third quarter, second year,
Intermediate Graded Course. The following is a sample of his satire:

> Lesson I. Ike Walton, the Fly Fisherman
>
> Bible Material: Peter the Fisherman
> Golden Text: "I go a-fishing"
> Lesson Truth: Don't fish on Sunday
> Lesson Hymn: "Pull for the shore."

So much opposition arose that it is doubtful if any
extra-biblical material would have been admitted had
it not been for a compromise that was finally effected
whereby two courses were authorized, the one to
contain only Bible passages and the other to admit
outside subjects for study. The Southern Baptists
and Southern Presbyterians were the leading denominations to insist on outlines containing only biblical

materials, while the syndicate of northern denominations accepted the extra-biblical lessons.

2. Liberal lesson helps

The Graded Lessons were subject to another unfortunate innovation from which the Uniform Lessons had thus far been immune, and in consequence suffered a further division of their forces. Some of the writers for the syndicate set forth in the lesson helps liberal views which eliminated the miraculous, and raised questions as to their belief in the supernatural origin and character of the Bible. This provoked so much controversy that the Northern Presbyterian General Assembly, in 1913, appointed a committee of investigation with power to act. The result was the withdrawal of this denomination from the syndicate and the inauguration of the Westminster Graded Series, which limited the lessons to biblical material. Denominational writers were selected to prepare the lesson helps.

A radical departure of the new series was the abandonment of the closely graded plan for the departmental lesson, which was in reality a compromise with the Uniform Lesson for the entire school. The small enrolment in the majority of Sunday Schools made it difficult to divide the pupils into so many separate classes. Moreover, there was a lack of enthusiasm and unity in the school arising from the fact that many different lessons were being taught at the same time. The group plan recognized the department rather than the grade as the unit of the Sunday School, and provided a uniform lesson for its constituents. As a departmental lesson permits a correlated worship program, as well as basic instruction for the expressional sessions of the Christian Endeavor or B. Y. P. U. groups, it proved the most practical of all plans of study, and its popularity eventually led the International Sunday School Association to adopt it and place it on equal footing with the closely graded type of lesson.

V. Improved Uniform Lessons

In 1914 the International Lesson Committee was reorganized to provide a larger representation from the denominations. Instead of the entire committee being elected at the conventions, now

(1) Eight members were elected by the International Sunday School Association.

(2) Eight members were elected by the Sunday School Council of Evangelical Denominations.

(3) One member was elected by each denomination represented in the Sunday School Council.

The introduction of so many new representatives on the committee changed the attitude toward the Uniform Lesson, which had enjoyed unquestioned prestige from the day of its inauguration. In fact, there were many who were in favor only of the closely graded lesson and the departmental lesson which was proving such a success in the Westminster Graded Series. For the sake of harmony, the advocates of the latter course agreed to give their support to a modification of the Uniform Lesson. A common portion of Scripture, golden text and daily Bible readings were retained to preserve the uniform character of the lesson. Separate captions were selected for the four age groups—Primary, Junior, Intermediate, Senior and Young People, Adult—

which with appropriate helps would give the lesson departmental distinction.

Ever since 1918 this series has been known as the International Improved Uniform Lessons, but the concessions made in recognition of the graded principle have been so insignificant as to occasion little change in the character of the series. Even though the committee permitted the Primary and Junior departments to select different Scripture portions, the necessity of maintaining the other uniform features made changes impractical if not impossible.

In the first cycle of this series (1918-1926) 202 lessons were taken from the New Testament, compared with 105 from the Old Testament, and 60 per cent of the former were chosen from the Gospels. While the Gospels were thus used repeatedly, not a single paragraph was taken from fourteen books of the Bible, and only 15 per cent from seventeen others. The failure of the "improved" lessons to solve the problems of the Primary department or to make use of a larger portion of the Bible has subjected them to the same criticisms the uniform plan has received from the beginning.

VI. International Group Lessons

The failure of the International Lesson Committee to adopt a departmental lesson or to change the character of the Uniform Lesson sufficiently to embody its values led to a demand that a competent committee be appointed to investigate and report on the merits of the three types of lessons. Under the chairmanship of Luther A. Weigle, a committee of seven was commissioned to survey the entire field of curricula. Questionnaires were sent to 627 carefully se-

lected persons, including publishers, editors, superintendents, department specialists, directors of religious education, and college and seminary instructors of Sunday School subjects.

The investigations and recommendations of this
commission were conclusive, especially as to the value
of the departmental lesson. The paragraphs of its
report relating to this subject are given in full:

1. There is general commendation of such improvement of the Uniform Lessons as has been secured by
their departmental adaptation. The figures submitted to
the commission indicate that the use of the Uniform and
Improved Uniform Lessons, though growing in some denominations, is on the whole not keeping pace with the
growing enrolment of the Sunday School.

2. The International Graded Lessons are rapidly
growing in circulation and are giving general satisfaction
both in their original graded form and as departmentally
adapted.

3. There is a widespread demand for courses graded
by age groups.

4. Many of our correspondents voice the conviction
that neither the Uniform Lessons nor the Graded Lessons
impart a complete enough knowledge of the Bible or give
to the pupil the disposition and the ability to use God's
Word intelligently. At the same time the need is expressed for enough extra-biblical material from nature
and from present-day social life to give the pupil a religious attitude toward the world in which he lives, and
for enough extra-biblical historical material to give the
pupil an adequate impression of the continuity of God's
presence and purpose in history.

5. Your commission recommends that a new system
of lessons be constructed to be officially known as the
International Sunday School Lessons: Group Graded
Series, and that the present system of graded lessons which
is to continue without revision be known officially as the

International Sunday School Lessons: Closely Graded Series; that we recognize as short popular titles for these two systems the following:

    a. International Group Lessons

    b. International Graded Lessons

  6. It is also recommended that the new system of International Group Lessons shall replace the Improved Uniform Lessons beginning January 1, 1924.

The recommendations of the commission were adopted in 1922, and for a time it looked as though the Uniform Lessons would be discarded entirely when the International Group Lessons would be ready for use. But so strong was the allegiance to the old series and so vigorous were the protests against abandoning it, that it was finally decided to continue it for a time. Thousands of editors who had been accustomed to making the Uniform Lesson a weekly feature of their columns found it difficult to make room for several departmental lessons, while there were certain commercial publishers whom Dr. Betts described as men "whose only watchword is *profits,* and who find it more advantageous to sell the Uniform Lesson Series than either of the graded series." Thus while officially buried, the Uniform Lessons remained in the field, and before the popular Group Lessons could fully take their place something happened that gave them a resurrection and a partial return to their former prestige.

VII. Experience-Centered Lessons

We have seen how the enlarged Lesson Committee introduced an element that strongly favored the graded principle in place of the uniform plan. This element, which almost entirely represented the liberal rather than the conservative thinkers of their respective denominations, grew in prestige, until their influence dominated the committee and led to drastic changes in the curriculum. Certain factors, however, were responsible for these new theories of curriculum making which changed the thinking of the Lesson Committee.

1. Contribution of John Dewey

Few modern educators have commanded greater attention and enlisted a larger following than Dr. John Dewey, of Columbia University. Will Durant says of him, "There is hardly a school in America which has not felt his influence." Walter Albion Squires adds, "Dr. Dewey's influence in education is not only nation-wide, but world-wide." As a student of Pestalozzi, Froebel and Herbart, he carried their theories of child training even further, to lay the foundation of a new education based almost entirely upon individual experience. "The aim of education," says Dr. Dewey, "is the reconstruction and reorganization of experience which adds to the meaning of experience and which increases ability to direct the course of subsequent experiences." The key word to this definition is *experience*. But the weakness of Dewey's theory is that its field is limited to the discoveries of the individual. To undervalue the achievements of the past discredits the whole heritage of culture as illusion. A world-view has little or no place in his system.

2. The three project schools

As a means to gain education by experience, three project schools have arisen. The constructive type consists of something to be done, requiring constructive or creative ability. It may demand manual labor, and this is the original and the best type of work. Motor activity is stressed. Busy work, hand work, construction work are motor responses which this school designates as projects.

The problematic type centers around the intellect rather than the hands. In every project there must be a problematic situation which demands reasoning from particulars to generalization. The problematic type project seeks to promote thinking in the pupils, but it seems to be interested only in one aspect of the thinking process—induction.

The purposeful type is not an organized achievement as the constructive type, or a program for directing inductory reasoning as in the problematic type, but it is a unit of activity or experience that involves wholehearted purposefulness on the part of the doer. Any experience may be a project—making a table, listening to a story, hearing a radio—provided a wholehearted purpose is involved in the experience. This type has little place for general principles, but following the Dewey theory of learning exclusively from individual experience, substitutes the student's immediate psychological experiences for the experiences of the race.

Working on this theory, an experience-centered curriculum is a curriculum carrying not the carefully considered experiences of the race, but the experiences of the individual. "Religious education following this theory," says Walter Scott Athearn, "eliminates the Bible and other religious knowledge from its curriculum and seeks to build its curriculum out of approved social experiences of immature students."

3. The project method in religious education

At the annual meeting of the Religious Education Association in 1917 a well-organized movement was started to introduce the project method of teaching into the field of religious education. Professor W. C. Bower, of the University of Chicago, pleaded for the reconstruction of the curriculum of the Sunday School on the basis of the Dewey formula—that Sunday School lessons should be made up of social projects. Professor Bower's appointment as a member of the Lesson Committee gave those who promoted the project program a strategic position for the propagation of their educational idea.

"With skillful administration, sincerity of convictions, and laudable zeal," says Dr. Athearn, "they made many converts for the position they represented." As a result, the leading denominations discarded the curriculum which had been adopted after the painstaking investigation of Professor Weigle's committee, and began furthering experience-centered lessons. "The new curriculum," says Dr. Athearn, "prepared under the influence of this group, which is now finding its way into the Sunday Schools of influential Protestant denominations, is notable for the absence of religious content. The experience-centered curriculum turns out to be an ethical cultured curriculum which cannot be distinguished from humanism."

4. The revival of the Uniform Lesson

The abandonment of the International Group and Graded Lessons for the experience-centered lessons left the orthodox constituency of the denominations without a Bible-centered curriculum. When they reminded their publishing houses that no provision had been made for conservative thinkers in the Sunday Schools, the educational boards, rather than assume the expense of reprinting the International Group or Graded Lessons, suggested a return to the old Uniform Lessons. Therefore to avoid the use of experience-centered lessons with their limited Bible content, thousands turned back to the Uniform Lessons with all their shortcomings.

VIII. All Bible Graded Lessons

The crisis in Christian education that confronted the Sunday School through the introduction of experience-centered lessons was sensed by the classes in curriculum making in the Christian Education Course of the Moody Bible Institute. In 1925 these students, under the direction of the author, began making a critical examination of all existing curricula, with the purpose of constructing a new series that would provide comprehensive, consecutive and complete Bible instruction. After eight years of investigation, criticism and experiment, they offered to the public, in 1933, the result of their work—the All Bible Graded Series.

In presenting these lessons to the Sunday Schools certain fundamental facts were recognized as essential principles in the preparation of this project.

(1) *"The Bible and the Bible alone is the religion of Protestants."*

These words of Chillingworth were the sum and substance of the greatest religious movement in history, and express the foundation and fundamentals of the Reformation. Throughout all these centuries

the Bible has been recognized as the very heart of
Protestantism.

While not oblivious to the importance of such
extra-biblical material as would provide instruction
in missions, temperance, Bible geography and church
history, the first objective of this new course was
the study of biblical material, leaving extra-biblical
material to such auxiliaries as the Vacation Bible
School and Week Day Church School. The All Bible
Graded Series recognizes the Sunday School as the
chief educational agency of the Church, and the Bible
as the first and foremost subject in the curriculum.

(2) *All Scripture is profitable for instruction.*

The Bible is not merely a library of sixty-six books;
it is better to call it a book of sixty-six chapters.
The study of every one is essential to an understanding and appreciation of the whole. The Bible is a
literary unit. It tells the human story. It tells that
story without unnecessary details or omitted essen-
tials. It starts at the beginning and concludes at the
end. Every book, every chapter, and every verse con-
tributes to the progress of the narrative. There is no
superfluous material.

To omit large portions of the Bible in our study
is to create wrong impressions and cause diversity
of opinions. As long as information concerning God's
Word is limited merely to detached portions, there
will be confused thinking among Protestants, and the
multiplication of heresies and fads. The Bible is a
harp of a thousand strings. Play on one, to the exclusion of its relationship to the others, and you will
develop discord. Play on all of them, keeping them
in their place in the divine scale, and you will hear
heavenly music all the time.

(3) *The lesson should be adapted to the
capacity of the pupil.*

Dr. G. Campbell Morgan, in *The Bible and the
Child,* says: "If the Bible is to be taught, the one
supreme necessity must ever be that we remember
the child's interest must be held. That is being recognized today, and different lessons are being prepared
for the different departments."

All educators are agreed that the graded principle
must be adopted in the Sunday School if pupils are
to secure a comprehensive knowledge of the Bible.
The Word of God contains moral and spiritual truths
which can be adapted to the understanding and need
of the individual from infancy to old age. The All
Bible Graded Series conforms to the psychological
and pedagogical laws which govern the development
of the child and adolescent. The lessons were planned
so that the Bible is unfolded to the school boy with
the same care that mathematics is developed in his
elementary and high school training. Each lesson was
chosen to fit precisely into the needs and understanding of the growing child.

(4) *Bible instruction can be made personal
and practical.*

Modern educators have made a mistake in thinking that expressional methods can be improved by
changing the content of the lesson. The Bible is the
changeless book for the changing age, and the Scriptures can be applied to meet the needs of each individual. It is not the content of the lesson so much
as the preparation and training of the teacher that
determines whether the pupil will apply the instruction to his own life. It is not the remote lesson writer,

but the local teacher who can best prescribe for the needs of the individual pupil. There is no question that a better trained teacher will mean not only better acquisition of the truth by the pupil, but above all, better appropriation and application.

The manuals of the All Bible Graded Series were written for the purpose of making the teacher a real *educator,* and the pupils real Bible *students.* Most lesson helps, unfortunately, have been a substitute for the Text itself, and in many Sunday Schools Bibles are not in use at all. The All Bible Graded manuals are *guides* to Bible study, and are especially appreciated by pastors and teachers who are eager that their pupils should "search the scriptures" and become independent investigators of the Book of books.

(5) *Bible instruction should parallel*
Christian anniversaries.

We have sufficient Bible authority (Exod. 13:14) to adopt the rule that the time to impart instruction is when the child's interest and curiosity are aroused. For this reason, as far as possible, the Church year has been observed in this series, so that lessons appropriate to both Christmas and Easter are introduced without interrupting the sequence of study. Reviews also conclude topics rather than periods of study.

(6) *Repetition should not impede progress*
or lessen interest.

Some repetition of Scripture is necessary in order to clarify and complete knowledge, but no pupil will attend with interest a series of lessons which is offered for a second time. As pupils graduating from the public schools look forward to taking up *new* subjects in the high school, so pupils in the Sunday School should be provided with *new* studies in the Intermediate and Senior departments, if we would have them remain in Sunday School. By selecting material from the unexplored portions of the Bible, the All Bible Graded Series sustains interest during the teen age, when 65 per cent of the girls and 75 per cent of the boys drop out of Sunday School.

A pupil attentively studying the 780 lessons provided for the fifteen year course will have a better knowledge of the English Bible than can be obtained anywhere today outside of a Bible institute. Churches that adopt this course will have established for their children and their communiity a veritable School of the Bible.

The first lessons of the new course appeared in October, 1934, and since then the series has enjoyed a remarkable growth. More than seven and a half million manuals have already been published, which does not include the translation into other languages.

---

1. Give some statistics to prove the popularity of the Uniform Lessons.
2. What were the earliest objections to the Uniform Lessons?
3. Compare the Lutheran Graded Series with the Christian Nurture Series.
4. What were the Constructive Studies in Religion?
5. What five distinctive principles were observed in the Completely Graded Series?

6. How did the graded supplemental lessons come into existence?

7. How was sentiment created in favor of graded lessons by Mrs. J. Woodbridge Barnes?

8. What resolutions regarding graded lessons were adopted at the Louisville Convention?

9. What syndicate was formed for the publication of the first International Graded Lessons?

10. What success followed their publication?

11. Describe the controversy over extra-biblical material.

12. How did the departmental lesson come into existence?

13. What change took place in 1914 in the International Lesson Committee?

14. Why have the International Improved Uniform Lessons failed to solve the problems of the curriculum?

15. Describe the work of the committee commissioned to survey the entire field of curricula.

16. Discuss John Dewey's contribution to education.

17. What were the three project schools that have arisen from the promotion of education by experience?

18. How did Dr. Athearn evaluate the experience-centered lesson?

19. Show how the experience-centered curriculum movement brought about a revival of the Uniform Lesson.

20. What five essential principles in curriculum making were observed in the preparation of the All Bible Graded Series?

13

BETTER TRAINING FOR TEACHERS

W E HAVE already observed the great improvement that was made in public school teaching through the founding of the normal schools. We have also seen the vain efforts of far-sighted Sunday School leaders to provide training equally as effective and efficient for religious schools. Following the tragic disappointment of the Chautauqua movement, teacher training was carried on for several decades by institutes.

These schools were intended to instruct teachers in the principles and methods of teaching. They did not, however, hold continuous sessions. They were flexible in size and in fields represented. Moreover, there was no standard program or order of procedure. Often they took a wide scope dealing in matters of organization and administration rather than in specific instruction and training of the teacher. While not intended to be permanent, these institutes continued for many years to be the only existing means of promoting higher ideals and a better knowledge of the best methods of reaching or developing the child mind.

I. Oliver, Hamill, Moninger, Hurlbut

The first attempt to offer a standardized course came in the brief manuals prepared by four authors, Oliver, Hamill, Moninger and Hurlbut. These books provided an entire course, the content dealing with the Bible, the pupil, the teacher, and the school. Their brevity made a popular appeal, and in some churches teacher training took the form of a mass movement in which many adults besides teachers enrolled for study. Unfortunately the manuals were merely outlines to be supplemented by able instruction. The absence of competent teachers made it impossible for thorough work to be accomplished by the students. It was not so much the use as the misuse of these training manuals that limited their value. Like the catechisms, the manuals constituted the total curriculum material and the teacher drilled the students in their memorization. Had competent teachers been available far more could have been accomplished.

II. The Southern Baptist Miracle

"The most amazingly successful movement in religious thought and activity since the first century, with the possible exception of the missionary movement," says Roland Q. Leavell in *An Unashamed Workman,* the biography of his brother, "is the development of the Sunday School enterprise during the first twenty-five years of the twentieth century." And nowhere was this movement more pronounced than in the Southern Baptist Convention.

According to Dr. Leavell, the most unbelievable Sunday School conditions existed in the South before 1900. While the majority of churches maintained a Sunday School, advanced ideas in organization and teaching were unheard of. Training for Sunday School teachers was but poorly defined even in the minds of those who were actually in the work of promoting school activities. Most pastors did not know what was meant by the term. Not a study course had ever been taken; not a diploma awarded;

not a seal given. No church maintained a regular teachers' meeting.

Sunday Schools in 1900 were conducted entirely upon the class basis. The one standard by which the efficiency and success of the teacher were measured was by the number of persons in the class, regardless of age. Men were usually conspicuous by their absence from Sunday School. It was deeply ingrained into their conscience that Sunday School was for women and children. This was the situation at the beginning of the twentieth century when "the Baptists of the South were hardly out of the log cabin stage of their development as a denomination."

1. The teacher training movement

In 1900 the honored president of the Southern Baptist Church, Dr. J. B. Gambrell, electrified the annual convention by a most stirring address. He said, "For years we have organized and evangelized. We have preached, but we have never taught. I believe that the most significant of all modern movements is the work of teacher training." It was upon his recommendation that the denomination adopted the slogan, "A certificate for every teacher," and all the resources of the denomination were concentrated upon this movement. Many of that denomination now count teacher training to be the crown and glory of the work of that Church.

Larger classes and training schools became the order of the day. As early as December, 1906, a training school was opened in the First Baptist Church of Nashville, Tennessee, for the workers in the city and county. Dr. B. W. Spilman, Dr. John R. Sampey and Landrum P. Leavell taught and brought the in-

spirational addresses. The report of the Sunday
School Board to the Southern Baptist Convention
the next year declared: "It gave us the best Baptist
work we ever had in Nashville, and well revolution-
ized our Sunday School conditions in the city."

Meanwhile Dr. Harvey Beauchamp was conduct-
ing separate training schools in Fort Worth and
Dallas, and the effect of his work in these two cities,
and even throughout Texas, was apparent. In 1910
a dual training school for Fort Worth and Dallas
was launched. The same teachers and speakers were
engaged in both cities, traveling on the fast inter-
urban from one class to the other. In an almost in-
credibly short time the school had become an established institution, teachers and officers by the
thousands receiving training.

This successful venture involved a calling out of
Sunday School specialists who would serve as field
men. Dr. Spilman and Landrum Leavell aroused
enthusiasm in the training classes of Nashville, together with Dr. Prince E. Burroughs, pastor of the
Broadway Baptist Church in Fort Worth, who had
received some vision of teacher training through the
successful movement in Texas. These three men not
only acted as field representatives throughout the
Southern States, but were also instrumental in preparing the first textbooks.

The Sunday School Manual, prepared by Spilman,
Leavell, and Burroughs, offered brief survey studies
in management, teaching, pupil study, and Bible.
Seven additional books elaborated on these four basic
studies. A diploma was awarded for the completion
of the manual; a large red seal when three more
books were finished; while the large blue seal com-

pleted the diploma and was awarded for the study of
the remaining four books of the course. In 1914 a
postgraduate course, consisting of five advanced
books, was added.

2. The marvelous results

The achievements and fruits of this training work
were manifested quickly among the churches. During
1905 and 1906 the number of Sunday Schools in
Texas increased by 900, while the enrolment in the
state gained 50,000 pupils. In 1902, the beginning of
teacher training, the Southern Baptists had 10,404
Sunday Schools with an enrolment of 712,012 pupils. In 1916 there were 18,075 Sunday Schools with
an enrolment of 1,760,802, an increase in fourteen
years of 250 per cent. The growth in the next
decade was even greater. According to government
statistics, the Southern Baptist Sunday Schools
gained one million pupils between 1916 and 1926,
an increase larger than the Northern Methodists,
Lutherans, Disciples, Episcopalians, and Presbyterians combined. The evangelistic effort that was put
forth by the trained teachers resulted in large acces-
sions to the church and Sunday School. In 1931
this denomination added more members to its rolls
than all the other major denominations put together.

The relation of this marvelous increase to teacher
training is apparent when we consider the amazing
enrolment in classes and the number of awards issued. Up to 1935 there had been 566,000 diplomas
awarded and 1,356,000 seals. The circulation of the
normal course books up to this time had been 1,316,-
043 volumes. This did not include some 400,000
sold to churches in other denominations. The work

continued with gratifying results. Between 1934 and
1941, 391,681 individuals received awards and
nearly a half million manuals were sold.

The course at present comprises some fifty books,
in which seventeen are devoted to Bible, four to
administration, five to teaching, six to doctrine and
evangelism, fourteen to departmental work, two to
Daily Vacation Bible School, and seven to general
studies. A diploma is now given for the completion
of the four fundamental books. The red seal is attached to the diploma on the completion of four more
books, the blue seal for the second four, and the gold
seal for the third four. Workers obtaining the gold
seal may pursue their studies further and secure the
postgraduate diploma.

3. Points of strength and weakness

The training course of the Southern Baptist Convention has been the outcome of much experiment.
The workers were blazing new trails. Many problems
confronted them. Would mature people, busy with
the cares of life, buy books, study them in class,
take written examinations, and seek awards? The
question was often and anxiously asked from 1901
to 1910. Gradually the conviction grew that not
otherwise could workers be really and effectively
trained. Slowly as the years passed it became evident
that those earnest and eager to serve as Sunday
School officers and teachers would undergo any rea-
sonable pains to secure the equipment they needed.

The success of the Southern Baptist program—
and it must be recognized as a success from the far-
reaching results it has obtained—lies in the simplicity
of its requirements and in the enthusiasm of its pro-

motion. Instructors made their appeal to the heart as well as to the head. They did not overlook the fact that the emotions were to be stirred as well as the intellect reached. Moreover, teaching materials were offered at a minimum expense. While this course lacked the scholastic standards that were to be attained by other teacher training agencies through the adoption of a specified unit period of study and recitation and the requirement of institutional training, yet the larger enlistment that this course commanded more than made up for the lack of scholastic standards.

While the Southern Baptist Convention, as well as the International Council of Religious Education, is to be commended for what has been accomplished in improving the quality of teachers through Sunday School and community classes, at no time has this training even compared with that given public instructors in state normal schools. As Dr. Athearn has well said:

> Teacher training programs now promoted by departments of church schools of various denominations are well intended, but they are largely futile. The training of church school teachers cannot be achieved by promotional agencies. It is an educational task which can be solved only by academic agencies.

Even Dr. P. E. Burroughs, who more than anyone else has been responsible for the million awards already issued in teacher training classes of the Southern Baptist Convention, admits the superiority of institutional work. He says:

> When our work is done in accredited colleges our students should receive exchange credit, but when the work is done in the field, as it must often be done, we

would readily wish that our students entering institutions should take the courses in full as they are offered there.

III. New Standards

While the Southern Baptists were moving forward by leaps and bounds in improving their teaching efficiency, the churches in the North were not idle. There was growing dissatisfaction of the approved outline studies of Oliver, Hamill, Moninger and Hurlbut. This was intensified by the larger use of graded lessons. Teachers who had received no better knowledge of the Bible than the International Uniform Lesson were being called upon to give instruction in portions of Scripture with which they were not familiar. The leading promoters of the new lessons, which contained nearly twice as much Bible as the Sunday School had been in the habit of studying, had quite overlooked the fact that no preparation had been afforded the teachers. In fact, the demand for a completely graded course of lessons came before the teachers were ready for it. The lessons had been outlined, but the teachers had not been trained before the clamor for graded instruction was so largely substituting it for the old Uniform Lesson. Therefore, nothing could be more evident than the need of a training course that would provide adequate knowledge of the Bible.

1. First Standard Courses

In 1910 the International Sunday School Association set up the First Standard and the Advanced Standard Courses. The First Standard Course called for fifty lessons divided as follows: Bible, 20; pupil, 7; teacher, 7; school, 7; and 9 lessons relating to any of the above. This course could be finished in one year, but most classes required more time. The Advanced Standard Course required 40 lessons of Bible; 10 on the pupil; 10 on the teacher; 10 on the school; 10 on the church; 10 on missions; and 10 more relating to any of the above required subjects.

At the Thirteenth International Sunday School Convention in 1911 it was reported that 27,008 had completed the First Standard Course, while 570 diplomas had been awarded for the Advanced Standard Course.

The new courses were a great improvement over the outlines of Oliver, Hamill, Moninger and Hurlbut, but they still lacked effectiveness. At the International Sunday School Convention held in Chicago in 1914, Dr. Walter S. Athearn, chairman of the Committee on Education, strongly urged a revision of standards. He said, "We deceive ourselves. We think that we are training teachers by this process when in reality we are simply doing the work which must be done over again if the Church ever gets down to the business of doing real school work." He revealed that 51 per cent of the enrollment had failed to complete the course and that the results were inadequate when compared with the energy and time expended.

2. Second Standard Courses

In 1915 the standards were revised. By agreement, all former standards were abolished and only one Standard Course was adopted. Instead of lessons, the term "unit" was substituted. A unit was defined as "a recitation period of not less than forty-five minutes based upon a lesson assignment by an approved teacher, the lesson assignment to require a minimum

of one hour lesson preparation." The new lesson
course was as follows:

Year I	*Units*
The Pupil	10
The Teacher	10
Teaching Values of the Life of Christ	10
Organization and Administration of the Sunday School	10

Year II	*Units*
Teaching Values of Old Testament	10
Training of the Devotional Life	10
Teaching Values of New Testament	10
The Program of the Christian Religion	10

Year III	*Units*
Specialization in the Methods of a Particular Department	40

The new Standard Course was longer than the
old Advanced Standard Course and more than
twice as long as the old First Standard Course. The
main value was not so much the increased time as
the added efficiency brought about through the adoption of a specified period for preparation and recitation. It will be noted that the Bible content material
"was practically eliminated from the course, on the
assumption that this was being adequately presented
in the graded lessons." Although the theory that
training should deal more with methods than with
teaching material was correct, those who revised the
curriculum undoubtedly were influenced by the program of the secular normal schools. Nevertheless,
the weakness of the Sunday School in comparison
with the public school rendered conditions altogether
different. Had the Bible been taught as thoroughly
and effectively in the Sunday School as secular sub-

jects were being imparted in the public school, there would have been little criticism. But this first step, which was followed by later revisions, continued to reduce the study hours of the Sunday School's Text-book, and eventually led the whole teacher training program to disaster.

In connection with the 120 hour Standard Training Course, the International Sunday School Association provided the Advanced Course of 300 hours, which was later reduced to 192 hours. This course required as an entrance qualification a high school diploma and three units of the Standard Training Course—Child Study, Pedagogy and Sunday School Organization. Its specifications were as follows:

Required Subjects	Units
Biblical Introduction	24
Biblical Material	24
General Psychology	24
History of Religious Education	24
Correlation in Religious Education	24
Curriculum Making	24

The subjects of Correlation and Curriculum Making were for educational executives, but these two subjects could be substituted by 48 units of departmental study for those preparing themselves as department superintendents.

In addition to the above 144 required units, two of the following electives of 24 units each were to be taken to complete the 192 hour course:

> History and Progress of Missions
> Devotional Literature
> Religious Art
> Biblical Geography and Customs

Worship in Religious Education
Educational Evangelism
Music in Religious Education
Bible Story Telling
Dramatization and Pageantry
Recreational Leadership
Manual Arts
Week Day Church School
Daily Vacation Bible School

3. Third Standard Courses

The Advanced Training Course was never popular because of the difficulty of putting on its program outside of well established schools. For this reason, in 1926 another revision was made by the International Council of Religious Education, which in 1922 had become the successor to the International Sunday School Association. This changed the name of the Advanced Training Course to Leadership Course and offered nearly all of the subjects of the Advanced Course as electives without increasing the original number of hours. The 120 units of the Standard Leadership Course are arranged as follows:

Subjects	Units
Child Study	10
Pedagogy	10
O. T. Teaching Values	10
N. T. Teaching Values	10
Message and Program	10
Teaching Work of the Church	10
Departmental Work	30
Electives	30

While thirty units of departmental specialization are required, each student has the privilege of selecting one of nine departments for special study: Cradle Roll, Beginners, Primary, Junior, Intermediate, Senior, Young People, Adult, and Administration. One additional study in department specialization may be elected from a limited number of subjects in keeping with that study, but the student is permitted to complete his course with two general electives from a field of no less than thirty-two subjects.

In its revision of the Standard Leadership Training Course, the International Council of Religious Education failed to introduce the much needed additional Bible study for the demands of the graded lessons. Furthermore, evangelism and missions, so essential to the equipment of a Sunday School teacher, were not listed among the required subjects of study. The diminishing gifts to missionary effort, as well as the decrease in additions to church membership, which were the 'result of this oversight, did not gain favor for the new revision. The emphasis upon acquiring a knowledge of methodology rather than the contents of the Textbook led one educator to declare, "We are now training our young people to teach everything without giving them anything to teach."

But the most serious mistake of the International Council, the representation of which by this time was largely from the liberal constituency of the denominations, was that it ignored the excellent textbooks of such leading and successful denominations as the Southern Baptist Convention, and limited its approved texts to authors not acceptable to orthodox churches. The result of these blunders was that while the teacher training movement was going forward by leaps and bounds in the Southern Baptist Convention, it sadly lagged in the North where the denominations for the most part were affiliated with the Council.

IV. Training in Colleges

We have already noted that the higher educational institutions of America were founded by the Church, and that in 106 of the first 108 colleges the preparation of men for the Christian ministry was the chief occasion of their origin. We have also pointed out that until the founding of universities the state largely depended upon these church institutions for instructors in their public schools. Even with the multiplication of state universities there has not been a sufficient number of graduates to supply the growing needs of the state, so that the Christian college has continued to graduate a large number of its students for this purpose.

1. The neglect of the Church

In 1915 Dr. Walter S. Athearn made an investigation of present conditions of religious education in colleges. From questionnaires submitted, he received replies from 140 institutions, of which 62 classified themselves as denominational, 14 indicated no direct affiliation with a Church, and others designated in a variety of ways their relation to religion. The most surprising thing revealed by the questionnaires was the unanimity with which these colleges were responding to the state's demand for trained teachers. The Christian colleges were making a fine contribution to the public schools *where religion is not taught*. On the other hand, they had not been equally responsive to the urgent need for real teachers in the schools of the Church. Dr. Athearn in his report said:

Nearly all of the states grant certain concessions and privileges to colleges that conform to the standards established by the State Department of Public Instruction. Departments of education, chairs of psychology and pedagogy have sprung up in nearly all of the denominational colleges. In almost all catalogues examined there are listed such courses as history of education, educational psychology, child psychology, philosophy of education, school administration and management, methodology, etc. The church colleges may well be proud of their splendid contribution to the training of the secular teachers of the nation, but they have not been equally responsive to the pleading of the churches for teachers of religion.

There is no denying the fact that thousands of graduates are going out from denominational colleges to serve the state as public teachers or to settle down for their life work apart from the Church. For the most part there are no distinguishing marks by which the local pastor can tell them from the graduates of state universities who are not prepared in knowledge, insight, or inclination to become constructive leaders in the religious life of their communities. As Dr. Athearn so aptly puts it, "No student should be allowed to graduate from a Christian college without being prepared for lay service in the local church." This training should be included even though the student majors in science, language, history, mathematics, or other traditional fields.

Today the state universities rest upon local high schools. They supervise the work of these secondary schools. In like manner the state normal is adequately providing for the needs of the elementary schools. Why then should not church colleges rest upon local Sunday Schools and be the centers of standardization and supervision of the educational work of the local

church? Why cannot church colleges train Sunday
School teachers and church officers just as state
schools prepare instructors for secular institutions?

2. A major in Christian Education

With the revival of Christian education at the
opening of the present century it is not surprising
that chairs in Bible began to appear in colleges, and
some institutions went so far as to offer a major in
religious education. In 1921 a joint commission from
the Council of Church Boards of Education and the
Sunday School Council of Evangelical Denominations
established a course in religious education of thirty
semester hours. A diploma was recommended for
one-fourth of the four-year college course, or thirty
semester hours, while a certificate in religious education would be granted to students who upon graduation had completed a total of twenty-four semester
hours of work.

The required work for a diploma was as follows:

Subject	Semester Hours
Bible	6
Teaching Values of Bible Material	3
Curriculum	2
Christian Religion	3
Educational Psychology	3
Introduction to the Study of Religious Education	3
Teaching the Christian Religion	4
Organization and Administration	3
History of Religious Education	3
	30

Of the twenty-four semester hours necessary for a
certificate in religious education, nineteen were dis-

tinctly specified, but five could be elected from the required subjects for a diploma. The specified courses were:

Subject	Semester Hours
Bible	6
Christian Religion	3
Educational Psychology	3
Introduction to the Study of Religious Education	3
Teaching the Christian Religion	4
Electives	5
	24

This was a long step toward providing training for church school teachers that would parallel the splendid preparation of the normal schools for public school teachers. Unfortunately, the comparatively few who secured the teacher's diploma or certificate were but a drop in the bucket to supplying the needs of 175,000 Sunday Schools. Moreover, the vastly superior training that these college students were receiving in comparison with the courses of the Southern Baptist Convention and the International Council qualified them for full-time paying positions. Instead of serving as teachers in the Sunday School, they were drafted for the most part to serve as educational directors in the church. An institution was needed that would function more like the normal school, and one which would provide a shorter curriculum than a collegiate course; also one definitely suited for the training of Sunday School teachers.

V. The Rise of Bible Institutes

The solution of this problem of the Church was to be found in the Bible institute movement. The man who was responsible for it was born in 1837, almost at the same time that Horace Mann was establishing the first state normal school at Lexington, Massachusetts. Bishop Vincent must have been well acquainted with Dwight L. Moody since both were outstanding Sunday School leaders of that day. Mr. Moody not only had the largest Sunday School in Chicago, but we have already seen how he became a national figure at the conventions, and together with B. F. Jacobs and William Reynolds organized every county in the state of Illinois—an achievement that has never since been equalled.

Little did Bishop Vincent imagine that his dream of institutional preparation for Sunday School teachers would be realized in the founding of the Moody Bible Institute in 1886. In fact, it is not likely that Dwight L. Moody himself fully comprehended the large service that was to be rendered to the Sunday School through the great movement he began.

This school was first called the Chicago Evangelization Society, which would hardly suggest that it had any relation to the Sunday School. After the death of the founder the institute was given his name. Even then it was not at once seen how far-reaching was D. L. Moody's plan and program. The *plan* of the Moody Bible Institute has been the institutional instruction of which Bishop Vincent had fondly dreamed. The *program* of the Moody Bible Institute has been the training of lay workers, especially in the knowledge and use of the English Bible, and instruction and experience in personal evangelism.

But how fitting is this institutional training for the Sunday School teacher!

> He is a lay worker.
> He is a Bible teacher.
> He is an evangelist.

Of course, this is not all that the Sunday School teacher needs to prepare himself for his task. He must study child psychology, pedagogy, Sunday School methods, and many other subjects. The General Course of the Moody Bible Institute today has more studies than the curriculum of the state normal school, and requires a period of eighty-eight weeks to complete. At the time of Moody's death, the physical equipment of the institution he founded was worth nearly $400,000. Under the leadership of the late Dr. James M. Gray, 1904-1935, the institution added building after building, until today there are twenty-four, including the twelve-story Administration Building. For the centennial observance of the birth of D. L. Moody, Dr. Richard Ellsworth Day wrote *Bush Aglow,* the life story of this great Christian educator. Dr. Day states:

> The Bible Institute incarnates more fully than any other of his institutions Moody's unique personality, dynamic power, great purposes, and deathless devotion to the Book.

The Moody Bible Institute has enrolled (April, 1943) 23,061 resident day students; 21,809 evening students; 102,901 Correspondence School students, making the incredible sum total of 147,771 persons.

The success of the Moody Bible Institute in Chicago as a training school for lay workers gave rise to similar institutions throughout the United States and Canada. Today they are as numerous as normal schools, and there is scarcely an unoccupied area where Sunday School teachers do not have within reach an institution in which they can adequately qualify themselves for their work.

VI. The Evangelical Teacher Training Association

While Bible institutes were multiplying with amazing rapidity throughout the length and breadth of the United States and Canada and even in foreign countries, there was no unity in fellowship or common standard in curriculum. Some organization was necessary to bind these training schools together and to assist them in enlarging and improving their work.

On a memorable afternoon in May, 1931, a small group of representative men met in the offices of the *Sunday School Times* in Philadelphia. Dr. James M. Gray and Clarence H. Benson represented the Moody Bible Institute; Dr. Charles G. Trumbull and Philip E. Howard, the *Sunday School Times;* Dr. Lew W. Gosnell, the Bible Institute of Pennsylvania; B. Allen Reed, the National Bible Institute; Dr. Calvin C. Ellis, Juniata College. This group met informally to consider three propositions:

(1) Should the training of Sunday School teachers be abandoned to those agencies which were then furthering it in church and community classes?

(2) Should a compromise be effected and a plan of co-operation furthered?

(3) Should an i n d e p e n d e n t organization be launched?

After carefully and prayerfully weighing each of these propositions, a unanimous conclusion was reached. It was decided that the only possible course was a new association that would not only serve the orthodox constituency of the denominations, but would put teacher training on a higher plane than any existing agency was then doing. That was the beginning of the Evangelical Teacher Training Association.

The Association at first confined its sphere of activity to a few of the leading Bible institutes and operated under the name of the International Bible Institute Council of Christian Education. However, when requests for admittance were received from colleges and theological seminaries, Dr. Trumbull suggested the more suitable name, Evangelical Teacher Training Association. The preamble of its articles of organization fully suggests its purpose:

> We, representatives of Bible institutes, colleges and seminaries in the United States and Canada, in order to foster a closer co-operation among evangelical Christian institutions; to certify to the public our deep interest and concern for Christian education; to provide and promote a common course in teacher training which will give adequate attention to instruction in Bible, personal evangelism, and missions; to recognize and encourage the use of textbooks of approved orthodoxy, do hereby associate ourselves under the following articles of organization.

The third article of organization specifies a uniform course of teacher training known as

1. Standard Training Course

The Standard Training Course is available only to students regularly enrolled in one of the co-operating institutions of the Association. It offers a period of 432 hours—the hour unit being defined as a reci-

tation period of fifty-five minutes and a preparation
period of an hour and a half. The studies of the
course are distributed as follows:

	Hours
Bible	144
Personal Evangelism	36
Missions	36
Department Specialization	48
Bible Geography	12
Biblical Introduction	15
Child Study	15
Pedagogy	15
Sunday School Administration	15
Electives	96
	432

The teacher's diploma, which is issued to all completing this course, contains the names of the co-operating institutions, and is signed by the officers of
the Association.

This course is not only five times the length of the
Standard Leadership Course of the International
Council of Religious Education, and provides adequate instruction in Bible, personal evangelism, and
missions, but in addition is arranged so that it can
be completed in one year in the day school or two
years in the evening school of many of the co-operating institutions.

2. Preliminary Training Course

While it is possible for the co-operating institutions to provide a decidedly superior course in a
briefer period than other existing agencies, because
of circumstances, many are unable to enroll in them.
For the benefit of community or church classes the

Evangelical Teacher Training Association prepared a Preliminary Course of 96 hours—an hour unit being defined as forty-five minutes of recitation and one hour preparation. The subjects of this course are distributed as follows:

	Hours
Old Testament Law and History	12
Old Testament Poetry and Prophecy	12
New Testament	12
Child Study	12
Pedagogy	12
Sunday School Administration	12
Sunday School Evangelism	12
Missions	12
	96

On the completion of each unit the student is awarded a registered certificate of credit signed by the approved teacher. To be approved the teacher should be a graduate of the Standard Training Course, or an instructor in one of the co-operating schools of the Association. This certificate of credit is accepted as completed work toward a diploma by some of the co-operating schools.

A teacher's certificate is awarded by the Association as soon as the student has completed the units of Bible, child study, pedagogy, and Sunday School administration. Sunday School evangelism and missions are postgraduate work, and on completion of these two units recognition is given by a gold seal on the teacher's certificate.

In the first decade of the Association the number of co-operating schools grew from five to 106. Teachers' diplomas awarded numbered 5,405, one institution alone being responsible for more than one thousand of these. For the units of the Preliminary Training Course 26,057 certificates of credit were awarded, and 129,954 manuals issued. This does not include the copies of translations in other languages.

VII. Summary

The teacher training program of the Sunday School was thoroughly investigated recently by George Paul Skoda in a thesis submitted to the Northern Baptist Theological Seminary for the degree of master of religious education. He found the three Protestant teacher training agencies in the United States to be the International Council of Religious Education, the Evangelical Teacher Training Association, and the Southern Baptist Convention. This critique is of special value because of the fact that Dr. Skoda had not previously received training from any of these agencies. After presenting the plan and purpose and a brief history of the Evangelical Teacher Training Association, he makes this interesting comment on the doctrinal statement to which all members of the Association subscribe:

> It is evident from the above that the Association did not organize on an all-inclusive basis. It wished to maintain, defend, and propagate the "faith which was once delivered unto the saints." It wished to uphold the divine verbal inspiration of the Bible, the orthodox and conservative evangelical views of God, of Christ, of the Holy Spirit, of the fall of man, and the avenue of escape through the regenerating work of Christ. It was not a broad, all-inclusive program, but a limited and definitely bounded field of endeavor. It wished to have the teachers trained in the Word of God and be fully prepared in fields of personal evangelism and missions. It was, in

other words, an endeavor to train teachers in a distinctly conservative and fundamental theology—a clear break from the evident liberal tendency of the New Standard Leadership Course of the International Council of Religious Education.

That many other institutes, colleges, and seminaries were likeminded is evident in the rapid growth of the Association. In 1930 there were but five Bible institutes; in 1932 the number with colleges and seminaries, now permitted to enter, rose to sixteen; by 1935 there were fifty, and at the close of 1936 there was an active membership of seventy-one schools, with a total, including affiliated institutions, of seventy-eight. [Since Dr. Skoda prepared his thesis twenty-eight new schools have been added.] This tremendous growth suggests that at least a portion of the American Protestant religious world, though it desires an ever-increasing scholarship, is not willing to have it at the expense of orthodoxy. The emphasis which the Evangelical Teacher Training Association has placed on the Bible, personal evangelism, and missions in its Standard Training Course gives it a distinctiveness which bids to make it outstanding in the field of religious education. The total of 216 hours in the above three subjects forms its bulwark.

But Dr. Skoda sees more in the Evangelical Teacher Training Association than a movement for definite orthodox instruction. After describing the new pedagogical and efficiency standards which make the training of the Evangelical Teacher Training Association distinctive, he goes on to say:

It is evident that in its stand for definite orthodoxy the Evangelical Teacher Training Association does not expect to make it at the expense of scholastic rating. Not only are the high standards already in existence being maintained, but there is a forward movement to create new and more efficient levels of teacher training. The continuous and consecutive work carried on in well equipped institutions makes for greater efficiency, and, at the same time, enables the student to complete a much longer course in a shorter time. The rapid growth of the Association indicates somewhat the favor with which its policies are being received by the American Protestant religious world.

Organized to defend the "faith which was once delivered unto the saints," the Association has admirably fulfilled its intentions. Not being denominational in character but interdenominational, it can co-operate and carry on with all the members of the various denominations that desire a fundamental and a conservative teacher training course. In fact, the wonderful demonstration of Christian unity in the associational activities has been one of its remarkable successes. With the curriculum emphasis rightly proportioned between teacher training methods and the necessary factual knowledge of subjects to be taught, the course bids to assume a place of ever-increasing importance in the field of religious education. It is truly the realization of Bishop Vincent's dream of having an efficient training course for Sunday School teachers compared with that of the normal school which trains public school teachers.

---

1. Criticize the Oliver, Hamill, Moninger, Hurlbut training manuals.

2. Describe conditions in the Southern Baptist Convention before 1900.

3. What circumstances brought about the great training movement in this denomination?

4. What marvelous results followed this widespread training of teachers?

5. Name the points of strength and weakness in the Southern Baptist courses.

6. Outline the First Standard Course of the International Sunday School Association.

7. Give Dr. Athearn's criticism of this course.
8. Compare the Second Standard Course with the First Standard Course.
9. Why was the elimination of Bible content a serious objection?
10. What was the Advance Training Course?
11. Outline and criticize the Third Standard Course.
12. What important fact did Dr. Athearn's college questionnaire reveal?
13. What recommendation did Dr. Athearn make regarding students in Christian colleges?
14. Outline the suggested college major in Christian education.
15. Why could not this excellent course solve the teacher training problems of the Sunday School?
16. How did D. L. Moody realize the dream of Bishop Vincent?
17. Show how well the Moody Bible Institute is equipped to train teachers and what it has already accomplished.
18. How did the Evangelical Teacher Training Association come into existence?
19. What is the preamble to its articles of organization?
20. Compare the Standard Training Course of the Association with the Standard Leadership Course of the International Council.
21. Outline the Preliminary Training Course of the Association.
22. What progress was made in the first decade of the Association?
23. Give George Paul Skoda's evaluation of the three Protestant teacher training agencies in America.

14

FROM SUNDAY SCHOOL TO
CHURCH SCHOOL

"OVER IN HUNGARY," wrote a student who had just arrived in America and had enrolled in the Moody Bible Institute, "we used to envy the enterprise and effort of American missions. We felt ashamed of our offerings and our representatives so meager in comparison, but since I have been in this country I feel quite differently. It is true that the American Church takes a deep interest in the children of other nations, but they sadly neglect their own. In our schools in Hungary, religious instruction is a daily matter. It is taught as frequently as geography and arithmetic, and no pupil is released from the classes in which it is required."

This evaluation of religious instruction in America is most significant. In recent years the trend has been to divorce religious instruction entirely from the public schools and to turn over this phase of the work almost entirely to the Church.

Even the home, which is regarded as the world's greatest university, has ceased to function. Before the days of automobiles, movies and other attractions, people spent more time in the family circle, and there was larger opportunity for character building. Important as is the instruction by parents, the home today has the child fewer hours than formerly. Industrial life, which occupies so much of the time and thought of the American people, also robs the children of much of the home association necessary for religious culture. The most lamentable of all is the fact that the best of parents, even if so inclined, are often not well fitted to give religious instruction.

Therefore, since the beginning of the twentieth century, the burden of the entire program of religious education has been shifted by both home and school to the Church. Under these conditions it is quite evident that the Sunday School, despite its increase in efficiency, does not provide sufficient time for this important task. In most Sunday Schools the session covers a single hour out of 168 hours of the week. When "opening exercises" instead of worship services occupy the first part of the hour, the actual class study constitutes the period of effective instruction. The time consumed in getting ready to teach, in attention to records of attendance, and other fussy occupations, further reduces the actual period of instruction.

"To call the teaching content of the modicum of minutes that remain a sufficient supply of Christian education for the ordinary normal boy or girl," says Dr. Donald R. Gorham, in *Christian Religious Education,* "is a ludicrous miscarriage of common sense." Many religious educators, while still emphasizing the need for Sunday School enlargement and improvement, came to believe that this agency had to be supplemented by other activities. The first successful supplementary agency was

I. Daily Vacation Bible School

Not since the birth of the Sunday School had any movement in Christian education been so intensely practical and so signally successful as the Daily Va-

cation Bible School. In less than thirty years, the
first school, founded by Dr. Robert G. Boville, was
multiplied in America by ten thousand, with more
than a million pupils, and every country on the globe
had been invaded. Like the Sunday School, its success was largely due to the practical plan of its founder to meet an appalling need.

With compassion similar to that of Robert Raikes,
Dr. Boville had a burden for the idle children of our
large cities, released from school and factory only to
run riot upon the streets to the extreme annoyance
of all decent people. But while Raikes' purpose was
to provide these groups of "miserable little wretches"
with the elements of both secular and religious knowledge, Dr. Boville sought to give them Bible instruction so conspicuously absent from the public school.

A passionate lover of little children, Dr. Boville
was a young Canadian minister who had been called
to the superintendency of the Baptist City Mission
Society in New York. Riding downtown to his office, in the summer of 1901, he saw myriads of little
boys and girls living on the crowded sultry streets,
block lanes, and filthy alleys, in danger of their lives,
to say nothing of their morals. The public schools
were closed and the mothers were away working in
shops and factories. Nearby were empty churches
with cool, pleasant rooms, closed for the summer.
Pouring out of the schools and colleges were thousands of unemployed students and instructors. Recog-
nizing the enormous economic waste of child life, of
church property, and of student energy, Dr. and
Mrs. Boville brought together these three factors on
the East Side for a daily school that combined worship, work and play.

The morning hours and the discipline of the public school were employed to advantage. The program gave a larger place to worship and expression than that enjoyed by pupils in the Sunday School. Larger opportunities were also given for consecutive and correlated instruction. In fact, the new educational agency was patterned more after the public school than the Sunday School.

1. First vacation school

The first summer Dr. Boville obtained permission to use five church buildings, and had posted on the door of each a notice stating that the school was free to all children up to fourteen years of age. College student staffs were selected and placed in charge. An average of two hundred children was registered in each school. The following year other churches became interested, and soon other cities.

In 1905 Dr. Boville resigned as superintendent of the Baptist City Mission and became leader of the entire Vacation School enterprise. In 1907 the National Vacation Bible School Committee was formed, and in 1911 this committee was incorporated as the Daily Vacation Bible School Association. In 1912 there were 141 cities in which Vacation Schools were operated.

2. Denominational promotion

Like the Sunday School, the Daily Vacation Bible School started as an independent movement. In the early years it was largely confined to the neglected children of the congested districts of the larger cities. It was in most cases a missionary enterprise. By 1910 the Presbyterian Home Mission Board had come to appreciate the value of the new movement for reaching the neglected children of America, and included the school as a part of its program. In 1915 the Baptists of the North took up the work, assigning its promotion and supervision to the American Baptist Publication Society, thus linking the movement with the denominational program of religious education.

One by one the other denominations followed, and within a decade almost every major denomination had officially recognized the movement. The recognition and support of the Church gave a new impetus to the movement, and it spread more rapidly than ever. By this time the Vacation School was no longer considered an experiment, nor was its value limited to mission children. Religious educators came to view it as important, and thousands of self-supporting churches conducted Vacation Schools as regularly as they operated their Sunday Schools. When once the appeal was pressed home to every church, "Give your children a chance for more religious education," schools began to multiply on every hand.

3. World-wide acceptance

Growth of the movement was phenomenal. In 1923 the International Association of Daily Vacation Bible Schools became an auxiliary of the International Council of Religious Education, and in 1928 it became an integral part of that organization. By 1921 there were 2,534 schools, 15,555 teachers, and 270,000 pupils, with an estimated expenditure of $270,000.

Missionaries and Sunday School leaders now began to adopt the new agency as a part of their educational program, and soon Vacation Schools were to be found on every continent. Missionaries found the new plan of daily instruction far more satisfactory than the weekly Sunday School in dealing with native children, and schools began to multiply on the foreign field. In 1937, Korea reported 1,116 schools, 6,529 teachers, and 118,403 pupils. The Philippine Islands came second, with more than 20,000; while China and India each had approximately one-half that number attending the schools. The report that year listed 3,500 schools, 10,572 teachers and 183,-635 pupils in foreign lands.

4. Evaluation

The Vacation School has come to stay. The fact that children are out of doors so much more in summer multiplies their temptations and increases their need of guidance. Juvenile delinquency rises 52 per cent when schools close, and street accidents increase 50 per cent.

The popularity of the automobile in America has created a serious problem for the Sunday School. Parents who are not deeply interested in the church or impressed with the importance of the Sunday School have formed a habit during the summer months of taking their children away for weekend excursions. For this reason Sunday Schools today experience a summer slump in attendance. The Vacation School, to a large extent, has offset the heavy withdrawals from the Sunday School. In addition, the unparalleled growth of forty years has demonstrated other ways in which the Vacation School is proving to be an indispensable agency.

a. *Reaches the spiritually illiterate*

Probably the greatest problem before the American Sunday School today is to reach the great mass of children who are receiving no systematic religious instruction. Two out of every three Protestant children are not enrolled in Sunday School and seem hardly likely to be. Statistics indicate that about one-fourth of the pupils in Daily Vacation Bible School have not previously been reached. Therefore, the summer school frequently means an increased enrollment for the Sunday School which is willing to follow up these new contacts.

b. *Improves the Sunday School*

Many churches are content with what they are accomplishing in the Sunday School, but not those who have witnessed the larger and better possibilities of the Daily Vacation Bible School. Pastors who have made careful comparisons of the schools and have given every opportunity for the advancement and improvement of both, have gone on record as saying that two weeks of intensive work in the Vacation School is accomplishing as much as the entire year in the Sunday School.

(1) *Best hours of the day*

In the Vacation School the entire morning is given to the children. As the sessions in most instances begin directly after the close of the public school for the summer, the pupil readily enters into the church program of the entire morning, accepting the afternoon release and freedom from homework as a sufficient guarantee of a vacation from studies.

(2) *Continuous program*

It is hardly to be expected that pupils would become proficient in reading, writing and arithmetic if their instruction were limited to a once-a-week session. The study of the Bible day after day makes it possible to progress more rapidly, since less is forgotten in the shorter interval between lessons. To permit longer periods to intervene not only requires for review purposes the time that should be spent in advance study, but it lessens the importance of the subject in the minds of the pupils.

(3) *Correlated curriculum*

Worship is a very important phase of religious education, but the average Sunday School does not give more than 6 per cent of its program to this exercise. Worship is not only given an adequate place in the day's program of the Daily Vacation Bible School, but the theme for these devotional services has a distinct bearing on the lesson that is to follow.

(4) *Adequate time for expressional activities*

Despite the fact that the pupil is far more likely to assimilate instruction which he reproduces, few Sunday Schools devote much attention or time to expressional methods. Whereas, 90 per cent of the period is given to information, no more than 4 per cent is devoted to expression in the average Sunday School. In the Vacation School the proportions are much more nearly equal. Manual expression especially is stressed, since its educational value is so superior to oral recitation. The instruction is reproduced by writing, drawing and handcraft. Knowledge clarified and confirmed by the construction of maps and models cannot be forgotten.

(5) *More attention to teacher training*

The fact that the Vacation School program is more an imitation of the public school system than a duplication of the Sunday School, has called for a higher standard of teaching. That Dr. Boville recruited college students for his first school has established a helpful precedent for a better preparation of religious instructors. In fact, the Vacation School in its program has so nearly equalled the efficiency of the public school that only untrained teachers and inadequate housing facilities have prevented it from wholly measuring up to the high standards of public instruction.

II. Week Day Religious Instruction

A boy attending one of our American public schools recently said to his father, "Dad, that religion of Osiris was a great thing, wasn't it?"

Dad looked up from the evening paper. "Where did you hear about the religion of Osiris? I never heard of it."

"In school today," answered the son. "It was the greatest religion the world ever knew. It saved the Egyptians from barbarism and they saved the world."

"What about our religion in America?" asked the father.

"Oh, we have not had anything about that in school," Johnny answered.

Incidents like this, which can be multiplied today, raise the grave question whether or not the Church can prosper if left out of our increasingly attractive and effective schools, and whether our nation can survive when its schools are not grounded for morals and patriotism in a religious faith. A generation ago in Britain the teaching of religion in the day school was a subject of fierce and bitter political contro-

versy. Today its need is so apparent that educators
and clergymen co-operate to make suitable provision
for it. Men of different theological outlook and different ecclesiastical loyalties have joined hands in an
endeavor to transform the methods of religious teaching, and they have succeeded. The result is that religion is now being taught in the elementary schools
much more efficiently and effectively than ever before.

Considering the origin of our magnificent public
school system from the intensely religious foundations of our Puritan fathers, it is tragic to discover
its irreligious character today. We have the Bible
in the American courtroom. It is customary for witnesses and prospective jurors to take a religious oath
on the Bible before giving testimony. The Bible has
found its way into the penitentiaries. One state gives
a Bible, at public expense, to any convict who asks
for a copy, while in Ohio and Illinois the government
supplies copies of the Bible for every cell. Chaplains
are employed at the expense of the government for
the American Army and Navy. Engraved on the
national seal used by the President of the United
States on all official documents is the significant fact
that God watches over and aids in the building of
the nation. Even on our currency, America's religious faith has been attested and widely circulated
by the confession, "In God we trust."

Considering then how closely the Bible has been
interwoven into the national life and leadership of
America, foreigners are naturally surprised to discover that it is not given an official place in the training of our future citizens. The Bible is recognized
in the courtroom, but not in the schoolroom! It is

provided for the insane, but not for the ignorant!
It is taught to criminals, but not to children! It is
prescribed for our currency, but not for our curriculum!

In 1905, at an interchurch conference held in Car-
negie Hall, New York, Dr. George U. Wenner read
a paper on the subject, "Religious Education and
the Public Schools." A great deal of discussion was
provoked and a resolution was adopted recommending, for the favorable consideration of public school
authorities throughout the country, the proposal to
allow children to be absent from the public schools
on Wednesdays, or some other afternoon, for the
purpose of attending religious instruction in their
own churches. This was the beginning of a movement
for weekday religious education. Authorities differed,
however, as to how this could best be carried out.
Three distinctive schools have come into existence.

1. National Christian schools

For years Catholics, Jews and Lutherans have conducted parochial schools, and it is well known that
Catholics especially place primary emphasis on their
schools. They not only teach religion, but all subjects from the religious point of view. However, a
group of spiritual people had a vision of an interdenominational school patterned largely after the
public school, giving the Bible a place, but not to the
exclusion of a well-rounded secular education. Consequently, the National Christian Schools have come
into existence largely with this purpose in view.

Although not denominational in character, this excellent system was made possible through the interest
and generosity of the Dutch Reformed and the larger

Christian Reformed Churches. While the pupils come chiefly from these denominations, fully one-fourth of the total enrolment consists of pupils from other Protestant churches. These schools are located largely in Michigan, Illinois and Iowa, where these two denominations are especially predominant.

The Chicago Christian High School compares favorably with any public institution of secondary learning, and in addition, its activities and curriculum have an underlying Christian motivation. It offers a regular program of high school work, including home economics for girls, shop courses for boys, as well as vocal and instrumental music. In addition to a normal schedule of subjects, each student has two hours a week of Bible study and two hours of athletics. The school is fully accredited by the North Central Association and other accrediting agencies.

2. Chattanooga schools

In 1922 Dr. J. P. McCallie, headmaster of the McCallie Boys' School and chairman of the Religious Work Committee of the Y. M. C. A., asked the directors to back him up in getting the Bible taught in the public schools of Chattanooga, Tennessee. They suggested co-operating with the Y. W. C. A. It was discovered that there was already a committee working on this matter. Representatives of the Y. M. C. A. and Y. W. C. A. approached the Pastors' Association and secured unanimous approval of their plan. A Bible Study Committee, representing the Y. M. C. A. and Y. W. C. A., the Pastors' Association and the public schools, selected and has been supporting a full-time teacher for one of the Chattanooga high schools and another teacher for the elementary grades and junior high school. All classes are taught during school hours in the school building with full school credit.

Since 1922 some twenty teachers have served as instructors. All of them have been true to the missionary motive and faithful to the Word of God. The wonderful effect of this Bible course is due to the enthusiasm and character of these teachers, as well as to the untiring efforts and wholehearted support of Dr. McCallie.

While the Bible Committee selects the teachers, plans the courses and raises the funds, the school authorities are responsible for discipline and good scholarship. The Bible is taught once a week in the elementary and junior high schools from the fourth through the eighth grades, and every day in the senior high schools. In the fourth, fifth and sixth grades, the regular teachers prepare the ground for subsequent instruction by reading *Hurlbut's Story of the Bible* and by hearing memory work required. In this way the Bible teacher can accomplish much more than the thirty-minute period each week might indicate.

Although the course is elective, so that parents may request a child's absence from class, the average enrolment for Bible instruction is nearly 100 per cent. It is the most popular elective in the public schools of Chattanooga. The Bible is the only textbook used, and each pupil is encouraged to have a copy at school.

The budget has been apportioned among the churches, some of which respond liberally. In addition, individuals subscribe with annual payments, and auxiliaries contribute regularly. The Parent

Teacher Association collects a love offering before Easter in all of the public schools, and pupils, parents and teachers have given with increasing liberality until a sum of more than three thousand dollars is now contributed to the total budget of over nine thousand dollars. No tax funds are used for salaries, but Bible teachers are allowed the use of public school time and property.

3. Week Day Church School

The Week Day Church School movement had its beginning in 1913, when an experiment was conducted, offering the public schools of Gary, Indiana, religious instruction on released time. Dr. W. A. Avann, pastor of the First Methodist Episcopal Church, called the ministers of the city to meet with William E. Wirt, superintendent of schools. Dr. Wirt offered to release the pupils from public schools for religious instruction provided the churches would assume the responsibility for the buildings and the teachers.

By 1914 several denominations had accepted this offer, and religious instruction on released time began in their churches. By December, 1915, 619 pupils were enrolled. The movement proved so popular that in 1918 five Protestant denominations united to form a Board of Religious Education. Churches were instrumental in interesting their denominational boards in the movement, and with the addition of corporation subscriptions as well as church support, a budget of approximately twelve thousand dollars was raised.

As the Gary plan made the most popular appeal, since it asked nothing more from the State than re-

leased time, other cities took up the plan. In Van
Wert, Ohio, a full-time director was employed and
86 per cent of the children in the elementary grades
enrolled. Dayton, Ohio; Evanston, Illinois; North-
field, Minnesota; Corydon, Iowa; Oak Park, Illinois;
Denver, Colorado; Kansas City, Kansas; Malden,
Massachusetts, and many other places followed. In
Waxahachie, Texas, 95 per cent of the public school
pupils were enrolled, and in Kansas City, fifteen thousand pupils in their weekday schools.

The last government report (1941) showed that
approximately five hundred communities of all sizes
in all parts of the country now release children during school time for religious education. These em-
brace 455 school systems. In February, 1941, it was
estimated that more than one million children in
forty-one states of the Union were granted released
time for religious education. The major development
of the movement has taken place during the last
twenty years and especially during the last five years.
Because this plan appears to be the most popular,
if not the most promising, it will be given further
consideration.

a. Legal problems

Has the State a legal right to dismiss children from
public schools for religious instruction? This question
has been raised by those who hesitated to start a
movement that would be unconstitutional. However,
the United States Supreme Court has handed down
a decision in this matter which is far reaching.

In 1922 the state of Oregon adopted a bill which
provided that after 1926 all private and parochial
schools in the state should be abolished. It sought

by this legislation to compel parents to send their children to schools conducted by the State. This would make it impossible for private and parochial schools to exercise a right inherent in American citizenship. When the matter was carried to the United States Supreme Court in 1925, that body declared the law unconstitutional on the ground that "it interferes with the liberty of parents and guardians to direct the upbringing and education of children under their control." The court said further:

> The fundamental theory of liberty upon which all governments in this Union repose, excluded, in general, power of the State to standardize its children by forcing them to accept instruction from public teachers only. The child is not the mere creature of the State. Those who nurture him and direct his destiny have the right, coupled with the high duty, to recognize and prepare him for additional obligations.

This decision of the United States Supreme Court is the final ruling concerning the question of released time. Parents may request of school authorities the opportunity for another agency than the public school to contribute to the education of their children. Roman Catholics, Lutherans, Jews and Mormons have been accorded this privilege for years. There is nothing unconstitutional about it and nothing that violates the principle of freedom, civil or religious.

This ruling of the Supreme Court of the United States prepared the way for legislative authorization for release of public school pupils during school hours for religious education in Iowa, Kentucky, Maine, Minnesota, New York, Oregon, South Dakota, West

Virginia, Hawaii and the Philippine Islands. Rulings of state attorneys authorized the release of public school pupils for weekday classes in Illinois, Nevada, Pennsylvania and Idaho. Court decisions in Vermont, Kansas, and Washington permit the release of pupils, or place certain prescriptions upon the program. Opinions from state boards of education in Connecticut, Delaware, Nebraska, New Jersey, Rhode Island, Ohio and Utah left the decision as to whether or not pupils should be released, to the jurisdiction of local school officials. As weekday classes are now reported in thirty-eight states, it appears that in some communities pupils are being released without any special legislation or court ruling.

b. Curriculum problems

There are two outstanding types of Week Day Church School where children are released on school time.

(1) Denominational Interchurch School

In this type of school the churches unite for the purpose of obtaining released time from the public school, but conduct different programs in the respective churches. The curriculum in this case is generally suited to the denominational program of Christian education. All co-operating denominations, including Catholics and Jews, are therefore able to offer a course of study that is in keeping with the doctrines of their church.

(2) Interdenominational Community School

In this type, churches pool their efforts by appointing a joint committee that is responsible for securing a centrally located place for instruction, as well as the necessary teaching staff. This plan, while far more economical and providing more efficient teaching, creates the problem of adopting a curriculum which is satisfactory to all co-operating churches. Catholics and Jews and many Protestants are unwilling to expose their children to instruction which to be inoffensive must be so broad that it may even eliminate the fundamental doctrines of the Christian faith.

Were the Week Day Church School the only agency, it might be advisable, if not essential, to agree upon a curriculum that would be satisfactory to all churches. However, instruction in the Week Day Church School should at least parallel what is being taught in Sunday School and other educational agencies of the church. The principle of correlation in education is so vital that it is doubtful whether community classes can ever be substituted for church instruction. Moreover, most churches, especially the Catholic, are vitally concerned about the future relationship of their children to the church. For this reason it would seem that the denominational interchurch school type, even with its disadvantages in efficiency and economy, is the more practical.

c. *Evaluation*

Valuable as is the Daily Vacation Bible School, it cannot measure up to the larger possibilities of the Week Day Church School. Granted that much instruction can be imparted in an intensive program of several weeks of concentrated daily instruction, this can never take the place of around-the-year education. We have seen in ancient and medieval times that religious instruction was a daily matter, and it is inconceivable that its importance will ever be recognized when secular subjects are taught daily and

the Bible spasmodically. Moreover, American people
are coming to realize that character building is just
as important a part of the public school curriculum
as those subjects which broaden the mind.

In making a statement to the Board of Education,
Dr. Ben Graham, superintendent of Pittsburgh
schools, said:

> The most important objective in high school education
> today is the development of the character of our American
> youth. In the Pittsburgh high schools for several years we
> have emphasized character training not only in regular
> classroom instruction, but also in special instruction pre-
> pared specifically for improvement of character. In our
> democracy, Church and State are separated, and religious
> freedom is guaranteed to every man. In order to encour-
> age the continuance of religious education during the high
> school period in the training of youth and at the same
> time preserve the true spirit of religious freedom, your
> superintendent recommends and plans for religious educa-
> tion.

Dr. Graham's plan was to give to every pupil who
devoted three hours a week to religious instruction
in his own church, two credits out of a possible
thirty-six toward high school graduation or college
entrance. The most striking feature of this proposition is that attendance at Sunday School and attendance at morning worship made up two of these
hours.

Such a plan, which puts the responsibility of the
instruction upon the individual church, is undoubtedly the most satisfactory from every point of view.
The real problem has been to bring the church to
assume this obligation. Many of the comments expressing interest in the weekday program specified

such conditions for accepting it as, "If the churches finance the problem," "If all the churches will agree on a time for the class," "If the church will organize a 'going' program," "If manned by competent teachers," and "If satisfactory instruction is given."

It will be seen from the foregoing that the success of the Week Day Church School largely lies with the church's assuming the responsibility for providing a bigger and better program of religious education. The church must reorganize its educational program and enlarge and magnify its teaching force. The church must bring the Sunday School up to the public school standard of efficiency and correlate its instruction with the weekday session. It means a real and definite program for all sessions, a properly trained teaching force, and suitable housing facilities.

III. The School of the Church

As the responsibility for religious instruction was more and more shifted to the church by the home and the school, additional agencies sprang up within its walls to share with the Sunday School the work of the teaching ministry. We have already seen how the Christian Endeavor Society became an important factor in providing for the neglected expressional activities. In addition to this organization, temperance and missionary bands, societies, and circles with service organizations of many names were introduced as a part of the parish life of some churches. To these were added in more or less standardized form the Cradle Roll, the Home Department, Boys' Brigade and Boy Scouts, the precursors of a multitude of early adolescent training agencies.

In 1904 Professor George Albert Coe, in his book *Education in Religion and Morals,* sounded a call for a reinterpretation of the Sunday School functions as well as the correlation of the agencies of expression and instruction within the church, together with such educational leadership of these local forces as would make the church a school. At the Boston convention of the Religious Education Association in 1905, Dr. W. C. Bitting restated Coe's vision, admitting that its realization presented many unsolved problems.

The General Assembly of the Presbyterian Church in 1908 made an important contribution toward a unified program of education in the local church. Its annual minutes stipulated that:

> There should be organized a school of the church which should embrace the supervision and unification of all the educational activities within the congregation. The present Sunday School is a most important member of the Church School, but it is not the whole of it, nor is it independent of the other members.

In June, 1910, Professor Ernest D. Burton voiced the concept still more clearly and fully, adding as an essential feature, a committee or board of religious education which should have general oversight of all the educational activities of the church.

1. Conflicting educational agencies

The work of the teaching ministry has not been materially strengthened through the multiplicity of supplementary agencies to the Sunday School. They compete with each other for time, interest, activity, and even for money from the same group of church members. Many of these organizations originated not as integral parts of the church program, but as movements from without the church. Each creates its own program for its own purpose, and demands the cooperation of the churches. Each had a distinct course of study with no relation to the others, except that they are all in the field of religious education.

There is also overlapping in social activities. The leaders of each agency plan for the social life of its members as if they represent the only organization in the church which makes provision for this need. Often this results in giving to some groups too many social activities to the neglect of other essential features.

In addition to the overlapping of subject material and social activities, each agency has a distinct plan of organization and administration. Each society has its own president, with full quota of officers and committees responsible for the promotion of the work in that particular group. It is practically a physical impossibility for most children and adolescents to belong to all these educational activities; and even if they did, there is so much omission and duplication in the instruction that the net value is very small.

It has already been pointed out that the introduction of the Christian Endeavor Society was an important addition to the educational program since it stressed the expressional phase of religious instruction that was largely neglected by the Sunday School. However, unless expression can be built upon information, it is of little value. In most young people's meetings, instead of participants giving expression to truths already learned, they conduct a ready-made, "cut and dried" program. The "discussions" are frequently memorized instead of being expressions of impressions which have been made upon them. Others read extracts because they have not acquired the information about which they are to give expression. Facts may be read and some information may be given which is not presented in any other organization, but the object of the young people's meeting as an expressional service is hindered because its members must use new subject matter in preparing its programs. In public school the pupil studies his lesson in the morning and recites it in the afternoon. In the Sunday School the pupil often secures information without being called upon for expression. In the Christian Endeavor Society he is called upon to give expression on some topic with which he is not familiar.

2. A new nomenclature

It is quite evident that since the Sunday School is no longer the only agency in the church that gives Christian instruction a new nomenclature is in order. Professor Walter S. Athearn was the first to suggest the title "Church School," and that name was used in his text on Sunday School organization and administration. However, Church School has been to many simply a more euphonious name than Sunday School. In fact, there seems to be a difference of opinion, since the names Sunday School, Sabbath School, Bible School and Church School are all being used today for the same major agency of the church. Sabbath School is suggestive of those denominations which believe that Saturday should be observed as a day of rest instead of Sunday. The name Bible School has been confused with Bible institute and Bible college, which of course are doing a more thorough work in Bible instruction than the Sunday School.

Church School can be and should be used as an all-embracive term to include the Sunday School, Vacation School, Week Day Church School and Christian Endeavor. The use of the name Church School is a recognition of the fact that other educational agencies exist beside the Sunday School, even though it is the largest and most important. Church School is the sum total of all educational agencies that today constitute the school of the church.

3. A Council of Religious Education

A lack of administration and supervision has characterized the educational undertakings of the church. Sometimes this lack has been well-nigh total insofar as supervision is concerned, and often the only administrative activity has been an annual meeting of the teachers and officers of the Sunday School to elect officers. The Sunday School superintendent has seldom been qualified to supervise the work of the teachers. He has only been a presiding officer for the "opening exercises," and has felt that when he has made provision for the teacherless classes, he has done all that is expected of a superintendent.

Most Sunday Schools have come to occupy a semi-independence, if not a total independence, of the church. They manage their own affairs, elect their own officers, choose their own teachers, raise their own funds, and decide every detail of the program without consulting the church. Under these circumstances the Sunday School can hardly be called the school of the church.

In recent years churches have found a happy solution to these problems by creating a council, whose members represent all existing educational agencies. This body has usually been called the Church Council of Religious Education, and is helpful even when the educational program of the church does not extend beyond the Sunday School. Churches are beginning to see that their educational work is an important task, and have determined to bring some sort of unity out of a chaotic situation.

a. *Membership*

The Church Council of Religious Education not only includes representatives from the Sunday School, young people's society, missionary societies and all other educational agencies, but delegated members from the official board. The pastor also serves as member ex-officio. Where the Sunday School continues to be the major enterprise of the church, this organization is not only represented by the general superintendent, but also by the department superintendents. Where all of the members of the council are chosen for their interest in religious education and for their demonstrated ability to carry on some phase of educational work, such a body is qualified to give efficient administrative attention to the teaching ministry of the church.

b. *Duties*

The most important task of the Council of Religious Education is to prepare the educational program. It plans and sponsors all educational activities, as well as provides necessary housing, equipment and finances. Extension work is not neglected, as this council is authorized to organize branch Sunday Schools. A committee has charge of the public school contacts where it is possible to arrange for Week Day Church School.

The selection of officers and more particularly teachers, has often led to conflict with competing organizations. This council is a clearing house, whose duty it is to prevent overworking and overlapping of competent leaders.

4. A correlated program

The selection of a Council of Religious Education is the first step toward a correlated program. It goes without saying that the program of religious education should be a unit no matter how many different organizations contribute to it.

A long step toward the development of a unified program of education for the individual church has been made by the organization which has come to be known as Correlated Schools of Religious Education. In these schools the work of the Sunday School, Week Day Church School, Christian Endeavor Societies, and club activities is brought under the Council of Religious Education. These organizations have a central program of information with which the worship services and the expressional activities are correlated. They strive together, without overlapping or competing, for the attainment of certain common goals.

Especially for children and adolescents of the school age, under the correlated school plan, the Week Day Church School becomes in reality the weekday session of the Church School. The Sunday School becomes the Sunday session, the Christian Endeavor meetings the expressional session, and the Daily Vacation Bible School, the summer session of the Church School. All of these sessions are parts of the school of the church. Their organization is uniform and the department is the unit of organization. Intermediates, for instance, are recognized in their educational agency as the junior high age group. Instead of each educational agency planning social activities for its group, the Council of Religious Education arranges for the needs of each department, so that children and adolescents of all ages share alike in the instruction, expression and social activities.

5. An educational director

While a Council of Religious Education is able to provide unity, none of its representatives as a rule have sufficient time or training to work out an efficient and effective correlated program. For this reason a new profession has been created in recent years, which seeks to give the church the teaching and training of which it has long been deprived.

Since the beginning of the century there has been a movement to provide trained specialists who are responsible for the entire educational program. Formerly, churches engaged an assistant pastor to take charge of the young people's work. Today, they are employing an educational director to supervise the teaching of the children and the training of the young people. The director's activities do not conflict with, but rather complete, the work of the pastor. The latter continues to be the head of the church, and is responsible for the services of worship and adult activity. But he recognizes in the director a professionally trained specialist whose division of work is the educational program. This dual ministry, which so harmoniously completes the work of the local

church, and enables it to give equal emphasis to each
of the four functions for which it is responsible, may
be seen from the following diagram:

Worship
Teaching } The Educational { The
Training }   Director { Pastor
Service

The directors of religious education were first recognized as a distinct group at the quadrennial convention of the International Council of Religious
Education in 1926. Those in attendance met in a
group at a special session, and reported the findings
of their conference as follows:

1. We, the ministers and directors of religious education, are pleased to note the evolving of a new
program in religious education which is life-centered,
dynamic, unified, comprehensive and flexible.
2. We recognize the consequences of such a program
as:
   a. Making the local church director of religious
   education the unifier of that program for his
   church.
   b. Freeing the director from the domination of
   all superimposed programs, whether interdenominational, denominational, organizational
   or otherwise.
   c. Requiring a higher standard of professional
   and technical training on the part of the
   directors and ministers of education in local
   churches.
   d. Making the director a creator, a producer, and
   experimenter, rather than a mere follower.
3. Further, we regretfully confess to a neglect of adults
in our program of religious education, and are committed to a new consideration of adult education as
urged by the leaders in that field.

4. We subscribe to the necessity and advisability of dignifying our program of religious education by trying to equal the standards of the public school in punctuality and regularity of attendance.

5. We commend to ourselves and to all other directors of religious education the use of the yardsticks of educational measurements now made available.

Perhaps the most important service rendered by the educational director is the development of an efficient teaching staff. Despite the multiplied agencies for teacher training, the majority of teachers are still inadequately prepared for their task. The training program is being extended to the home, and now parents, the first and most important instructors, are being prepared to teach their children in those early impressionable years.

In addition to training the teachers, the educational director is able to arrange a program that provides correlated, accumulative and complete instruction, and at the end, definite recognition and promotion. The instruction of the Sunday School is correlated with the expressional session of the Christian Endeavor Society, thus perpetuating and completing an organic unit of instruction. The educational director has charge of the Daily Vacation Bible School, and in consequence its program supplements and correlates the instruction received on Sunday. He also supervises, if not imparts, the instruction given in the Week Day Church School, so that it not only conforms to the denominational doctrines of his church, but is also made a part of the unified program of instruction.

With the assistance of an educational director the church today is not only able to make a Sunday

School hour 100 per cent efficient, but by correlating the Christian Endeavor Society and making it the expressional session of the Sunday School, the educational period can again be doubled. When the Daily Vacation Bible School is made the summer session of the Church School, and weekday instruction is unified and correlated with a unified curriculum, more valuable hours are added to the child's instruction. Finally, the educational director organizes a children's church, which provides a service of worship better adapted to the needs of the young than that given in the average church service.

Protestant children in the United States receive each year approximately one thousand hours of secular education, but those enrolled in Sunday School cannot possibly be credited with more than one hour a week. Untrained teachers, ungraded lessons and irregular attendance reduce this period to approximately seventeen hours of real religious instruction annually. Now, with a Council of Religious Education to unify the program, and an educational director to provide and supervise the curriculum, the average church has been able to increase its teaching and training ministry from 17 to 256 hours a year. This may be seen from the following tabulation:

	Hours
Improved Sunday School	52
Correlated Expressional Sessions	52
Children's Church	52
Summer Session of Church School	60
Week Day Church School	40
	256

There is no question but that the educational director, who alone is capable of correlating a curriculum and adapting it to the needs and development
of the pupils, can best solve the problem of religious
education today. Neither the public school nor the
home can be depended upon to assume the full responsibility for this training, though they should
serve as supplementary agencies. On the other hand,
a correlated and complete program sponsored by the
church and ably directed by a trained specialist is
proving to be highly effective.

---

1. How does religious education in America compare with Hungary?
2. What is Dr. Gorham's estimate of the Sunday
   School hour?
3. Write one hundred words on the beginning of
   the Daily Vacation Bible School.
4. Give statistics to indicate the rapid growth of
   the new agency.
5. Evaluate the Daily Vacation Bible School.
6. Compare the Vacation School with the Sunday
   School.
7. Give several reasons why one would expect the
   Bible to be taught in the American public
   schools.
8. What are the National Christian Schools?
9. Describe the Chattanooga schools.
10. Write one hundred words on the Week Day
    Church School.
11. What was the Oregon decision of the United
    States Supreme Court?

12. Compare the two outstanding types of Week Day Church School.

13. Why is the Week Day Church School superior to the Vacation School?

14. What is the real problem of the Week Day Church School?

15. What forward step in education did Professor Coe suggest in *Education in Religion and Morals?*

16. Criticize the supplementary educational agencies of the church.

17. What nomenclature is correct—Sunday School, Sabbath School, Bible School or Church School? When should that term be used?

18. Why is a Council of Religious Education in a church desirable?

19. Who compose the council and what are the duties of its members?

20. What is a Correlated School of Religious Education?

21. What is the relation of the educational director to the pastor?

22. Give the findings of the directors of religious education at the quadrennial convention of 1926.

23. What is the most important service an educational director can render?

24. Show how under a council and an educational director the church can increase its teaching and training ministry from 17 to 256 hours a year.

15

FROM CONVENTION TO COUNCIL

MUCH credit for the success of the Sunday School must be given to those who were instrumental in promoting it. We have seen how Robert Raikes through his publication first gave publicity to the movement. We have also observed how the American Sunday School Union, founded by laymen, with its governing board excluding any but laymen, was able to further this movement apart from the Church. Businessmen have been more willing to use promotional methods for religious activities and agencies than the clergy, and their identification with the Sunday School has meant much to bring it before the people.

After the American Sunday School Union, the convention proved to be the outstanding instrument of promotion. The enthusiasm aroused at these great gatherings was invaluable in furthering the work. Everybody came, everybody sang, and everybody seemed to feel that the convention had been well worth while. The appeal was made to the heart fully as much as to the head, and every one present could be reached by the program.

Some were inclined to criticize the emotional emphasis of these conventions. Even Bishop Vincent went so far as to say that the Sunday School of his day was strong in the heart but weak in the head. Could he have lived to see the cold intellectual atmosphere that was to prevail in the gatherings of the

twentieth century and to have witnessed the dead-
ness and decline in Sunday School interest, he surely
would have reversed his crticism. Religion is a matter of the emotion fully as much as of the intellect.
Love emanates from the emotions, and a familiar
passage in the Bible assures us that the understanding of all mysteries and of all knowledge amounts
to nothing unless it is accompanied by love. We
speak of the importance of rational religion, but investigation shows that love enters into our decisions
fully as much as knowledge. William Jennings Bryan
said that the decisions of the heart are more to be
depended upon than the decisions of the head.

Undoubtedly the Sunday School was brought to
the commanding place it occupied in the thought and
interest of Christian people at the beginning of the
twentieth century, through the extension and enlargement of the convention movement.

I. The Convention

1. International conventions

The National Sunday School Conventions have
already been traced, and it was found that in 1872
the large representation from foreign countries led
to the change of nomenclature. Therefore, the Sixth
National was also the First International Sunday
School Convention. The progress of the Sunday
School as shown in the achievements of the first nine
International Conventions has also been surveyed.
Conventions now remaining for our considera-
tion are:

a. *Tenth International Convention*

This convention met at Denver, Colorado, in
1902. The first session was a memorial service, com-

memorating the life, work and character of B. F. Jacobs, the acting chairman of the International Executive Committee, who had died just three days before. Rev. B. B. Tyler, D.D., of Denver, the second clergyman in the history of a convention movement so honored, was chosen president. W. N. Hartshorn, of Boston, was unanimously elected as a successor to Mr. Jacobs. Delegates registered numbered 1,186, representing fifty-five states, provinces and territories. The president of the British Sunday School Union, F. F. Belsey, was a distinguished guest.

As was pointed out in an earlier chapter, the plan of lesson selection was one of the great themes of discussion. The final action taken at the convention was the adoption of a resolution which read:

> That at this time we are not prepared to adopt a series of advanced lessons to take the place of the Uniform Lessons in the adult grades of the Sunday School.

b. *Eleventh International Convention*

This was held in Toronto, Canada, in 1905. Sixty states, territories and provinces were represented, and the registration of delegates was larger by far than that of any previous convention. The delegates numbered 1,958, of whom 318 were pastors, 351 superintendents, 856 teachers, and 252 other officers. The mayor of Toronto, Thomas Urquhart, in welcoming the delegates, stated that while there were 35,000 attending the public schools of Toronto, 50,000 were enrolled in Sunday Schools.

Justice J. J. Maclaren, of the Court of Appeals, Ontario, was chosen president. The treasurer reported that more than $55,000 had been received during the past three years, and that $72,668 was pledged for the coming three years' work. Charles G. Trumbull, editor of *The Sunday School Times,* in an address, said:

> At thirty-three cents a Sabbath, which was the established rate when the Sunday School teachers were paid, the American Sunday School Union congratulated itself that its volunteer teaching force was contributing $903,697 annually toward education. Today on the same evaluation the Sunday School officers and teachers of the United States and Canada are contributing $26,717,210 annually.

This convention considered the action of the previous assembly at Denver, and instructed the Lesson Committee to prepare an advanced course of lessons in addition to the Uniform Lesson and the Beginners' course.

c. *Twelfth International Convention*

This convention was held in Louisville, Kentucky, in 1908. The main sessions were held in the Armory Building, the attendance reaching over 5,000. The motto of the convention, "We Would See Jesus," was conspicuously placed above the platform in electric lights, an innovation which has been followed by subsequent conventions.

At the opening session there was a fitting memorial service for Dr. John Potts, whose death the preceding year had climaxed twenty-five years of service on the Lesson Committee, eleven years of which he was chairman. Hon. John Stites, of Louisville, was chosen president. The treasurer's report showed that the convention had received $108,000 during the triennial and that about $110,000 was pledged for the new triennial. The reports of all departments showed great advance, and the general note of the convention was one of optimism and encouragement.

Without doubt the leading action of the assembly was in regard to the lessons. As has already been observed, by this time there was a great demand for a thoroughly graded course, and the convention instructed the Lesson Committee to prepare such a course of lessons to be used by any Sunday School which desired it.

d. *Thirteenth International Convention*

This assembly was held in San Francisco, California, in 1911. Its motto was, "The Open Bible and the Uplifted Cross." W. N. Hartshorn was chosen president. Dr. J. Wilbur Chapman delivered the daily devotional addresses. His general theme was "Soul Winning and Christian Service." The opening day was devoted to home missions and 567 Chinese, Japanese and Koreans participated in the exercises. King George and Queen Mary were crowned in London on the third day of the convention, and congratulations were cabled to their Majesties. On the fourth day 10,000 Sunday School men paraded, each carrying a Bible furnished by the Gideons.

All departments of Sunday School work were discussed by experts in the general assembly and at the departmental conferences. An emphatic stand was taken in favor of having the Bible in the public schools of the states and provinces. A demand was made for uniform divorce laws, and a ringing note was uttered in behalf of international arbitration. The convention gave evidence of a greatly increased interest in both denominational and interdenominational Sunday School work. It was also seen that a new era in Sunday School journalism had been entered. The convention realized the wish of its program builders which was stated by its president, that the delegates "might be seized with the conviction that the Sunday School is the supreme agency within the church to induce Bible study."

A great temperance mass meeting was held at the Coliseum Sunday afternoon, with addresses by outstanding speakers. This was the first step of the united Sunday School movement toward prohibition, which was to result in the adoption of the Eighteenth Amendment to the Constitution of the United States in 1919.

e. *Fourteenth International Convention*

While World War I had already started in Europe, its effect in the United States and Canada had not been sufficiently felt to interfere with a convention being held as scheduled. An eight day convocation was therefore called in the summer of 1914, in Chicago, Illinois.

Howard M. Hamill was chosen president. The program consisted of 167 sessions with 378 participants, indicating it was distinctly a convention of conferences. There were sixty-five group meetings in addition to the sixteen sessions of the main assembly. This plan was carried out in order that the delegates might learn of the tremendous growth of the department as an organization unit and appreciate in a larger way the importance of specialization.

An International Convention had been held in Chicago twenty-seven years before. At that time the total enrolment in the Sunday Schools of the United States and Canada was 9,650,648, and now, in less than three decades, it had grown to 18,441,036.

At the opening session of the convention Marion Lawrance read telegrams of cordial greeting from Woodrow Wilson, president of the United States; William Jennings Bryan, secretary of state, and Josephus Daniels, secretary of the Navy. Following this the delegates rose and sang with great enthuiasm "My Country 'Tis of Thee."

An interesting part of the convention was the exhibit of Sunday School material by the various publication houses interested in furnishing Sunday School equipment. The exhibit was the eye-gate of the convention, and its completeness and striking characteristics ranked it as a Sunday School educative factor of inestimable value.

The International Bible Class parade of men and older boys occurred Saturday afternoon. Nearly every group of marchers carried a banner bearing some sentiment referring to Sunday School work. The strength of the growing prohibition feeling was evident from such slogans as, "The Saloon Must Go," "Mr. Sunday School, Booze Undertaker," "We Will Bury Booze in Wisconsin." In the midst of the Wisconsin delegation was a float bearing a dummy representing a corpse, with the sign, "The Bier That Made Milwaukee Famous." Saturday evening a historical pageant of the Sunday School was given. It portrayed in a series of twenty-one progressive episodes the origin, growth and development of religious education of youth from patriarchal times to the modern graded Sunday School. At least 550 people of all ages took part, from Cradle Roll babies in arms to gray haired members of the Home Department.

f. *Fifteenth International Convention*

Up to this time International Conventions had been triennial, but the entry of the United States into the World War in 1917, together with the conflicting but not competing gatherings of the World Sunday School Conventions, made it desirable for quadrennial assemblies to be held. For this reason the Fifteenth International Convention was held in Buffalo, in 1918.

Like the preceding gathering in Chicago, it was essentially a departmental convention. Instead of devoting most of the time to addresses by noted speakers and giving half hour periods to department and division leaders, entire afternoon sessions were devoted to group conferences. As many as twelve conferences were held simultaneously in an afternoon.

The convention motto, "Thy Kingdom Come," was printed in massive red letters on a canvas hung from the iron rafters of Elmwood Music Hall. Two thousand fourteen delegates were registered, a wonderful attendance for war times. Every state in the Union was represented, except Texas, Wyoming and New Mexico; and every province in Canada, including Newfoundland. Cuba, Alaska and South America sent delegates, while Japan, Korea, India and the Philippines sent distinguished visitors. President Wilson and the Duke of Devonshire, governor general of Canada, replied to telegrams, pledging the full support of the convention to them "in their efforts to make the world safe for democracy."

The outstanding feature of the convention was the educational program launched by Professor Walter

S. Athearn, chairman of the Committee on Education of the International Sunday School Association. Professor Athearn believed that the time had come for a co-operative program of the Church with the public schools, based on psychological, scientific child study and teacher training. He admitted that the project would require a budget of millions of dollars and that the financial problem would stand in the way of its early adoption. However, this was the first recognition given by the Sunday School convention to the growing place of weekday religious instruction in the thinking of the Church. It was to prepare the way for a change in nomenclature so that the Vacation Bible School and Week Day Church School would be recognized as important educational agencies.

The statistical report showed that the Sunday School had made a remarkable record despite the difficulties encountered by war conditions. The total gain in Sunday School enrolment for the four war years had been 2,208,761, or more than half a million a year. Nearly 63,000 conventions had been held during this period, an average of forty-three conventions every day in the year. Another remarkable record was that of 1,582,575 additions to the Church from the Sunday School, or an average of 7,600 for every Sunday during the quadrennial. These statistics would indicate that the Sunday School was an outstanding factor in maintaining the morale of the people during the colossal conflict of the nations, if not in actually winning the war. Sunday School influence also prepared the way for the enactment of the prohibition amendment to the Constitution of the United States the following year.

2. World conventions

While more than half of the Sunday School enrolment was on the Western Hemisphere, the growth of the movement in other countries soon made it apparent that a world convocation should be called.

a. *First World Convention*

This gathering, held in London in 1889, was the result of conferences and the desire for co-operation between a group of American Sunday School leaders such as B. F. Jacobs, William Reynolds, E. K. Warren, J. H. Vincent, Marion Lawrance, E. Morris Fergusson and Joseph Clark, and such British Sunday School men as Sir Francis Flint, F. F. Belsey, Rev. Carey Bonner, Rt. Hon. Lord Kinnard and Sir John Kirk. The total number of registered delegates was 904, of whom 440 were from Great Britain and Ireland, 360 from the United States, 69 from Canada, and 35 from other countries. The Sunday School enrolment for the world at that time was reported to be 19,715,781. Interest seemed to center about India, and before the convention adjourned, the British Sunday School representatives had engaged Dr. James L. Phillips to be their Sunday School missionary to India.

b. *Second World Convention*

This convention was held in St. Louis in 1893 and was a combination of the International and World Conventions, the program of the latter occupying the last three days. The joint enrolment of the two conventions was 882, fifty-five of whom were from Great Britain, Germany, Sweden and India. One delegate represented Burma. Dr. Phillips was present from India and made a stirring appeal in the interest of Japan. The amount of $223, most of which was thrown upon the platform at Dr. Phillips' feet, was raised spontaneously for the purpose of placing a secretary in Japan. As a result of this passionate appeal, T. C. Ikahara, a native Japanese, educated in America, was employed to become secretary for Japan. Through his enthusiasm and efforts, a few years later Frank L. Brown and Dr. H. M. Hamill visited the Orient and effected organizations in Japan, Korea, China and the Philippine Islands.

c. Third World Convention

London again was host to the gathering from the continents in 1898. Delegates from North America chartered the Cunard ship *Catalonia*. The voyage was made memorable by a fire in the hold of the vessel. The delegates were called out of bed at midnight and stood on deck until daybreak while the valiant crew, assisted by many passengers, fought the flames.

The convention enrolled 1,154 delegates, 299 of whom were from North America, representing 30 states and provinces. Most of the delegates were from Great Britain, though Austria, Belgium, France, Germany, Holland, Italy, Norway, Sweden and Switzerland were represented.

Weekday religious instruction, which prevailed in most of continental Europe, had retarded the Sunday School movement and at this convention action was taken to interest the Protestant countries in the furthering of the Sunday School.

d. Fourth World Convention

This was held in 1904 in Jerusalem, which proved to be a very popular center for the convocation. The

North American delegates, numbering 817, sailed from Hoboken on the North German Lloyd Steamship *Grosser Kürfürst,* and they lived on shipboard except during their excursions in the Holy Land and in Egypt. Stops were made at missionary ports and inspirational meetings were held along the journey. This wonderful trip was made possible by three great leaders, E. K. Warren, W. N. Hartshorn and A. B. McCrillis. Probably never before had so many prominent Sunday School leaders been gathered together as were represented on this voyage. The British group also chartered a ship, *The Victoria Augusta,* and brought 485 delegates.

The convention was held in two tents just outside the north wall of Jerusalem, at the edge of Calvary, overlooking the Mount of Olives. There were 1,526 delegates registered, from 25 countries and 50 religious denominations. The outstanding result of this great convention was a world-wide recognition of the value of the Sunday School in mission fields.

e. Fifth World Convention

This gathering was held in the historic city of Rome, Italy, in 1907. There were 1,118 delegates, representing sixty-six countries. A notable meeting was held in the Colosseum under the direction of C. R. Blackall, and a remarkable exhibit was arranged in the convention building. En route to Rome, many of the delegates from the United States visited cities in North Africa, and became so enthusiastic over the missionary possibilities in that part of the world that they pledged generous support to Bishop Joseph C. Hartzell, of the Methodist Episcopal Church, for work in this new field. The result of the convention was that the missionary vision of the leaders was broadened and a great impetus given to a world-wide Sunday School program.

f. Sixth World Convention

This convention came to the United States and was held at Washington in 1910. It was without doubt the largest Sunday School convention up to that date. More than two thousand five hundred delegates registered and there were thousands of visitors. Nearly every state and province in North America was represented, and many delegates came from abroad. Congress recognized this great assembly by adjourning its sessions in order to permit the members to participate in the men's parade. President Taft was present with Mrs. Taft.

Joint secretaries were elected at this convention, Rev. Carey Bonner, of London, and Marion Lawrance, of Chicago. This was the beginning of paid secretarial leadership. Seventy-five thousand dollars was raised for three years' work. With this financial support, Frank L. Brown was sent to the Orient, Arthur Black to South Africa, and Rev. H. S. Harris to South America for Sunday School investigation.

g. Seventh World Convention

Zurich, Switzerland, in 1913, was host to this, the best represented convention up to that time. Delegates were sent from fifty-one countries, representing seventy-five religious denominations. Altogether 2,607 delegates registered, including 221 missionaries, 47 pastors, 601 Sunday School superintendents, and 983 Sunday School teachers. In preparation for this convocation, two pre-convention events of unusual importance took place. Marion Lawrance visited thirty-five cities in England, Ireland, Scotland and Wales, and addressed seventy-seven thousand people in the interest of the Sunday School. H. J. Heinz with a party of twenty-nine persons made a tour through the Orient, visiting Japan, Korea and Russia by rail, and on to the convention at Zurich. This was the first world Sunday School tour of the kind, and created immense interest not only in Japan but throughout the world. As a result of this tour two delegates from Tokyo were present at Zurich and extended the invitation for the next convention to come to Japan.

The main features of the program, which occupied eight days, were the reports of six great commissions organized for the purpose of studying Sunday School work as to its present conditions and future possibilities. Six fields of investigation for these committees were continental Europe, South Africa, India, the Orient, Latin America and Mohammedan lands.

h. *Eighth World Convention*

Seven years elapsed after the Zurich convention before the war-afflicted nations were able to get together. Despite the fact that the energies of three million Sunday School officers and teachers were engaged in war service, during this period there was an extension of Sunday School work in every land, especially in the United States. Peace finally having been declared between the nations, the Sunday School workers of the world gathered in Tokyo in 1920. This was the first time that a world convention had been held in a pagan land, but a great impression was created by the Christian forces. It is probable that no country has ever provided a welcome more warm-hearted or entertainment more lavish. From the time of arrival in Japan until the last of them left the island empire, courtesies were showered upon the delegates, the Japanese being delighted to think of them as the guests of the nation.

The first of three municipal receptions during the convention was given by the city of Tokyo in Hibiya Park. The mayor shook hands with the visitors and it is estimated that the municipality expended $12,500 for the entertainment. The Japanese also financed an excursion to Kamakura, the famous seacoast town thirty-three miles south of Tokyo where stands the colossal statue of Buddha, the finest bronze image in the world. The third municipal reception was given by Yokohama. The delegates were taken to that city by special train, personally welcomed by the mayor, and provided with entertainment and refreshments. The Tokyo Municipal Tram Car Company provided a pass for every delegate, which was good from October 5 to 31.

The great assembly hall which had been built expressly for this gathering burned to the ground only a few hours before the opening session. Had it occurred at any other time, there might have been serious loss of life. What could have been a tragedy became a blessing in disguise. The fire gave to the World Sunday School Convention and its work a publicity it never could have had in any other way. It also developed a spirit of sympathy, not only among the Japanese friends, but throughout the whole world. Messages of sympathy were received from President Wilson, Hon. Lloyd George, President-elect Warren G. Harding, the Archbishop of Canterbury, and many others. The feeling in Japan was intense. It was one of genuine sorrow, and was so frequently expressed, that it had a marked effect on the proceedings of the convention.

The Young Men's Christian Association building was secured for the opening session, but as its auditorium was inadequate to accommodate the crowds, the Japanese government tendered the use of the Imperial Theater, which proved adequate in every respect except in its limited seating capacity. Its commodious stage accommodated the large choir of one thousand voices and many hundreds of others who took part in the pageants. The cost to the convention committee per day was two thousand five hundred dollars, but this building was the only auditorium available.

In the big parade Sunday afternoon all of the delegates and some twenty thousand Tokyo Sunday School children marched to Hibiya Park and later through the principal streets of the city. It was a notable scene in this great heathen city and one long to be remembered. Over the park floated a big balloon upon which was inscribed, "World Sunday School Convention. God is Love." Flags and pennants waved from the hands of every enthusiastic parader.

The fact that all addresses had to be interpreted greatly lengthened the sessions, so that this assembly has gone on record as being the longest Sunday School convention ever held. Altogether there were 1,814 accredited delegates from five continents and seventeen countries. Most of these carried the convention to others on their return trip. Delegations visited Osaka, Kobe, Kyoto and other points in Japan, and where returning ships stopped at foreign ports, arrangements were made for brief presentations of the program. Echoes of the convention were thus heard in Korea, China, India, Egypt, Palestine, Europe and America.

Although only one-half of one per cent of the Japanese people were Christians the convention created a deep impression throughout the empire. The Sunday School Association of Japan, through stereopticon and motion pictures, carried the program to sixty cities of the empire. Up to that time there had been tacit and sometimes open opposition to Sunday School attendance. But the public school teachers from that time encouraged Sunday School attendance in many places. The opening of the universities and the school buildings in Tokyo and throughout Japan for addresses by delegates was a marked indication of the favor of the Japanese educational leaders.

i. *Ninth World Convention*

At the convention of 1920 in Tokyo, there were many invitations for the next quadrennial meeting. However, twenty-six years had intervened since a world gathering of Sunday School workers had been held on British soil. In 1924 representatives from fifty-four nations gathered at Glasgow and there was a total of 2,810 registered paid delegates and many hundreds of visitors. The sessions were held in St. Andrews Hall which, packed in every corner, presented an impressive and inspiring spectacle in the draping of the galleries with the flags of many nations. The convention was not only a Sunday School event of the first magnitude, but also a mighty instrument for the fostering of better relationships.

One of the most interesting features of the

public sessions was the series of "Glimpses of the World Field." As representatives from twenty-seven foreign countries spoke of the Sunday School work being carried on in these widely scattered lands, there was given to many a new vision of the greatness of the Sunday School movement. The widespread extent of the work came home with peculiar power as one native Christian after another told, sometimes in broken English, of the labors in which they were engaged.

The world-wide view was further emphasized by the exhibition which proved so successful and helpful an adjunct of the convention. The missionary section included many rare curios, some of them, such as Livingstone's magic lantern, being of special local and general interest. For the first time at a world convention the motion picture was used most effectively.

Another outstanding feature was the pageant. It was almost impossible to cope with the crowd seeking admission. Hundreds, and it is believed even thousands, were turned away disappointed. Having more than five hundred participants with representatives from seventy-four countries, the pageant could not have done other than make an impression by its very magnitude. But it had been designed for a special purpose and that purpose was kept steadily in view. It was meant to help all who saw it to realize more fully what so many pastors and parishioners are tempted to forget, the immense and far-reaching importance of the Sunday School.

One other spectacular exhibition impressed the convention. The Saturday morning session was devoted to the presentation of juvenile organizations for boys and girls. The Boys Brigade, the Girls

Guildry, the Boy Scouts, the Girl Guides, and the Girls Life Brigade were all presented. In certain instances the speakers were accompanied on the platform by members in full uniform designating their respective organizations. In the afternoon there was a great parade of the juvenile organizations and a large crowd witnessed their maneuvers and demonstrations.

The convention broke all records in its receipt of messages from rulers of the world and leading personalities of different nations. As these expressions of interest came from kings and rulers, the convention stood while they were being read, and nation joined with nation in applause at the close.

The keynote of the gathering was "The Healing of the Nations." The addresses largely centered about the uplifted Christ and His all-important place in world peace and evangelism. The address of Dr. Luther A. Weigle on experiences in lesson course making reflected the work of the special American Committee of Inquiry into the curriculum needs of the Sunday School. Dr. Weigle pointed out that world unity does not involve the principle of lesson uniformity and that educators on the mission fields were already expressing their conviction that a uniform lesson that afforded the same material for all the pupils in the school from the youngest to the oldest was no longer adequate. The progress and success of graded instruction in America led to the appointment of a Curricula Commission to make a comprehensive study of lesson syllabi throughout the world field. A World Survey Commission was also appointed to make a comprehensive study of national organizations and their needs.

Probably the most outstanding action of the convention was its reorganization into a federation of national and international units. Up to this time the World Sunday School Association had been composed of individuals who were deeply interested in extending Sunday School work throughout the world. In the mind of the delegates the time had come for the Association to become a federation of national and international units on a world basis, governed by an executive committee composed of representatives elected by these units. Under this provision there were approximately thirty-five nations federated in the World Association. Of these the North American unit and the British unit were the only two that were not only self-supporting but contributors to the work in other fields. The International Council of Religious Education was recognized as the North American unit while the British Committee, including England, Scotland, Ireland and Wales constituted the British unit.

j. *Tenth World Convention*

Los Angeles, California, was host to the World's Tenth Sunday School Convention which met in 1928. There were 7,631 delegates representing no less than fifty-one nations. Some five thousand more paid admission in order to gain entrance to a single service. At the great Sunday evening gatherings, at least thirty thousand others were present. Thus more than forty thousand people attended the convention. Of the seventy-five speakers provided for the main session, forty-eight came from abroad. The theme selected for this occasion was "Thy Kingdom Come" and the addresses centered about this topic. In addition, considerable attention was given to the curriculum of the Sunday School and the foundation laid for the experience-centered lesson which had already met with favor among the more liberal group of educators in America.

But beside the inspiration of the general sessions, the convention was still more remarkable for other features. For two days preceding the opening session, the officials of Sunday School Associations from all parts of the world sat in conference concerning the problems with which religious education must deal in carrying out this world commission. There were popular conferences held in four centers according to the plan outlined. The interest in these conferences was profound. The largest attendance was at the meetings which considered the work among children. At least twelve hundred people were in attendance.

Another outstanding feature was the series of ten area meetings held Friday afternoon, dividing the entire world into ten sections. Delegates to the convention and others who were interested, gathered in auditoriums of ten downtown churches and heard speakers present the needs and progress of the work of religious education around the world. During the convention various countries made graphic presentations of the Sunday School work in foreign lands. China staged a demonstration which depicted some of the many problems to be faced. Korean delegates gave a vivid representation of forty-four years of growth from no Christians in 1884 to 260,000 in 1928.

The staff of the International Journal of Religious Education issued daily for free distribution to all delegates a helpful eight-page paper which made announcements which could not be given from the platform, reported the news of the previous day, and spoke of good things to come. An anthem was written for the convention as well as a prayer hymn. The Executive Committee approved the proposal to change the name of the World Sunday School Association to the World Sunday School Council of Religious Education. The new nomenclature, however, was never popular and the old name was retained at subsequent conventions.

k. *Eleventh World Convention*

It was the insistent invitation of Sunday School leaders in Brazil over a period of twenty-two years that finally brought the convention in 1932 for the first time to South America, and indeed for the first time south of the equator. Coming at a time of marked transition in the thought-life of forty million Brazilians and sixty million other Latin Americans, it made a vital contribution to the progress of evangelical Christianity in this part of the world. There were 1,626 delegates registered, representing twenty-three countries and coming from every continent. To have held so representative a convention far from the accustomed paths of travel and in the midst of many languages, difficulties due to war, revolution and the world-wide depression, proved to be an achievement that speaks well for the vitality of the Sunday School forces around the world.

The opening address by President W. C. Poole, D.D., of London, presented the convention theme, "The Living Christ." At the conclusion, children led a procession of delegates to the platform where the banners of the nations were assembled. Each child in his own language sang "All Hail the Power of Jesus' Name" and united in the Lord's Prayer. One afternoon the convention divided into language groups. The sessions were arranged to be conducted in Portuguese, Spanish, English, German, French and Japanese. The climax was reached when on the closing evening all assembled to hear "The World's Challenge in Christian Education."

The exhibit which proved to be a popular contribution to all the later conventions was especially impressive. Teaching materials and methods from five continents were presented. Dr. Chester S. Miao of Shanghai, China, brought some very recent productions of literature in the way of textbooks, also samples of art pictures rich in indigenous color and setting. While in earlier years the exhibits were largely contributions from Europe and North America, native leadership in foreign lands was now presenting an indigenous curricula. There were no less than thirty-one North American publishers contributing material and funds to the exhibit, while thirty-five British houses and societies were represented.

1. *Twelfth World Convention*

Sunday School representatives had not met on the continent of Europe since the gathering at Zurich in 1913, so it was fitting that Oslo, Norway, should be chosen for the twelfth World Sunday School Convention in 1936. During this quarter of a century the whole state of affairs had been completely transformed. The great war had changed the map of Europe almost beyond recognition, and the post-war period in continental countries had produced problems as great as those of wartime.

The twelfth convention was the first to be held on Scandinavian soil. Two thousand seven hundred delegates, representing fifty nations were in attendance. Of these, 877 together with 300 unofficial Americans represented the largest delegation that has attended any world convention held outside the United States. His Majesty King Haakon VII honored the convention by his presence at the opening session. This is the first instance in which royalty has attended any of the conventions in any land, and the entrance and seating of the king, while impressive, was attended without pomp or ceremony. "Christ the Hope of the World" was the theme of the convention. From the first address by Dr. George P. Howard of Chile speaking on "Christ the Saviour," until the closing message of the president, Sir Harold MacIntosh, the contributions could be said to be Christ centered.

The great spectacular event of the convention was the open-air demonstration on Sunday afternoon. It was held in the festival place of the university, a spacious quadrangle opening on to the main street of the city, Karl Johan's Gate. When the service was opened a never-to-be-forgotten sight met the eye. Every inch of standing room was occupied; all the windows of the university had their quota of onlookers, and out in front there was a vast sea of faces stretching far beyond the quadrangle and right across the street. The police authorities' estimate of the number of auditors was twenty thousand. The principal address was delivered by Bishop Johan Lunde, Primate of the Lutheran Established Church. Dr. Toyohiko Kagawa spoke for Japan, Dr. Chester S. Miao for China and Rev. M. Franklin for India. The climax was Lady Kinniard's forcible address on "Jesus the Children's Friend."

The convention made much of its departmental conferences. As on former occasions, the children's division attracted the largest numbers. Adolescent work and teacher training and adult groups also were well attended. The Daily Vacation Bible School conference was well supported and considerable interest was shown in the group representing religious education in day school.

The Sunday School courses again occupied the attention of the convention, and it was discovered that not only the British Lessons Council, but representative groups of other countries were committed to the graded principle. Summing up the three days' conferences, the joint chairmen, Ernest H. Hayes of the British Sunday School Lessons Council and Dr. C. A. Bowen of the International Council of Religious Education declared that there had been a surprising agreement on the point that lesson courses must be graded. There had been little use revealed for a uniform lesson, and the need for relating the Bible and its teaching to modern life by extra biblical material was fully recognized.

The statistics of the Sunday Schools of the world which were released at this convention are as follows:

	Teachers	Pupils	Total
Africa	81,522	1,587,989	1,669,511
Asia	107,611	1,778,908	1,886,519
Australasia	91,013	884,972	975,985
Europe	794,427	8,636,809	9,431,236
Latin America	44,585	643,900	688,485
North America	2,026,737	20,607,046	22,633,783
TOTALS	3,145,895	34,139,624	37,285,519

II. The Association

The Sunday School convention was a democratic institution. Its purpose was to give the widest freedom of expression to representatives direct from the schools, each convention to be self-controlled and self-managed in its arrangements and proceedings. Its councils were advisory rather than legislative. The functions of the convention were limited to the gathering and collating of information regarding the Sunday Schools, suggesting improvements that could be made in the light of past experiences, and arousing greater enthusiasm for the work.

Before the end of the nineteenth century a movement was started to change the conventions to a permanently organized body, to be called "association." Outstanding Sunday School leaders opposed this effort in the belief that the democratic freedom of the common assembly would be seriously impaired. They feared the drift toward a permanently organized body or the assumption of any legislative powers, believing that what might be gained in stability of organization would be lost in interest and enthusiasm. They predicted that the representation of the individual schools would disappear and a free expression of views by the ordinary workers would be lost. Just how true their prophecy proved to be will be seen in the development of a centralized program which followed.

As early as 1825, and even before, Sunday School workers in each state began to form organizations which were then called State Sunday School Unions. The promoters for the most part were missionaries of the American Sunday School Union. These state unions were financed by voluntary gifts, and supplemented by appropriations from the American Sunday School Union. The financial efforts of these state organizations from 1825 to 1870 prepared the way for raising the funds necessary to maintain state Sunday School conventions which were formed in this period. Most of these state conventions became associations, incorporated in their respective states, co-operating more or less efficiently with the International Sunday School Convention. New Jersey was the first state to hold a convention. This was in 1858, and subsequently state conventions and associations followed rapidly.

In 1920 there were approximately three hundred full-time paid workers in the United States and Canada employed by the state conventions. In 1921 the New York State Sunday School Association employed five full-time staff workers at the central office and twenty full-time regional workers. The Pennsylvania State Association employed eight state workers on a budget of $60,570. In addition, the Philadelphia

Sunday School Association raised an annual budget
of $20,000 to sustain four full-time workers.

1. International Association

The success of the state associations created a
movement in the International Sunday School Convention for a more permanent organization. The first
official organizer for the international field was William Reynolds of Illinois, elected as field superintendent by the convention of 1887. He was assisted
from time to time by outstanding Sunday School
workers who were loaned by the state association.
In the convention of 1899 at Atlanta, Marion Lawrance was elected as general secretary for full-time
service.

After discussion and amendment, the Toronto convention in 1905 adopted the report of the Executive
Committee:

> That the name of this body be changed from "convention" to "association" is recommended, and that proper
> steps be taken for incorporation.

The convention thus recognized itself as a continuing body, leading the Sunday School forces of the
continent through an Executive Committee which
was now in effect a permanent board. As Dr. E.
Morris Fergusson points out:

> It could not then foresee that the move to incorporate,
> so cheerfully endorsed, involved the early and irrevocable
> transfer of its legislative power to this board, nor the
> effect of this transfer upon the committee and the denominations.

The incorporation act of Congress in 1907 decreed
that sixteen men would direct the affairs of the asso-

ciation. Not a word in the charter referred to a
convention. The body that had been included was
the Executive Committee.

The Louisville convention of 1908 considered itself
to be with undiminished powers the International
Sunday School Association. However, a convention
cannot be incorporated, and little did the delegates
at Louisville know how far the old power of the
international convention had passed away. Control by
a convention and control by an inclusive board of
managers were two different things. Would this
board in which all power had been invested prove
domineering, or would it still look to the convention
for guidance and counsel?

Between the Louisville convention and the next
international gathering at San Francisco a staff of
ten traveled over six hundred thousand miles and
made more than twelve thousand addresses. Every
state and province was organized, and all but four
had their general secretaries. The state and provincial
salaried workers numbered 154. More than 125 counties were organized and were holding annual conventions.

2. World Association

It was at the World Convention in Rome, 1907,
that the World Sunday School Association was organized. The need for financing Sunday School missionaries in distant lands required a more permanent
organization than the convention. As in the case of
the International Sunday School Convention, the
Executive Committee became the incorporate body
of directors. Marion Lawrance was the first general
secretary of the World Sunday School Association,

but in 1910 Frank L. Brown succeeded him. Mr. Brown had attained national recognition through building up the Bushwick Avenue Methodist Sunday School of Brooklyn, from eighty to three thousand five hundred, and for adding six thousand members to the church. His particular Sunday School experience, together with his executive ability and rare spirit, made him a very successful leader.

The Executive Committee of the Association is composed of fifty-seven members, exclusive of the officers. The world-field for purposes of administration was assigned to American and British sections of the Executive Committee; the American section assuming responsibility for Japan, Korea, the Philippines, South America and the Moslem fields, while the British cared for China, India, South Africa and Europe. The purpose and policy of the Association stated by the Rome convention were:

(1) That this Association shall hold conventions and gather information concerning the condition of Sunday Schools throughout the world by correspondence, visitation and other methods.

(2) That it shall seek to extend the work and increase the efficiency of Sunday Schools by co-operation with Sunday School and missionary organizations, especially in those regions of the world most in need of help.

(3) That it shall seek to improve as far as possible the methods of organization and instruction in the Sunday Schools, and promote formation of Sunday School Unions of the Association.

Since 1900, Sunday School Association Unions or Committees in affiliation with the World Sunday School Association have been promoted in approximately forty countries. It is the plan of the World

Sunday School Association to vitally relate these affiliated associations to the existing missions and church organizations in each field. Quadrennial conventions are now incidental to the larger work of girding the world with a chain of Sunday School organizations, with trained workers in each field.

III. The Council

About the time that the convention was yielding its prestige and power to the association, the General Conference of the Methodist Episcopal Church, leading denomination in America and outstanding sponsor of the Sunday School, decided to do its own standardizing and promoting of Sunday Schools, teacher training, and development of Sunday School specialization. This Methodist action formed a part of a general stirring of educational interests among the denominations between 1908 and 1911. There was a feeling that the International Sunday School Association in its close adherence to the International Uniform Lesson and other products of the nineteenth century was not alive to psychological and pedagogical advances in education. It was believed that the modern theories used in the public school should be applied to religious education. The new educational movements appealed to denominational workers who had no precedents to which they were attached. Therefore, the denominations felt that they must organize and promote for themselves if the newer methods were to have a chance in their churches.

1. Sunday School Council of Evangelical Denominations

In July, 1910, a preliminary meeting was held in Philadelphia with twenty representatives of eleven denominations present. This was followed by a second meeting, in October, at which fifty-nine delegates from nineteen denominations organized the Sunday School Council of Evangelical Denominations.

Besides annual sessions, the Council worked in four sections: editorial, educational, extension, and publication. "For the first time in the history of the North American Sunday School cause," says Dr. Fergusson, "the denominations as such were acting together." But in their statement of the aims and purpose of the organization, the new association made it plain that it was the real leader of the Sunday School cause. No lay-managed convention or association would be permitted any longer to set up standards for denominations to meet or impose upon denominational Sunday Schools a community-made program. "The denominationally thinking men of the Council quietly but firmly took the helm."

The denominational association gave attention to the preparation of standard courses of study for teachers, but left the preparation of material for these courses to each denomination. It supervised the selection of lessons for Sunday School study, and sought to correlate the entire work so as to avoid overlapping, yet leaving each denomination free in the conduct of its own work.

Up to this time the International Lesson Committee had been the exclusive instrument for preparing Sunday School curricula. The invasion of the Sunday School Council of Evangelical Denominations made it necessary to change the representation on the Lesson Committee. We have already seen in a former chapter that in 1914 the constituency of the Inter-

national Lesson Committee was completely changed.
Instead of the International Convention appointing
a committee as had been the custom since 1872, it
was now limited to the selection of eight members
of the committee. The Sunday School Council of
Evangelical Denominations contributed eight, and
each co-operating denomination had a representative. Thus the International Sunday School Association lost its authority to choose the majority of the
Lesson Committee, and there was diminished enthusiasm and interest in its plans within the rank
and file of some Christian workers.

2. Religious Education Association

An influential factor that contributed to the
launching of the Sunday School Council of Evangelical Denominations was the Religious Education Association, an organization which has exerted great influence on religious education in the last four decades.
This Association came into existence in 1903. Its
purpose was to gather together those who were firm
believers in the value of religious education as a vital
factor in character formation. While this group had
no organic relation to any church, its governing
board included clergymen who were outstanding in
their denominations as liberal thinkers. It also numbered among its members educators of outstanding
colleges and universities.

"These men," says Dr. Brown, "have not feared
to be known as radical in the field of religious education, and have exerted themselves in the task of
investigating and making known the experiments in
this field and the factors essential to success." The
organization attracted men of extremely liberal ten-

dencies and admitted to its membership Jews, Budd-
hists and representatives of all religions. Through
their magazine *Religious Education* they became a
powerful factor in molding public opinion. In their
constitution the Association declared that its object
was:

> To inspire the educational forces of our country with
> the religious ideal.
>
> To inspire the religious forces of our country with the
> educational ideal.
>
> To keep before the public mind the value of religious
> education, and the sense of its need and value.

Education in religion and religion in education
might be said to be the slogan of the Association. The
spiritual forces in religion were minimized and the
educational factors emphasized. The departmental
plan was also stressed, and in its annual conventions
there were sections for directors of religious education, department of universities and colleges, department of Bible teachers in colleges, department of
church schools, department of churches and pastors,
department of public schools, department of theological seminaries, and department of community
agencies.

While full credit must be given this Association
for creating new interest in religious education and
crystallizing the sentiment in favor of better methods,
its efforts to modernize the content of the instruction
accomplished more harm than good. The liberalizing
of the curriculum they believed was the necessary
sequence of directing more attention to the interests
of the pupil, and as the members for the most part
had modernistic conceptions of the Bible, their con-

tributions were at variance with those who accepted
the Scriptures in their entirety as the Word of God.

3. International Council of Religious Education

The two rival organizations, the International
Sunday School Association and the Sunday School
Council of Evangelical Denominations, maintained
friendly relations, but it was evident that no house
divided against itself could stand. For more than a
century the Sunday School convention movement
had provided free and democratic expression. The
denominational enterprise was transferring the control into the hands of a select few. Even in the International Convention when the appointment of delegates was made by the state and provincial associations, which was the case after the convention was
made an association, individual schools were often
left without representation. This was a situation
which the originators of conventions definitely
planned to prevent.

The Sunday School Council of Evangelical Denominations was even less democratic than the Association in providing for its constituency. As its representatives were largely denominational officials, the
situation led Dr. Athearn to publish in the *Christian
Standard* of Cincinnati an article entitled, "Shall the
American Sunday School Be Prussianized?" In this
he vigorously attacked what he accounted as attempts
to establish denominational control of the Sunday
School. Throughout this controversy the vast Sunday
School forces had no thought of division among their
numbers, much less of open conflict. Those who
understood the gathering struggle for dominance felt
sure that some way of conciliation might be effected.

So it proved. In 1918 the first steps were taken to bring together the two organizations, and in 1919 a joint committee met for two days in Detroit and agreed on principles which a united organization would recognize and follow.

The plan for reorganization provided that 50 per cent of the members of the Executive Committee of the International Sunday School Association should be territorial representatives selected as formerly to represent the International Sunday School Convention and the territorial state and provincial associations, while 50 per cent should be selected as official representatives of the co-operating denominations. It also provided that full-time paid workers of the International Sunday School Association and its auxiliaries should be admitted to the membership of the Sunday School Council of Evangelical Denominations.

The final chapter in the merger of these two denominational agencies for Sunday School promotion took place in Chicago in February, 1922, at the meeting of the Sunday School Council of Evangelical Denominations. This action was ratified at the Sixteenth International Sunday School Convention which met in June of the same year, in Kansas City. The merged body was called the International Sunday School Council of Religious Education, but later the word "Sunday School" was dropped. In order that neither group might dominate, Hugh S. Magill, the secretary of the National Educational Association, was called to head up the new group.

While the new International Council of Religious Education unified the denominations in their Sunday School, Vacation School, and Week Day School

activities, and soon received the recognition of leadership from no less than forty-four church groups, nevertheless in many other respects the merger has
proved to be disappointing. Many state and county
associations refused to drop "Sunday School" from
their title. Pennsylvania complied with all the merger
stipulations; nevertheless insisted upon retaining its
distinctive title as the Pennsylvania State Sunday
School Association.

Considerable opposition to the use of the word
"religious" in the nomenclature also developed. It
was contended that this term was equally applicable
to non-Christian creeds. However, repeated efforts
to substitute "Christian" proved unavailing. To
many this was accepted as unquestionable proof of
modernistic control of the Council.

The minimizing of the Bible content and the introduction of experience-centered lessons further ali-
enated the orthodox constituency of the churches.
State secretaries trained under the Association found
it hard to believe that in every official set-up the
denominational men were not trying to gain for their
side an effective control. As the main emphasis was
now on the annual meeting of denominational specialists, the amateur spirit which had kept alive Sunday School enthusiasm disappeared and the interest
in the old-time convention waned. The professional
spirit replaced the old zeal, passionate loyalty and
humble service, which characterized the voluntary
contributions of lay workers. Many came to look
upon the Council as a professional aristocracy in
which was vested certain rights and privileges and
to which due honor and obedience was to be
rendered.

The result was a marked lack of confidence of thousands who had been outstanding supporters of the old-time Sunday School convention. While the Council had the denominations behind it, there was a growing realization that it was without support of the majority of individual churches. James DeForest Murch says in his recent book, *Christian Education and the Local Church:*

> Friends of true Christian education, particularly in churches committed to the evangelical faith, have resented these trends in an organization which they would like to support wholeheartedly. This sector of American church life is growing rapidly. They have established numerous new institutes, seminaries and colleges, which in addition to other institutions loyal to the faith are increasingly the vital factor in the educational life of America. They have set up publishing houses, teacher training associations and national organizations. There is a growing feeling among these evangelical groups that, if the International Council cannot serve their interests, some new co-operative venture must be launched to take its place.

---

1. Discuss the value of the convention as a means for promoting the Sunday School.
2. When and where was the Tenth International Convention held?
3. What was Dr. Trumbull's testimony to the Sunday School teacher at the Eleventh Convention?
4. When and where was the Twelfth Convention held?
5. What was accomplished at the Thirteenth Convention?
6. Compare the Sunday School enrolment of the Chicago convention of 1887 and that of 1914.

7. Describe the exhibit, parade, and pageant of the Fourteenth International Convention.

8. What encouraging statistics were reported at the Fifteenth International Convention?

9. What was the outstanding feature of this convention?

10. When and where was the First World Convention held and how many registered delegates were in attendance?

11. Compare the London convention of 1889 with that of 1898.

12. Describe the Fourth World Convention.

13. How was North Africa related to the Fifth World Convention?

14. Compare the St. Louis convention of 1893 with the Washington convention of 1910.

15. What was accomplished at the Seventh World Convention?

16. How were the delegates entertained at the Eighth World Convention?

17. Describe the conflagration, the parade, and the impression created by the Eighth World Convention.

18. What were the accomplishments of the Ninth and Tenth World Conventions?

19. Describe the Eleventh and Twelfth World Conventions.

20. In what respects was the association different from the convention?

21. How did the state associations come into existence?

22. What loss was sustained when the convention became an association?
23. What is the purpose and policy of the World's Sunday School Association?
24. Why was the Sunday School Council of Evangelical Denominations organized?
25. How did the new organization affect the International Lesson Committee?
26. What was the Religious Educational Association?
27. Criticize its activities.
28. How did the International Council of Religious Education come into existence?
29. In what respects has the merger proved disappointing?
30. What is Dr. Murch's evaluation of the International Council?

16

THE CONCLUSION

SPEAKING in a small country church in England at the close of the world's last colossal conflict, Woodrow Wilson, then president of the United States, said, "It was such gatherings as this that won the war."

Undoubtedly the Church, in maintaining the moral stability of the nations as well as contributing sons for armed services, has been the outstanding factor in winning all wars where national righteousness and justice were at stake. But we believe if the Church had strengthened and lengthened its educational arm war might have been avoided entirely.

Were the Church today as much concerned in reviving the teaching ministry as Judah's good king Jehoshaphat was, and would imitate his educational program by multiplying Sunday Schools until they are as thick as schoolhouses, the fear of the Lord might fall upon the threatening nations so that they would make no war against us (II Chron. 17:7-10).

War for Great Britain and America has been inevitable. Never in the history of these English-speaking nations has there been less religious instruction in the home and in the school. Should we fail to recognize this appalling need and arrange to adequately meet it, even though we win the war, we shall certainly lose the peace.

We must come to believe that Christian education is the way out. We have tried force and it has failed.

Legislation has been tried and found inadequate. We have turned to secular education and seen that it is insufficient. These agencies are unavailing for producing character. We must begin with the child and indoctrinate him with the truths of the Bible by a process of teaching and training. The English-speaking people must give support to:

I. The Indispensable Sunday School

The Sunday School has done a wonderful work in the fractional bit of time allotted to it. Moreover, its power for good has won general recognition. As Lloyd George, the peerless premier of Great Britain, testifies, "Personally, I know what a Sunday School can do. All the best training I ever had was in a Sunday School. It has become the university of the people for the study of the higher and deeper knowledge of religion."

That the Sunday School is valued as the hope of America is the testimony of one hundred governors, congressmen, editors, educators, authors and master merchants whose utterances have been gathered by William E. Atkinson in *The Value of the Sunday School.* John M. Rankin, former governor of Louisiana, is quoted as saying: "I regard the Sunday School as among the most indispensable institutions we have." The former governor of Colorado adds, "If this country is to be the leader among the nations of the world, every effort should be made to develop among the young people those elements of Christianity which will fit them for success and leadership. This can best be done in the Sunday School."

President Wilson had this to say: "No study is more important than the study of the Bible, and there is no more effective agency for such study than the Sunday School." President Harding, alarmed at conditions in his day, warned that "it is time we give our attention to the religious instruction of the children of America." Roger Babson, that keen interpreter of the times, concludes by saying, "The need of the hour is not more factories, railroads, steamships, armies or navies, but more religious education."

Perhaps the best evaluation of the Sunday School has been given by Dr. Murch:

> It is impossible to segregate and enumerate the beneficent influences upon the home, the Church, the State, and our social order in general, which have been the direct or indirect result of the Sunday School. It placed a new premium on child life. Its evangelistic influence increased the membership of the churches many fold. It is said that in 1915 alone, 1,055,444 pupils of teen-age were admitted into church membership in North America from the Sunday Schools. Such reformation movements as the temperance movement, which wrote the Eighteenth Amendment into the Constitution of the United States, were largely promoted through the influence and co-operation of the Sunday School. People of the state developed a new conception of morality and changed the organic law of the land accordingly. Higher ideals in industry and business lifted burdens from labor. Peace and international good will were envisioned, and definite steps were taken for their achievement. It was freely prophesied that the millennium was at hand.

The blessings of the Sunday School have not been confined to America. They have gone forth like the gulf stream to warm the arctic climates of foreign soil. It is not too much to say that the Sunday School is the gulf stream of modern religious history. Lives in foreign lands have been warmed by the enthusiasm and fire of its love. Nearly all the progressive nations have the Sunday School in a high state of development and so make possible a greater measure of co-operative work, both within and without the nation, among all who love the Lord Jesus Christ. Out of this unifying force of the Sunday School come largely the beginnings of church life where the Sunday School often, if not usually, precedes the church. In not a few communities the golden days were before the churches multiplied and became competitors, for in the early days the community joined in a union Sunday School.

II. The Downgrade Movement

After more than a century of continued advance, the Sunday School movement came to a halt in 1916. By 1926 it was in full retreat, but since 1936 it has been a rout. In June, 1929, the author prepared an article for the *Moody Monthly* entitled "An Impending National Peril." In this he pointed out that within twenty-one years there had been a decline of 1,545,792 pupils in the Sunday Schools of England and Wales, and a falling away of 541,693 from the American schools in less than half that time. Statistics from the United States Census Bureau were quoted to show that sixteen states showed a decrease in Sunday School attendance between 1916 and 1926. Most of these states not only showed a marked increase in population, but in church membership as well, which made the failure of the Sunday School the more conspicuous and inexcusable.

The most alarming revelation was the denominational reports of smaller numbers enrolled in their

Sunday Schools than they had recorded as communicant members. One large denomination, which in 1900 reported nearly equal numbers in the church and Sunday School, indicated in 1928 that there were 348,826 less Sunday School pupils than church members. In Chicago, the church membership of that denomination exceeded its Sunday School enrolment by 11,560, despite the fact that in this metropolis there were 750,000 boys and girls growing up without any religious instruction. So much for 1929.

The reports for the next decade were much more discouraging. Government figures indicated that despite the increase in population, Sunday School enrolment had decreased 12.6 per cent between 1926 and 1936. The Methodist Episcopal Church reported a loss of 34 per cent, the Disciples 23 per cent, Northern Presbyterians 18 per cent, Northern Baptists 15 per cent. The Lutheran Church was the only one of the larger denominations that did not show a loss. That the retrograde movement was nation-wide was evident from the fact that only in the District of Columbia, Louisiana, Idaho, New Mexico, Utah and Nevada had there been any gains at all. Not a single one of the larger denominations now has a larger Sunday School enrolment than church membership. Methodists report nearly two million and Southern Baptists approximately a million and a half less; the Northern Baptists and Disciples a half million less in the Sunday School than on the church membership roll.

In the last two decades the Church has not only lost its missionary spirit of reaching the spiritually illiterate of America, but it has imperiled its own existence since '75 per cent of its recruits come from the Sunday School.

The only encouraging fact revealed from the statistics was that a number of the smaller denominations showed sensational gains in the Sunday School. The Assembly of God, for instance, led with an increase of more than 300 per cent; the Pentecostal Holiness Church, from 12,772 to 24,261; the Mennonite, from 87,897 to 113,136; the Nazarenes, from 109,237 to 136,227; the Wesleyan Methodist, from 39,053 to 46,575. As these denominations, for the most part, have carried on their educational activities independent of the International Council of Religious Education, it would seem that this leadership of the Sunday School movement is not proving as successful as in the old days of the convention.

III. The Mounting Crime Wave

Shortly before the outbreak of the present World War, Dr. Clarence Edward Macartney, speaking at the First Presbyterian Church of Pittsburgh on the subject, "Is America on the Road to Ruin?" produced some startling statistics. He proved that more people had been murdered in the United States in ten years than all the soldiers that fell in all the wars in which the nation had been engaged from the Revolution of 1776 to the colossal conflict of 1917.

It would appear that crime today is a more dangerous enemy than Germany, Italy and Japan. One million of the people of the United States are murderers, will be murderers, or will be murdered. We have sixty times as many murderers as Switzerland; twenty times as many as Great Britain; thirteen times as many as pagan Japan. In one year, grief was carried every twenty-two seconds into American homes by the commitment of 1,500,000 major crimes, such as murder, manslaughter, robbery and assault, and 14,000,000 minor offenses, such as forgeries, embezzlements and vice. We harbor three and one-half times more criminals than college students, and four times as many law-breakers as school teachers. Lawlessness in this nation has already reached such proportion that three out of four homes are destined to be the scene of a serious crime.

A national committee of prominent jurists, educators and statesmen reported findings of the prevalence of crime with this significant statement: "Crime in the United States has reached appalling proportions, and unless checked will carry the nation on to anarchy." Earl W. Evans, president of the American Bar Association, in an address before that body said that America was the most lawless nation in the world, and that its annual crime bill had now reached fifteen billion dollars. Shortly after his inauguration in 1929, President Hoover addressed representatives of the Associated Press on what he called "the dominant issue before the American people." He said, "Its solution is more vital to the preservation of our institutions than any other question before us. With us life and property are relatively more unsafe than in any other civilized nation."

Dr. W. S. Fleming, in his recent book, *God in Our Public Schools,* takes for his text Benjamin Kidd's dictum, "What you put into the schools will, in from twenty to thirty years, be a controlling force in the lives of the people," and applies it to present day conditions in America. He says:

> Religion left the schools in the '70's, and in 1890 crime was seen to be growing and religion suffering, just as the dictum said. If a rule will not work in reverse, it may well be doubted. If it works both ways, it is pretty reliable. If crime grows and religion suffers when religion leaves education, crime should decline and religion flourish when religion returns to education, allowing in each case a few years to take effect.

Dr. Fleming introduced statistics from the Department of Commerce to the effect that while crime increased in the United States 66.3 per cent from 1910 to 1938, it increased notably less in the five states where the Bible has been read daily in the public school.

The gradual disappearance of the Bible from the public school during the nineteenth century was only one factor that contributed to the appalling crime wave. The decline of religious instruction in the home and the lamentable dwindling of the Sunday School in the twentieth century have greatly aggravated the situation. Never in the history of the nation was there less Christian education in the home and the school than today, and it is nothing less than tragic that the church should fail to do its part in this hour of national crisis.

IV. Some Solutions to the Problem

The downfall of the most permanent, powerful and prosperous Republic in history may still be averted if all its religious forces are united in furthering a program for maintaining the moral integrity of the nation. The multiplicity of denominations and their diversified and divided efforts have sadly weak-

ened the power and prestige of the Church. Only
by universal recognition that the strategy of tomor-
row is to win the children of today and by united
effort in a program of religious instruction can we
hope to stem the tide of godlessness that threatens
to overwhelm the nation.

At the Fifteenth International Sunday School Convention in 1918, before the Sunday School had entered upon its disastrous decline or the crime wave
had assumed large proportions, Dr. Walter S.
Athearn said:

> We cannot maintain a Christian democracy unless we
> maintain a system of efficient schools. The price of our
> religious liberty is the sum required for the building of a
> system of church schools which will parallel our system of
> public schools. But this system does not work with the
> whole child. It is but half an educational arch. We must
> complete the arch by building a system of church schools,
> closely co-ordinated with the public schools. These two
> systems of schools—one supported by the State with
> secular leadership, the other supported by the Church
> with religious leadership—will form the only system of
> education that a country can have, in which the Church
> and State are apart. The building of this system of church
> schools is the task now pressing for completion.

1. Legislation requiring religious instruction

If character as well as intelligence is essential for
the preservation of a democracy, both religious and
secular subjects must be included in the curriculum of
the schools. Dr. W. S. Fleming, in *God in Our Public Schools,* says:

> Uncle Sam is not an atheist, nor a secularist, but a
> Christian. Sad to say he has adopted some pagan prac-
> tices, and must get right with God by restoring religion
> to the schools or perish through secularism and crime.

However, Dr. Fleming has no hope of the parochial school solving the problem. He says:

> They oppose the public schools as godless, and take their children out and still insist upon keeping the schools godless. They take their children out of the state schools and at great expense build schools of their own. We are inclined to commend their religious devotion. But when, with their children gone, they still fight to keep the public schools godless, we wonder quite a bit at their supposed religious devotion. Even if all the churches set up parochial schools there would still be in the sadly weakened public school the two-thirds of the children who never darken church doors, and from these would still come the dangerous elements we now have.

Even the plan for having children excused from school for one or two hours a week to attend religious instruction classes elsewhere, does not appeal to Dr. Fleming. He quotes from a bulletin of the United States Office of Education, dated July, 1941, to the effect that only 488 of such schools were reported in 1940, with an average daily attendance of 135,877. The plan, he declares, depends upon voluntary attendance, and it is folly to think that those who will not come to church on Sunday will come some other day during the week. He also is very insistent that teaching non-religious morals in these Week Day Church Schools or in the public schools will never get us anywhere.

> Man-made morals in the schools mean no God in the schools, and that would mean a nation without God, which means atheism, irreligion, crime, chaos, destruction.

Dr. Fleming contends, as many others have, that the only solution to the problem is to restore the

Bible to the public school curriculum. Undoubtedly
he is not familiar with Carl Zollman's *American
Church Law,* which says:

> If there is any one thing which is well settled in the
> policies and purposes of the American people as a whole,
> it is the fixed and unalterable determination that there
> shall be an absolute and unequivocal separation of Church
> and State and that our public school system, supported by
> the taxation of the property of all alike—Catholic, Prot-
> estant, Gentile, Jew, believer and infidel—shall not be
> used directly or indirectly for religious instruction, and
> above all that it shall not be made an instrumentality of
> proselyting influence in favor of any religious organiza-
> tion, sect, creed or belief.

Zollman recognizes that as long as the Constitution of the United States gives equal rights to all
religions, it is futile to expect that the Bible of the
Protestants, the catechism of the Catholics, or the
systematized instruction of any denomination can be
made a part of the public school curriculum.

The sooner the Protestant Church recognizes that
it is impractical, if not impossible, to legislate the
Bible into the public school curriculum, the sooner
can its energies be directed along more promising
lines. As Zollman so well points out:

> The result of the school controversy as it appears to-
> day is that all sides lost—a result not at all uncommon in
> such matters. The Catholics lost their subsidies, and hence-
> forth were forced wholly to support their schools. The
> Protestant denominations lost the teaching of their religion
> in the public schools, which henceforth was confined to
> purely secular subjects. The public school pupils lost a
> large part of the moral restraint which religion alone can
> impart. The churches lost many who should have become
> faithful members, and the State finds its burdens increased

and its citizenship degenerating. The consequences of a
godless education can be studied today at close hand in
any penitentiary, house of correction, or reform school.
They are vitally felt by every teacher from the kindergarten to the university, and by every businessman from
the corner grocer to the president of the most powerful
bank. They fill the courts with litigation, the jails with
inmates and the cemeteries with corpses.

Getting the Bible into the public school would
not fully solve the problem, for there still remains
the difficulty of providing capable instructors to teach
the Word of God. Normal schools do not offer a
course in Bible, and even if they did, it is certain that
all graduates could not teach it. The average Sunday
School teacher at least *believes* in the Bible even if
woefully ignorant of its contents.

If the curriculum of the American child is recognized as incomplete without religious instruction,
why not have some legislation requiring a public
school pupil to attend sessions of a religious school?
By the Oregon decision of the United States Supreme
Court, parents are invested with the right to determine the content of their children's curriculum.
Could they not by legislation be brought to see that
the nation regards character essential to its preservation? Catholics, Protestants and Jews have their institutions of learning. The parents of the thirty-seven
million spiritually illiterate children have a wide selection of religious schools in which to supplement
the secular instruction of the public schools. The
State can and must see that the Sunday School—
whether Protestant, Catholic or Jewish—looms up as
conspicuously in national thinking as the public
school.

2. Recognition of a divided Protestantism

Efforts to secure universal religious education in America have not only been hindered by the well intended movement of Protestants to legislate the Bible into the public school, but also their failure to recognize an irreconcilable division of their forces. Protestants can and must unite in the *furtherance of religious education,* but they cannot agree as to the *content of the curriculum.* Efforts on the one hand to broaden the curriculum to include extra-biblical material, or on the other hand to narrow it to exclusively biblical content, have been equally disastrous to unity. Dr. Betts clearly states the situation in *The Curriculum of Religious Education:*

> There is no use dodging the issue, it must be met. The literalist and the modern biblical scholar do not have the same Bible. The God and the Christ of the fundamentalist are not the God and the Christ of the liberalist. While many of the points of controversy are wholly incidental in that a belief in either position has no discernible influence on conduct or character, yet the two points of view at issue are at root too far apart to compromise upon them, and compromise but confuses thought and undermines faith.

It is amazing how many in Protestant denominations can agree as to the fundamentals of Christian instruction. Recently the *Moody Student* (April 16, 1943) printed a photograph of representatives from fifty-seven different denominations attending the Moody Bible Institue of Chicago. At the same time the International Council of Religious Education yearbook (1942) lists forty-two denominations that contribute to its support. But the doctrinal beliefs of those who attend the Bible institutes in the United

States and Canada and those who actively support the International Council are as far apart as the poles. Even the Catholic doctrinal position is not as remote from evangelical Protestantism as the modernists who deny the cardinal facts of Christianity. If the Catholics, then, are to be recognized as having a distinct type of religious education for their children, surely distinction should also be made between Protestants who base their instruction entirely upon the Word of God, and those who supplement it with extrabiblical material.

All Protestants today do not regard the Bible in its entirety as the Word of God, and for them it is essential that the International Council or some similar group exists. But those among all denominations who believe that "the Bible and the Bible alone is the religion of Protestants" must find their representation in a separate and distinct leadership. The International Council does not and never can represent more than a part of Protestantism.

3. A new appreciation of the Sunday School

We have already seen what a powerful influence the Sunday School exerted in the life of the nation. It has and probably always will be the outstanding agency for Christian education in America. It creates no problem with the public school. It permits instruction from every Protestant viewpoint. Modernists and fundamentalists can easily agree upon the value of the Sunday School. When they once unite in this common agency, unquestionable progress can be made in reaching the thirty-seven million unenrolled children and adolescents in America. The greatest difference between Protestants is their indifference to the great masses of boys and girls who are not receiving any religious instruction. As these will constitute the voting class in another decade, we can only continue to neglect them at the peril of our national existence.

Seldom do Sunday School pupils become criminals. According to a nation-wide survey made in recent years, the testimony of juvenile court judges proves that less than one out of two hundred offenders, or less than one-half of one per cent, are Sunday School members. A famous New York judge found that only three out of five thousand boys he had sentenced were attending Sunday School. A Toledo juvenile court officer declared that in a period of seven consecutive years not one boy who attended Sunday School regularly was arrested for any offense.

Probably no one is better informed on the crime situation in America than J. Edgar Hoover, head of the Federal Bureau of Investigation. "Of course, I believe in the Sunday School," he says, and continues: "Crime among youth would become practically negligible if the young people of America attended Sunday School regularly during their formative years. Surely no one cognizant of the true crime situation in the United States could be blind to the importance of the activities of this institution in reducing materially the army of youthful offenders and delinquents."

To restore the power and prestige of the Sunday School in America, five suggestions are submitted:

a. *Every church should regard the Sunday School as its main enterprise.*

It is far less expensive to operate a Sunday School than a parochial institution, but America will never

be made safe for democracy through a school maintained by the pennies of the children.

Senator B. L. Eddy of Oregon, in *Christianity and
Education,* says:

> The training of the young in the true faith is the
> greatest existing challenge to the Church of Jesus Christ.
> If the Church refuses to hear and accept the challenge,
> its influence will die out of the world. The alternatives
> which the Church faces are "educate or die." One of the
> first practical steps to be taken is to convince every
> Protestant church that it should raise for Christian educa-
> tion from fifty to one hundred per cent of what it raises
> for its minister.

> b. *Every church should enlist and train a larger
> number of its members for Sunday School
> work.*

In the apostolic Church, members were admitted
on the understanding that they were "saved to
serve." Everyone became a Bible teacher, and with so
many to sow the seed it is not surprising that in those
early days there were such bountiful harvests. Today
not more than 8 per cent of Protestant church members are teaching in the Sunday School, and many
of them are very poorly equipped for their work.
It takes so much less time and expense to prepare
a teacher for the Sunday School than the public
school, that one would naturally suppose the ranks
of the Sunday School and not the public school
would contain the larger number of qualified instructors. As Senator Eddy says:

> Why should not consecrated young people who do
> not enlist for full-time Christian service be led to prepare
> themselves for Sunday School teaching, which can be

carried on while following secular occupations? Perhaps
one reason why this idea has not appealed to more young
Christians is that Sunday School work is so haphazard,
such a hit-and-miss affair, which the average congregation
does not take seriously. In many churches the whole attitude toward the Sunday School needs changing.

c. *Every church should have something better
than the Uniform Lesson for its curriculum.*

It is inconsistent to hold persistently to the Word
of God in its entirely and then maintain a program
that never studies more than 35 per cent of it. As
Gerrit Verkuyl, in *Christ in American Education,*
says:

> In spite of two decades of pleading, urging and demon-
> strating on the part of our leading educators, the majority
> of our Sunday School members still receive Uniform Les-
> son quarterlies. The pupil who studies them is as rare as a
> white raven; but even if he did, what complete acquaint-
> ance with the Bible could he acquire! The six-year cycle,
> selected with a futile hope of fitting young and old, treats
> but a limited series of passages and these in each successive
> cycle. More effectively than any higher critics has the
> Lesson Committee eliminated the greater portion of our
> Bible.

Supplementary educational agencies have been
urged simply because the pupil, limited to the Uniform Lesson, was receiving only a smattering knowledge of the Bible in the Sunday School. Advocates
of placing the Bible in the public school have also
recognized that its instruction would be consecutive,
comprehensive and complete. The persistent use of
the Uniform Lesson has been the main stumbling
block to a better appreciation of the value of the
Sunday School.

d. *Every superintendent should reach his
constituency.*

The present enrolment of the average Protestant
Sunday School is only one-third of its constituency.
If each Sunday School is to serve the nation to its
full capacity, it must triple its enrolment. Let every
superintendent be elected upon the progressive platform of Sunday School extension, and let him make
it his first business to reach the neglected children
of the neighborhood with the moral and religious
instruction that will make them law-abiding citizens.

e. *Every church should start a branch
Sunday School.*

When a church finds its constituency limited in
the neighborhood of its location, it can perform a
patriotic service to its country and a missionary service for its denomination by organizing and supporting
a Sunday School in some other community. Churches
which have their members engaged in such a missionary enterprise are more easily and more directly
fulfilling the "go . . . teach" of the Great Commission
than those whose representatives are all serving on
foreign soil. You can *support* a missionary in a distant land, but you can *be* a missionary in the Sunday School.

---

1. Give the testimony of Lloyd George and President Wilson to the value of the Sunday School.
2. What does Dr. Murch say as to the accomplishments of the Sunday School?
3. What is the impending n a t i o n a l peril of
America?

4. Compare the Sunday School decrease of 1926-1936 with that of the preceding decade.

5. Give statistics to show the widening gap between Sunday School enrolment and church membership.

6. Why have some of the smaller denominations made sensational gains in the Sunday School?

7. Prove by statistics that America has a mounting crime wave.

8. To what does Dr. Fleming attribute the prevalence of crime?

9. What did Dr. Athearn contend was needed to maintain a Christian democracy?

10. What is Dr. Fleming's estimate of the parochial school?

11. Why is it impractical to legislate the Bible into the public schools?

12. What legislation could be enacted that would give no offense to any particular religion?

13. Show that it is impossible for Protestants to agree upon a curriculum. What is the one dividing factor?

14. Give several reasons why the Sunday School is still the best American agency for religious education.

15. Give five suggestions for restoring the power and prestige of the Sunday School.

BIBLIOGRAPHY

Athearn, Walter Scott—*The Minister and the Teacher*

Atkinson, William E.—*The Value of the Sunday School*

Bennink, B. J.—*The Church in the World*

Betts, George Herbert—*The Curriculum of Religious Education*

Boehmer, H.—*The Jesuits*

Bower, William Clayton— *The Curriculum of Religious Education*

Broadbent, E. H.—*The Pilgrim Church*

Brown, Arlo Ayres— *History of Religious Education in Recent Times*

Bunsen, Christian G. J.—*Hippolytus and His Age*

Burroughs, Prince E.—*Fifty Fruitful Years*

Coe, George Albert—*Education in Religion and Morals*

Cubberley, Ellwood Patterson— *Public Education in the United States*

Day, Richard—*Bush Aglow*

Deutsch, Emanuel—*Literary Remains*

Dexter—*History of Education in the United States*

Eddy, B. L.—*Christianity and Education*

Ellis, Samuel Robert—*Jesus, the Great Teacher*

Faris, John T.—*The Sunday School and World Progress*

Fergusson, E. Morris.—*Historic Chapters in Christian Education in America*

Fleming, W. S.—*God in Our Public Schools*

Ginsburg, Louis—*Students, Scholars and Saints*

Gorham, Donald R.—*Christian Religious Education*

Grice, Homer L.—*The Vacation Bible School Guide*

Haslett, Samuel B.—*The Pedagogical Bible School*

Hayes, Ernest H.—*Raikes the Pioneer*

Heaton, W. J.—*The Bible of the Reformation*

Hinsdale, B. A.—*Jesus as a Teacher*

Hodgson, Geraldine—*Primitive Christian Education*

Huffman, J. A.—*Youth and the Christ Way*

Hurlbut, Jesse Lyman—*The Story of the Christian Church*

Hyma, Albert—*World History*

Jacobs, Charles M.—*The Story of the Church*

Kuist, Howard Tillman—*The Pedagogy of Saint Paul*

Kurtz, John Henry—Textbook of Church History

Lankard, Frank Glenn—A History of the American Sunday School Curriculum

Leavell, Roland Q.—An Unashamed Workman

Lotz, P. H.—Current Week Day Religious Education

McKoy, Charles Francis—The Art of Jesus as a Teacher

Monroe, Paul—A Brief Course in the History of Education

Munro, Harry C.—The Director of Religious Education

Murch, James DeForest—Christian Education and the Local Church

Nichols, Robert Hastings—The Growth of the Christian Church

Ost, A. B.—The Bible and Our National Life

Painter, F. V. N.—Luther on Education

Paniel, K. F. W.—History of Christian Oratory and Preaching

Pasma, Henry K.—Things a Nation Lives By

Peloubet, F. N.—The International Question Book

Piper, David R.—How Would Jesus Teach?

Porter, Noah—Educational Systems

Power, John Carroll — Rise and Progress of the Sunday Schools

Price, J. M.—Introduction to Religious Education

Proudfit, Isabel—Noah Webster

Qualben, Lars P.—A History of the Christian Church

Quick, Robert H.—Educational Reformers

Read, Hollis—The Hand of God in History

Reu, M.—Luther's Smaller Catechism

Rice, Edwin Wilbur—The Sunday School Movement and the Amerian Sunday School Union

Ridpath, John Clark—Cyclopedia of Universal History

Sampey—The International Lesson System

Schaff-Herzog—Encyclopedia of Religious Knowledge

Schaff, Phillip—History of the Christian Church

Seeley—History of Education

Skoda, George Paul — The Teacher Training Movement (thesis)

Squires, Walter Albion—A Parish Program of Religious Education

—The Week Day Church School

—Educational Movements of Today
Thompson, W. Taliaferro—*Weekday Religious Education*
Trumbull, H. Clay—*Yale Lectures on the Sunday School*
Tyng, Stephen H. — *Forty Years Experience in Sunday
    Schools*
Verkuyl, Gerrit—*Christ in American Education*
Webster, Noah—*The Elementary Spelling Book*
Willyams, Jane Louisa—*The Waldensian Church*
Zollman, Carl—*American Church Law*

International Council of Religious Education:
    The Weekday Church School, Educational Bulletin 601
    The Standard Leadership Training Curriculum, Educa-
        tional Bulletin 503
Official Reports, Eleventh, Twelfth, Thirteenth and Four-
    teenth International Sunday School Conventions
*The Encyclopedia of Sunday Schools and Religious Educa-
tion*
The New England Primer, 20th Century Reprint
U. S. Government Publications:
    Week Day Religious Instruction, Pamphlet No. 36
    Week Day Classes in Religious Education, Bulletin
        1941, No. 3
    Religious Bodies: 1936, Vol. I, II, III